We Are Not Finished...

We may be the end-product of evolution as we know it, but we are not finished...

We know that we presently use only about a tenth of the powers potential to the human mind, and that we observe only a tenth of the physical universe there is. We are not finished until we attain the remaining nine-tenths, for that is the purpose of all creation.

We start the upward path as we turn within to the awakening of the Deep Unconscious Mind—activating psychic centres and channels as well as neural circuits to give direction and release of powers and perceptions previously rarely glimpsed.

We take a necessary evolutionary step, a giant step, with the first publication of one of the most renowned techniques employed in the practical Qabalah—the core of the Western Esoteric Tradition: *the art of Pathworking.*

Pathworkings are structured narrations evoking images and feelings, a progressive series of happenings that are visualized in a heroic journey of unfolding dimensions, carrying the reader/listener/participant from the mundane world to higher levels of consciousness.

The Paths have not been "invented," but *discovered*; they are psychologically—and psychically—real, and to traverse them is to awaken to your own Self, and to the beauty and power and glory of your own existence.

Pathworking engages the deeper levels of mind, the Unconscious—which is like a pre-programmed computer connecting us to the Source of All Life. Pathworking intensifies and strengthens communication between the levels of the psyche, and every word & phrase of the narrative is likely to trigger chain-reactions of associated images in many directions simultaneously—all in the Deep Mind, which is that part of the psyche that "dreams" continuously, whether we are awake or sleeping.

Pathworking opens new circuitry between the Deep Mind computer and the normal consciousness, providing new access between Inner and Outer, the Source and the Individual, the Self and the Personality. It is the building of "bridges" between the Lesser Universe that is Man/Woman and the Greater Universe that is All/the Source of our being.

The realization of one's full potential—magically, spiritually, practically—depends upon willful and directed contact with life's underlying archetypal realities. This is the object of Pathworking, for within each of us are counterparts to the universal archetypes by means of which we can draw upon the resources of the archetypal powers for our own growth, attainment, and even practical benefit.

Dedication

For our colleagues in Light,
Dr. Thomas G. Chisholm
and
Kathryn Anne Chisholm,
with love and appreciation

MAGICAL

STATES

of

CONSCIOUSNESS

About the Authors

Melita Denning and Osborne Phillips are both past Grand Masters of the Aurum Solis, a magical society founded in 1897, which has continued in active existence to this day. Melita Denning was head of the order from 1976 to 1987 and again from 1988 to 1997, when she passed from this earth. Osborne Phillips headed the order from 1997 until 2003. He resides in the United Kingdom.

MAGICAL
STATES
of
CONSCIOUSNESS

Pathworking on the Tree of Life

DENNING & PHILLIPS

Llewellyn Publications
Woodbury, Minnesota

SECOND EDITION
Third Printing, 2023

Cover background © iStockphoto.com / Peter Zelei
Cover design by Kevin R. Brown

The authors express their grateful thanks to Dover Publications for permission to use material from the following works:
Background Patterns, Textures and Tints, by Clarence P. Hornung. © 1976 by Dover Publications, New York.
Optical and Geometrical Allover Patterns, by Jean Larcher. © 1979 by Jean Larcher. Published by Dover, New York.

Llewellyn Publications is a registered trademark of Llewellyn Worldwide Ltd.

Library of Congress Cataloging-in-Publication Data
Denning, Melita.
Magical states of consciousness.
(Llewellyn's inner guide series)
Magic. 2. Occult sciences. 3.Consciousness—
Miscellanea. I. Phillips, Osborne. II. Title.
III. Series
BF1621.D46 1984 133.4's 83-82527
ISBN 978-0-7387-3282-4

Llewellyn Publications
A Division of Llewellyn Worldwide Ltd.
2143 Wooddale Drive
Woodbury, MN 55125-2989
www.llewellyn.com

Printed in the United States of America

Contents

The Sephirothic archetypes, sources of magical and mystical power. Their counterparts within us. The Supernals, the Planetary Spheres, and the Sphere of Earth: distinct types of power, magical states of consciousness. Strengthening the counterparts: increasing your magical potential, ensuring your balanced spiritual progress. The need to work with pure forces. Pathworking: sure guidance for the beginner, a psychic toner for the experienced magician. The influences upon the Paths: their power in guided meditation to inaugurate real shifts of consciousness. Insight of Qabalistic psychology shown in the traditional placing of these influences. How the foundation philosophies of the Western World relate to the Paths up to Tiphareth.

Congruous patterns: the inner plan of the individual, and the plan of the universe as humanly conceived. To reunite the individual point by point with the cosmic forces, a goal of initiation. Initiatory patterns of the Tree of Life. The "Composite Tree" in the Four Worlds. States of consciousness and gates of initiation. Entry into Tiphareth, a change not only of mode but also of level of consciousness. What dawning Briatic awareness brings you: the rational mind's true heritage. The Intuitive Mind and its part in the completion of human nature. The distinguishing mark of the adept. "Divine intoxication." The World of Atziluth. The meaning of initiations above Tiphareth. The true individuality of initiation through Pathworking: exploring the mystery of your own self.

Making a powerful magical technique more effective for more people. The deep levels of the psyche must be reached. The unconscious as a hive of bees: the "cell minds." The computer as a self-portrait of the human unconscious. True personal autonomy: know and play along with your inner computer, know the codes it will accept. Symbolism and associated ideas. The unconscious as synthesizer. Pathworking a series of fantasy adventures. Letting your computer/synthesizer play with the narrative. Characteristics of the dream-mind in sleep and waking. The magick of change and movement. Pathworking as a "training" game. Points for Pathworking readers and leaders. Importance of the change of level to enter Tiphareth in the World of Mind: Why Path 25 must be completed before 26 or 24. Life and Death in the light of the Sun Sphere. How the transition is made.

Reinforcing your awareness of pathworking's inner realities. How your unconscious personalizes and expands the narrative for you. The Correspondences as road signs. The Path as the way to a Sphere, and as an adventure in its own right. "Travelers upon the Paths" by nature. The deep mind as child. Assimilation of new experience through play. Let your rational consciousness share the fun: Your Journal of Dreams. Dream exploration of the Paths: quests, adventures, and secrets you can learn.

I. Symbolism relating to visualized temples: some necessary preliminaries before the Pathworkings. Description and explanation of Aurum Solis symbols occurring in visualized temples: the Two Pillars, the Bomos, the Banner of the New Life, the Mystical Tessera. Suggestions for substitution. Meaning of the number Eight. II—Furnishing and arrangement of place of working: the simple requirements not to be confused with what is to be visualized. The optional robe. Batteries and incenses. III—Programming the Deep Mind before Pathworking. Preliminary use of the mandala and the correspondences: two methods. IV—Opening and Conducting the Pathworking. The Formula includes the uniting of energy of participants,

directives to the Deep Mind, the invocation of the Hebrew
Divine Names for this Pathworking with the text for each Path.
How to read/receive the Pathworking. How it is to be closed.

Little fundamental difference between individual and group
Pathworking: chief differences relate to maintaining incentive
for individual without group support, and adapting practical
procedures where required. The robe specially recommended.
Setting up the place of working. Use of mandala and correspondences. *Circulation of Energy* (to replace *Uniting of Energy*).
Reading the Pathworking text for yourself. Visualization and
reflection. The Journal of Dreams, another activity specially
recommended to the individual Pathworker.

Each Pathworking text is preceded by its list of correspondences with reflective *Comments* on the Path's significance, and
mandala for use as directed in Chapters 5 and 6. Texts of Paths
32 through 27 are given at once in their entirety. Paths 26 and
24 follow, incomplete as required for their first reading for the
reasons given in Chapter 3. Path 25 comes next in its entirety:
finally, the texts for conclusion of Paths 26 and 24 in Tiphareth,
for use when those Paths are given *subsequent to* the working of
the 25th.

Why a Pathworking performed by itself, that is not in series as
given in the previous chapter, needs special magical care. Three
categories fo "selective Pathworking"—for a non-magical purpose, or as a source of inner power and development, or to
add power to a working of a different type. Tables of the Paths
whose use is recommended for inner development and for outward magick. The requirements to balance or to resolve the
forces activated by the Pathworking in these various cases: how
and when the balancing or resolution should be performed.

The sephirothic magical images for visualization in these balancing and resolution rites, with their descriptions: and the text
of simple rites of Yesod, Hod, Netzach, Tiphareth, Binah, and
Malkuth, as required after Selective Pathworkings in the circumstances which are described in Chapter 8.

Definitions and special applications of words occurring in the
text.

Introduction

The perception and control of changes in states of consciousness, whether for purposes of magical development or of life generally, is supremely important. It is now widely recognized that our state of consciousness, and in consequence the accessibility and direction of our entire mental and emotional potential—thus to a great extent our physical potential also—is affected by seemingly minor circumstances, and can by their aggregate be affected profoundly: imaginative stimuli, the inner impact of dreams, the colors, odors, and lines of association with which we surround ourselves. To many people who are interested either in maximizing or in controlling human potential, research into these matters has become an absorbing new study. To the student of Qabalah, who is interested in maximizing his or her own potential and in controlling his or her own spiritual destiny, the study and practice of these matters is likewise fascinating and of supreme importance, but is by no means novel. In truth, modern approaches and modes of interpretation can be applied with good effect to timeless knowledge, as they are in the pages of this book: but the deep psychology which underlay astrology of Chaldaea, the philosophic and mystical teachings of many lands and systems, can be traced here too. All have in their measure flowed into, or out from, the traditions of Qabalah.

In the glyph of the Tree of Life, each Sephirah represents one of the archetypal spiritual states, existent not only cosmically but in the depths of each person's own being: each Path with its attributed influence represents the changes of consciousness by which a specific one of those states can be attained from one or other of the Sephiroth which are placed lower on the Tree of Life. Knowledge and practice in achieving these controlled changes is thus a most potent means of spiritual progess, of inner initiation, and of establishing an effective relationship with the deeper levels of one's own psyche. It would be possible to experience the Paths in many ways, some taking perhaps a considerable span of time for each Path: but in matters of the psyche, duration of time is hardly ever needful for impact and effectiveness, whereas repetition of an experience is often of great value. Thus, in the traditions of the modern and magical Qabalah, the guided meditations known as Pathworkings have taken a vital place among techniques for training in spiritual growth and development.

The Pathworking texts and methods given in this book are based upon Aurum Solis teachings and techniques. At the same time, they are recommended to the individual student as well as to the group, to aspirants of whatever mystical leaning or commitment as well as to entirely independent seekers. In accord with the general practice of this Order, the texts are not heavily burdened with its own distinctive symbols and concepts: where these are inevitably introduced, however, explanations of them are given and suggestions are made as to alternatives.

The Order Aurum Solis is a representative of the Ogdoadic school of the Western Mystery Tradition. The systems of symbolism and methods of attainment of the Ogdoadic school have profoundly influenced Western thought at many points in its development: its great symbol, the eightpointed Star of Regeneration, and its use of the fivefold pattern of the House of Sacrifice, that is, the Qabalistic pattern of the psyche, as a schema of concepts in areas mystically relating to the human condition, are widespread in medieval, Renaissance, and modern art and literature. This Gnostic-Qabalistic system of initiation can be traced back historically for a thousand years, setting aside the question of its earlier roots.

It thus clearly predates the Rosicrucian school, and is one of the oldest surviving branches of the Western Mystery Tradition.[1]

Besides the Pathworkings up to Tiphareth, with the elucidations needed for the initial entry into that Sephirah and the World of Briah, this book contains the complete material required for effective working and understanding of these Paths. The particular formulation of the Tree of Life is explained, whereby Pathworking can lead not only from mode to mode of consciousness but also from level to higher level. The inner operations of the psyche are described, whereby the general words of a guided meditation which contains certain key concepts and images will become the true personal experience of each member of a group: no two experiences are exactly alike. You are shown how to discover the unending inner drama of the Paths at even greater depths in your own psyche by means of your dreams. An effective formula for opening a Pathworking is given, and, besides the texts themselves, there are reflections upon the inner meaning of each Path. The chief correspondences of each Path—the key concepts and images themselves—are listed out for meditation, and, additionally to the Pathworkings proper, an effective technique with the use of a specially designed Mandala is given to assure the meditator of easy entrance upon each one of the Paths. In addition, a chapter is devoted to the special uses of isolated (or "selective") Pathworkings, whether for purposes of "soul sculpture"—the enhancement or overcoming of particular qualities in one's own character—or in conjunction with magical procedures for other objectives. For use in connection with such isolated Pathworkings (even the working performed by a group as part of a magical festival, or by an individual for the sheer pleasure of it) simple rites are given, invoking the appropriate Sephirothic archetypal powers so as to resolve or balance those workings, as required. For the purpose of visualization in these rites, portrayals of the relevant Sephirothic powers are also given.

The "soul sculpture" uses of isolated Pathworkings, as well as the self-balancing upward progress of the workings taken in series, opens up

---

1. The teachings and history of the Order Aurum Solis itself are given in the four volumes of *The Magical Philosophy* series, also published by Llewellyn.

new and exciting prospects in therapeutic directions. Here is a technique which involves not only the conscious personality, but the physical neural circuitry itself (as the "adventure" situations of the Path narratives are designed to do), and which reaches down to the deep and unconscious levels of the psyche. In this way unaccustomed or unpracticed areas of the psyche and of the neural circuitry are activated, not in any haphazard manner but according to the system of a venerable and tried tradition. In Pathworkings properly performed, the patterns of inner activity here encountered will re-link whatever may need adjustment, through the conscious and unconscious functions of the psyche itself, to the veritable archetypes whose powers directly and indirectly set the norms of action and aspiration for the psyche. There is no conflict here between the potential of low-level and of high-level adjustment, since we are dealing with an initiatory system based on the primal structure of the psyche itself and designed for the coordination and integration of the entire psycho-physical person with all functions in their right hierarchy and balance.

As is shown in Chapter 3, the dream life of the individual can easily be brought into the procedure, so that any supposed danger of "stereotyping" is manifestly avoided, and the entire personality is introduced into the drama, the pilgrimage, the inner processional dance of Pathworking. As to the physical body, there can be no doubt of the benefits to it, too, from the psychic equilibrium, and from the harmonious neural impulses engendered by eventful narrrative, by the meditative state, and by ritual archetypally directed. Perhaps the great potential of Pathworking and its associated techniques for group therapy, and for clinical work, will be taken up by others who see, as we do, the powerful instrument for exploration and adjustment which here lies ready to hand.

Magical States of Consciousness is a complete guide to Pathworking, both as an art in itself and as a means of entering the Sephiroth, up to Tiphareth. The subject has many aspects and wide interest. It is the hope of the authors that it will be a fruitful means to inner adventure and understanding, and to true spiritual advancement, for all readers.

Bright Blessings,

D & P

Twin Cities, August 1984

chapter 1

Magical States
of Consciousness

In every person, the qualities which are essential for the development of magical powers and the acceleration of spiritual evolution are innate: yet even people who recognize these potentials within themselves and aspire to realize them, still need effective means of progess. One requirement is a form of training which will enable the aspirant to recognize, to select, and to direct the will effectively to life's underlying archetypal realities.

The tangled network of thoughts, feelings and sensations which fills day-to-day life constitutes a problem, since in its meshes attention, energy and resolve are scattered and dispersed. For dealing with this problem, one of the methods which has been recognized through the ages is an ascetic program of simplifying the aspirant's experience of life, and at the same time continually analyzing every inner response to the remaining stimuli ruthlessly into its archetypal components.

In both Western and Eastern cultures, such ascetic programs have had and continue to have their value: for our sources of power are not any quality nor component of the conscious personality, but the great archetypes which are present to (not part of) the depths of the psyche. Virtue or wide experience of life, deep learning or childlike simplicity:

these qualities have value to the aspiring mystic or magician insofar as, and only insofar as, they clarify our perception of, and contact with, the archetypal powers.

The archetypes with which we are here concerned are by no means all the possible archetypes which may subsist either in the collective Unconscious or in the Divine Mind. For millennia it has been recognized that there are an essential seven to which all that pertains to magical or mystical power, indeed all that pertains to human life, may be aggregated; adding to these another three, we have all that pertains to the universe both outer and inner, both cosmic and microcosmic, as seen by humankind. For, both physically and metaphysically, we can perceive only those phenomena which we have faculties to perceive. Though this be a truism, it is well worth stating because it simplifies at one stroke the task of explaining man's direct relationship with, and correspondence to, his universe.

These ten archetypal sources of power correspond to the ten Sephiroth, the "spheres" of the Tree of Life. To apprehend any of them directly in its spiritual reality is a work of consummate adepthood: to apprehend the highest of them directly is to pass beyond the lower worlds of existence into the realm of that pure being which is a continual becoming. Happily, however, there is another way of proceeding, and it is the way which magical and mystical practices have ever followed. Each of the Sephiroth has its counterpart within each one of us: and that counterpart is also a focal point for the power of the Sephirah in question, just as that very point on a mirror which reflects the light of the sun or of a powerful lamp will project its heat also. We can, therefore, work with these coutnerparts within ourselves—and for greatest effectiveness this working involves the body as well as the psyche—so as to come at the veritable powers of the sephirothic archetypes.

To work thus, by image and by enactment, by calling forth within the self the effect which is to be produced in the outer worlds—this, from the earliest traces we can find of humankind, has been the method of priest and of magician.

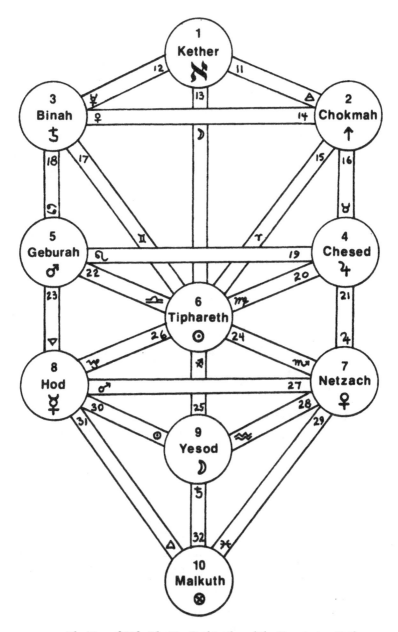

The Tree of Life: The Ten Sephiroth and the Twenty-two Paths

In respect of what is to follow here, it is necessary at this point to give only a brief indication of the nature of the ten Sephirothic spheres which are shown upon our diagram of the Tree. The highest Sephirah, Kether, is the primal and unconditioned source of all the rest. It is the initial point of positive spiritual energy in our universe, the First Cause, in whatever manner one conceives of it. It is also, to the individual person, that particular Divine Flame which is at once the source and the center of one's being. Next, and proceeding from this primal Cause, come the two great spiritual powers designated respectively as the Supernal Father—creative force in action—and the Supernal Mother—formative force in action, giving viability to, but also necessarily in some manner constricting, the energies of the Father. To the depths of the psyche, these Supernal Parents are represented by the high archetypes of Animus and Anima, lesser images of which are made manifest to the less profound levels of the personality with whatever cultural or individual bias and detail may be added.

Thus far the Supernals: they are vital to our understanding and use of the Tree as a whole, although we do no magical work directly with them. The Third Sephirah, that of the Supernal Mother, has however another and more accessible identity as the sphere of Saturn, the highest of the traditional planetary spheres. The power of the Mother, who is both dark and bright (as the Qabalists knew long before Freud discovered her ambivalence) is enthroned as it were behind the figure of Saturn who is ruler alike of primeval opulence and fecundity and of the barren rocks.

Saturn, Jupiter, Mars, Sol, Venus, Mercury and Luna: these, the seven traditional luminaries of astrology, are represented by the third through the ninth Sephirothic spheres. Their qabalistic characters are not entirely identical with their astrological influences, although qabalistic and astrological understanding can usefully supplement each other: but the differences need not detain us. The general nature of each of these spheres is sufficiently well known to everyone for a beginning, and more will be made clear in the course of this book.

The tenth and lowest sphere represents this planet Earth, or, micro-cosmically, our physical body: in either case it is seen to be the recipient of the influences of all the other spheres.[2]

Our chief magical concern, then, is with the seven Sephiroth which have been designated as "planetary": the third (in its lower aspect) through the ninth. Each of these is the source to us of a particular type of power, distinct from the others in character and in purpose. Among them these seven comprise the whole range of human life: it is note-worthy in this regard that the astrologers, exploring the significances of the "new planets" Uranus, Neptune and Pluto, have found that these can in general terms be regarded as higher octaves of functions already within the domain of one or other of the traditional seven.

As mystical or magical aspirant, therefore, you need to be able, at will, to place yourself in a state of attunement with each of these seven sephirothic sources of power: that is to say, you need to be able to induce in yourself the Magical State of Consciousness of each. Your first objective in so doing is to receive and to familiarize yourself with each, so as to individuate and strengthen the counterpart of each within the depths of your psyche. Thus you will nourish and increase your per-sonal magical potential, and at the same time ensure the balanced prog-ress of your spiritual development. Then, having strengthened those archetypal counterparts and enhanced your awareness of them, and having learned to attune yourself readily to the powers of the spheres, you will be able to draw upon the mighty resources of one or another of those powers, as may be required whether in magical workings or in daily life.

There are two great magical methods for achieving these states of consciousness. First, there is the art of Sphere Working. This consists of techniques of building up directly, and of magically empowering, the influences of a particular sphere, whether for the purpose simply

---

2. Each of the ten Sephiroth, considered at its highest level—in the World of Atzi-luth—represents an aspect of the Divine Nature itself. This does not make the Divine Nature less than infinite: only as much of it as is knowable to us is here outlined in attributes.

of meditating in it and strengthening oneself thereby, or for the potent performance within that ambience of some specific working.

There is also the art of Pathworking, the subject of the present book. These two magical skills can very effectively be combined, but it is most desirable that the newcomer to them should acquire proficiency in Pathworking before any attempt is made in Sphereworking.

The reason for this can be stated simply. In building up the ambience of a Sphere, there is no great difficulty in ensuring that all components are included which are necessary for the magical reality of the experience of that Sphere. It is quite difficult, however, unless certain precautions are taken, to ensure that no additional incongruous factor has crept in, which, being an impurity, would vitiate the whole power of the operation.

As in some procedures of medieval magick, a long period of preparation might be undertaken, including the preparation of the operator who would need meanwhile to eat only foods harmonious to the sphere of the intended operation, to wear only suitable colors and to meditate only on suitable subjects, lest body or psyche unwittingly bring something alien into the ambience. Or an exhaustive and exhausting magical banishing of every influence might be performed, necessarily including, as Crowley points out, "the very one which we wish to invoke, for that force as existing in Nature is always impure." (*Magick in Theory and Practice*, Chapter III.) For a simple Sphereworking, such massive precautions are needless if the operator has sufficient experience, and the sensitivity which comes with such experience, to throw out anything incongruous whether it be discerned as an objective or subjective factor: it is also needless if the Sphere is reached by means of one of the related Paths of the Tree of Life, for they are designed to lead the person who experiences them from the Sphere at the head of the Path, through a traditional and consecrated preparatory influence which belongs specifically to that one Path, and thence into the integrity of the Sphere which closes that Path.

The aspirant thus gains the experience of savoring the Magical States of Consciousness of the Sephiroth in fully safeguarded conditions: and when once a Sphere has been gained and its particular quality is known, the aspirant has right of entry to it thereafter by any magical or meditative means. At the same time, there is no reason against repetition of the Pathworking experience; the Paths can never be too thoroughly known, and repetition at no matter what period thereafter will usually produce unforeseen benefits.

The importance of knowing, and of employing, the sephirothic powers in their pure state cannot be overemphasized. Just as eating pure foods and breathing pure air will work through the body to benefit the whole person, so in a more subtle but even more vital manner, nourishing the psyche by contact with the sephirothic archetypes will benefit the whole person. To realize the truth of this, apart from personal experience, perhaps the surest way is to be convinced of the antithesis: not only the mere impotent confusion of everyday life but the real damage wrought in the entire personality by a marked failure to distinguish the sephirothic archetypes.

Crowley, who gives many counsels on the need to work with pure forces, at one point gives an illustration of the reverse confusion, based on the story of an unenlightened character in Dickens' *Oliver Twist*: he points out that the "spirit of the nature of Venus" and the "Martial or Saturnian spirit" which attend Bill Sykes in his course of love, hate and murder, "are not pure planetary spirits, moving in well-defined spheres ... They are gross concretions of confused impulses ... They are also such that the idea of murder is nowise offensive to the Spirit of Love." (*Magick in Theory and Practice*, Chapter XVI pt. 1.)

Another and even more striking example is shown by means of two drawings reproduced in one of the works of Carl Jung. Here the powers involved in confusion (in the unconscious acceptance of a particular individual) are those of the two Supernal Parents, represented in the functioning of the psyche as Animus and Anima. One of these drawings depicts two beings, mermaid and merman, who have one fish-tail by means of which they are joined back to back. Each of them looks out unhappily into vacuity, each evidently suffers from a desperate loneliness which cannot be cured so long as they are thus captive to one another. In the second drawing, their separation has been effected: each is now a complete being, and the arms of mermaid and merman are entwined about one another in a joyful embrace. It has to be realized that no matter how far distant from the conscious mind of the individual might be the events thus symbolically represented, the initial frustration and grief, and the subsequent sense of rightness, joy and fulfillment, would certainly influence the whole of the life of the person in question.

Pathworking, then, affords a sure and exact method by which the consciousness of even the beginner can be safely guided into the true experience of sphere after sphere: and it also affords an excellent psychic toner for all, even for the most experienced student of the practical Qabalah.

Here, indeed, we have a superb example of the Qabalistic system being directly and exactly brought into practical working, and being fully justified in the result. The distinctive feature of each of the Paths of the Tree of Life is the special influence which is operative upon it, additionally to the influences of the Spheres at its two ends. This special influence upon the Path can be designated in various ways, each of which opens up a new approach by which we can understand it. One such designation for each Path is a specific letter of the Hebrew alphabet, comprising its form and significance, its numeration, and even a consideration of certain Hebrew words incorporating it. Another designation is a corresponding planetary influence, zodiacal sign, or element as the case may be; while yet another is a specific card from the Major Arcana of the Tarot, again with its own character, significance and associations.

With each Path there are also associated its own colors, incenses, gemstones, symbolic beasts and plants, through the whole range of the "Qabalistic correspondences": many of these are traditional, and carry the power of long magical usage as well as that of their intrinsic fitness, but, when once the principle is assimilated, an up-to-date innovation based on sound magical reason is preferable to the use of a traditional correspondence which has outlasted either its suitability or its practicality.

Much the same observations apply to the texts of the Pathworkings themselves. A Pathworking is, essentially, a "guided meditation" designed to lead the participants into the Magical State of Consciousness of the Sphere which is approached, so that an authentic entry into it may be effected. To achieve this, it is necessary that in the course of the working itself the participants shall become so deeply immersed in the contents of the text as to be lifted, even at that stage, into a state of consciousness somewhat altered from the everyday level. This condition is, in fact, most often attained by the majority of participants in a Pathworking; and the further transition to the state of consciousness of the goal is proportionately facilitated. Something here depends on the leadership and the magical status of the reader of the text; but the main onus rests and must rest upon the text itself.

Every valid Order of the Western Mystery Tradition possesses, or can be presumed to have possessed in the past, its own series of Pathworkings, incorporating the essential traditional concepts but suited in spirit and in detail to the teachings and perspective of the individual Order: suited, too, to the generation for which they were composed. The teachings and perspective of Aurum Solis, while in a sense undoubtedly as distinctive as any, have at the same time been marked consistently by a conscious will to embody the pure mainstream Western Mystery Tradition, from the Ogdoadic viewpoint, certainly, but without singularity and without prejudice.

Even the current of magical thought and purpose, however, veers slightly with the times; and to remain faithful to its intention of attunement to the psychic ambience, the Aurum Solis has had to make adjustments to a number of its traditional texts, those of the Paths included. There have, therefore, been revisions in these texts: but the specific character of each Path remains unchanged. Above all, nothing has been changed needlessly or for the sake of conformity with what seems to be a passing fashion: neither has there seemed any good purpose in giving a "New Age" slant to that which is deeper than the tides of the ages. It has, however, seemed to be a good opportunity for removing any traces of heaviness or rhetoric.

The planetary influence, zodiacal sign or Element attributed to a Path is often the principal factor experienced by the participant. These attributions can be at first sight surprising, but they are never irrational or arbitrary.

It is precisely by passing through the experience of this attribution that the participant is conditioned for the transition to the culminating Magical State of Consciousness, in a way which could not occur if an attempt were made simply to transfer the consciousness directly from sphere to sphere.

Some meditative reflection upon the "why" of the conditioning influences on each Path is likely to afford a deeper insight into the nature of that Path than can readily be conveyed by the printed word. However, one or two examples may indicate a fruitful approach to the subject matter.

For instance: the diagram of the Tree shows Path 14, which unites Binah to Chokmah—the sphere of the Supernal Mother to that of the Supernal Father—as carrying the symbol of the planet Venus. The Hebrew letter is Daleth, "the Door," the Tarot Arcanum is The Empress. The significance is plainly of love, harmony, increase, and this is what we might expect. But, in the lower part of the Tree, what of Path 27 which similarly unites Hod with Netzach, the Sphere of Mercury with that of Venus, the Sphere of Magick with that of Nature? Despite the greater complexity in this part of the Tree, surely we might expect to find some almost equally harmonious influence here? But in fact, this Path 27 carries the sign of the planet Mars. The Hebrew letter is Peh, representing the mouth and tongue with a connotation of anger, and the Tarot image is The Tower Struck by Lightning. What can we learn from this?

The particular virtue of the Tower is that its inmates are thrown clear of it. An "explosion" takes place whose effects are, ultimately, altogether salubrious. Without it, the persons would be trapped in the outward shell of their situation, confused by material considerations, and incapable of attaining the Venusian peace and harmony of the resolution. From a psychological viewpoint, it is notable that the persons are flung to safety head downwards. To emphasize this circumstance, the tower itself is generally shown as being deprived of its "head," or crown, by the lightning strike. The suggestion here is that the harmony between Hod and Netzach is not effected by the superficial personality but by the deeper levels. The entrapping tower seems to be associated with a too fixed, or too materialistic, view of life. The emotions need to find a voice, in some cases even a voice of anger, to break the domination of this outer shell.

The attributions of the Paths can also be usefully compared with one another in relation to the pattern of the Tree. Their positions in relation to each other are not random, but they form the balanced pattern of a living organism rather than any mechanical symmetry of human devising. The makers of the Tree have explored *what* is, not set forth a simplistic scheme of what by human standards *should be*.

Thus, when we compare the attribution of Path 31 (from the Earth Sphere, Malkuth, to Hod, Sphere of Mercury) with that of Path 29 (from Malkuth to Netzach, Sphere of Venus) there may at first be some surprise that while the one is elemental Fire, the other is not elemental Water but the watery zodiacal sign of The Fishes. Since Hod is an abode of Science (among other things) and Netzach an abode of Nature, a reason for the more "animate" attribution in the approach to the latter Sphere easily presents itself. In each case, however, the Hebrew letter of the Path warns us that in moving from everyday consciousness to the mentality of the destination, a progress has to be made which may seem like a regression. On Path 31 we have *Shin*, "the Tooth," the Devourer. The intending scientist and the intending magician alike must put aside that mundane possessiveness which clings to sentiments and prejudices as well as to material things: all the emotional and self-indulgent clutter of life is, on this Path, only food for the hungry tooth of Fire.

On Path 29, that of The Fishes, the Hebrew letter is *Qoph*, "the back of the head." If one is to be "in the swim" with the forces of Nature, the austerely purified intellectual force which lifts one towards Hod would be completely out of place. It is of interest that the pituitary gland, situated in the midst of the brain, is concerned with such physical functions as the circulation of blood, bodily growth, and the action of giving birth: while, as a more obvious association with the image of The Fishes, the name of the pituitary gland derives from a traditional association with the "phlegmatic," cool and stolid temperament.

To pursue our comparison of Paths, when we approach Hod and Netzach respectively from Yesod, the change in the attribution of the Path in each case is at once intelligible. We are now setting out not from the Earth Sphere, but from the Sphere of the Moon, the Sphere of imagination, even of fantasy, which rules the astral world. The approach to Hod is now by the Path, not of Shin but of Resh: not of Fire but of the Sun. Here we have not simply a passive purification and reconstitution, but also inspiration and the force of personal creativity. Similarly, in proceeding to Netzach not from Malkuth but from Yesod, we are no longer on the Path of Pisces but on that of Aquarius: no longer of passive immersion in the currents of natural life, but with an implication that we should take a creative part in the interrelationship thus established. (True "moral responsibility" does not subsist in the Paths below Tiphareth—a point which could clear up many thorny theological problems—but on this 28th Path the constraining power of the Supernal Mother is reflected with particular force.)

The present book does not cover the full range of twenty-two Paths. Intended as it is for practical use, it is limited to those Paths upon which the proposed method—that of guided meditation—is of proven, true and traditional worth in magical practice: that is to say, on that whole series of Paths, counting down from 32 through 24, which together lead the aspirant to the attainment of the Magical State of Consciousness of Tiphareth, the Sun Sphere. The opening of the consciousness of this Sphere marks so salient a point in the inner development of the individual, that a complete change of approach in the presentation of materials for the Paths above Tiphareth is customary: while, however, even mages and mystics of many years' standing can benefit from time to time by a "refresher course" in the Paths below Tiphareth, and can always find further aspects therein for meditation.

With each of the Paths has been associated in magical tradition one of the great philosophic schools of pre-Socratic to Renaissance times: schools whose teachings are in truth timeless. So long and earnestly have the philosophers debated their claims throughout history, that plainly their differences would have been resolved long ago if they could in fact be resolved in purely philosophic terms. The real basis for these irresolvable differences (when once the mere misunderstandings, which Wittgenstein indicated, have been removed) lies not in the realm of the rational intellect but in the personal psychology of the philosophers.

The allocation of the different schools, in broad terms, to the different Paths of the Tree is therefore a valid concept, and, so far from discrediting the philosophies, it prevents their discrediting each other and gives them a new and perennial value. For, no matter what may be the personal bias of soul of each one of us, nevertheless every one of the Paths exists somewhere in our composition: and the more completely, by study and reflection, we can bring them in a balanced manner into consciousness, the more channels of communication we shall open up within ourselves and the greater measure of life, at all levels, we shall be fitted to enjoy.

For those who may wish to explore the philosophic attributions of the Paths up to Tiphareth, they are as follows:

32. Orphism: the step from the domination of the material world, into the realm of vision, symbol and mystery.

31. Stoicism, particularly the philosophy of Heraclitus.

30. Alchemy: the discipline of the psyche through the natural order.

29. Epicureanism, as Epicurus intended it.

28. Humanism: control of the natural order by enlightened human understanding.

27. Drama as *katharsis*: violent cults of the Mother, as that of Attis.

26. Aristotelianism, especially of the Nicomachean Ethics.

25. Mystical cults of Dionysus. The continuity of this Path from the Orphism of Path 32 has a philosophical, not a chronological significance. The intersection of Paths 27 and 25 represents that vital relationship between the cults of Dionysus and of the Mother which Euripides saw to be symbolized by the timbrel.

24. Gnostic teachings on the Great Mother. Death and rebirth as philosophic imagery may be traced back to the pre-Socratic Leucippus (the atomist), if a concept so basic to human thinking can be given an origin.

chapter 2

The Paths and Initiatory Progress

In the foregoing chapter an observation is made which, while it can pre-eminently be demonstrated and applied through the Qabalah, also forms the basis of other systems of initiation, spiritual development and magical practice in both East and West. This observation is that the inner plan of the human individual—body and psyche—and the pattern of the universe as humanly conceived (or of some essential spiritual pattern in the universe) are in nature and essence the same. From this perception it is but a natural magical step to conceive a procedure to reunite the cosmic and microcosmic patterns so as to perfect, renew or activate the one by means of the other.

In some instances this operation may be visualized as performed within the person: but this inward operation is intended, step by step or at the last, to reverberate with a cosmic spiritual counterpart with whose force the energies of the operator are thus united. This is the method of some forms of yoga, for example, including Kundalini Yoga.

In other instances the practitioner dramatizes, narrates, visualizes— or any combination of these—a progressive series of happenings. These events, which may involve deific or heroic characters, are considered initially as taking place in some remote era, locality or level of being. The practitioner, with any other participants, is carried along by the narrative and, when the outcome is reached, will receive its archetypal force for whatever purpose the operation is performed. This force can be transferred to another person (as in a rite of healing) or even to a material object (as in charging a talisman). It is also one of the great methods of effecting an initiation.

Coming to Qabalistic usage specifically, the Tree of Life, which is a compendium of plans of the major and minor workings of the psyche, offers a range of initiatory patterns both major and minor. The major patterns have been utilized at different times by different Orders—mystical, philosophic, occult, of some specific religious affiliation or of none—and changes have undoubtedly occured in the practical application of these patterns, for both the human requirements and the interpretations of the Tree have varied.

It is to the Tree as it exists within each individual—that is, to the "microcosmic Tree"—that the initiatory patterns are particularly related, since it is upwards through the levels of the candidate's own nature that initiation must lead. For initiation is always the revelation, the making accessible, of something which is already an integral part of the candidate's spiritual heritage: it is never the creation of anything new.

This initiatory process moves "upwards" in two senses. It is not only a progress "upwards" through the Sephiroth from Malkuth towards Kether, as could be indicated upon any diagram of the Tree. It is at the same time a progess of consciousness up through the Four Worlds: and it is here that the concept of the "Composite Tree" has to be introduced. The Composite Tree has been known and recognized in Qabalistic thought and writing for many centuries, and progress through it is organized upon a definite plan.

At the lowest level of this plan, the Sphere of Earth is considered as this planet upon which we live, in its material aspect only, with the various animal, plant and mineral bodies which are portions of it: our own physical bodies included. In Qabalistic terminology, this is the Sephirah Malkuth in the World of Assiah.

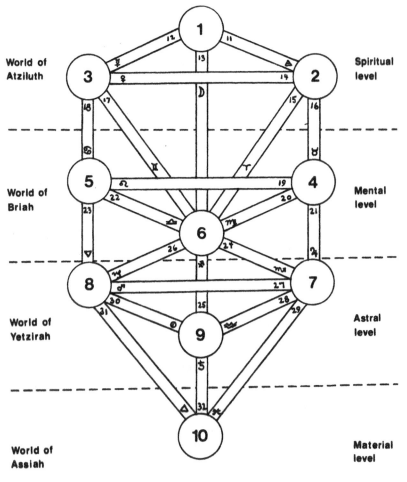

The Composite Tree

Our consciousness ascends from this level (to which in practice it is never naturally confined) to the Sephirah Yesod: and at the same time it passes through the gate of that Sephirah into the World of Yetzirah, which comprises the whole wide range of the astral, including its lower level which is sometimes termed the "etheric" world. In terms of our own nature, the World of Yetzirah includes everything from those sensory perceptions which enmesh with their physical causes and effects, through the instincts and emotions up to and including our highest emotional feelings no matter what their spiritual or esthetic causation.

Having entered the World of Yetzirah through the Gate of Yesod, you can move (and this book gives you the means to move by the tried and traditional "Paths") into the two other "States of Consciousness" which are comprised in the astral world. There is no need to remain in a state of dream-consciousness, of illusion and fantasy, or to be governed entirely by your sensations, instincts and impulses: you can "travel" to the Sephirah Hod, which is the sphere, or mode of consciousness, represented by the planet Mercury: that is to say, the Sphere of knowledge, and pre-eminently the Sphere of scientific, mathematical and magical knowledge, of the acquisition and employment of such knowledge. And you can "travel" to the Sephirah Netzach, which is the "sphere" or mode of consciousness of the life forces, the powers of nature.

In the plan of Pathworking, when you have overcome the fears, frustrations and nostalgias of the 32nd Path so as to give your emotional-instinctual nature the freedom of the Sephirah Yesod, you are qualified next to achieve Hod, the Sphere of science and magick: first from Malkuth, the Earth Sphere, by the 31st Path which confronts us with the hard concept that if life is regarded as the *materium* of an objectively-realized "trial by fire", then we ourselves are in the crucible along with the rest. Then, reaching the same destination from the dream-region of Yesod, you attain it by methods (still familiar to the present-day scientist) of analogy, symbol and hypothesis in soaring flights of the mind which often avail more than a thousand earthling collations of data.

Similarly, when you travel to the Nature Sphere of Netzach: even though all your journeying is still in the astral world, you will go first from the Sphere of Earth by the 29th Path, through miry ways and as it were under the light of the waning moon. You will thus gain the vision and the gladness of the unity of all life, but this has been a fact from the beginning and it may not, in itself, suggest a motive for further action: the "materialist" approach from the Earth Sphere does not prompt creativity. Then, however, you will take the 28th Path, again to Netzach but from Yesod, and to the experience you have will be added the airy breath of romance and of inspiration to give wings of initiative to your vision.

Another "initiation"—another revelation to you of the powers within you—is to be made at this purely astral level of your being, and that is the journey from Hod to Netzach by the 27th Path. Why is this Path so explosive? There are various considerations involved, all valid at different levels of being; but the one which seems most appropriate to indicate here is the radically different *attitude of mind* encountered betweeen these two Sephiroth. Even when a person does not deliberately take refuge in knowledge as a defense against reality, it is a fact that knowledge can deaden the psyche to the impact of truth. Any false refuges in mere knowledge have to be broken down completely if we are to experience the forces of life in their fullness.

This, it should be noted, is a simple statement of fact. Nowhere in these Paths below Tiphareth—not even in the Paths which lead directly into that Sephirah—is there, strictly, any question of "moral obligation." The Paths, and the philosophies concerned with them, below Tiphareth are entirely occupied with the observation and experience of natural cause and effect. Nor is there a question of any one of the modes of consciousness which are associated with the Sephiroth being "better" than another. The astral awareness into which we enter in Yesod is developed into a mode of knowing and doing in Hod, and into a mode of feeling and being in Netzach (to state the matter in very general terms). The undifferentiated astral perception, the "dream mind" of Yesod, is adaptable to some purposes which are particular to that Sephirah, purposes for which the modes of consciousness of Hod or of Netzach would not take its place: but the modes of consciousness of all three of these Sephiroth, which in the composite Tree belong to the World of Yetzirah, are essential to our functioning in the fullness of our nature. Their assimilation is thus necessary before we can progress further.

It is not proposed here to comment on the 26th, 25th, and 24th Paths: what needs to be said beforehand of them will be given in the next chapter. Here remains to be stated that with entrance to Tiphareth a complete change takes place, not merely in the mode of consciousness as with any Sephirah, but also in the level of consciousness. For Tiphareth is the Gate of the World of Briah. From the astral world, the World of Yetzirah—the world of imagination, of the use of sensory data and of deductive reasoning—the initiate now crosses the threshold of the great World of Briah: the world of "Mind" in its truest sense.

The rational mind, the Ruach, properly belongs to the World of Briah. However, in its "uninitiated" state—that is, before the consciousness has passed through the Gate of Tiphareth—the rational mind can function only as the organizer of Yetziratic materials since these alone are accessible to it. These materials include personal experience, which comprises sense data and an awareness of our impulses and emotions: also what we learn from others whether we classify that learning as scientific, historical, magical, metaphysical or any other. Upon all these materials—personal experience and acquired knowledge—the rational mind can work with great elaboration and subtlety: but it cannot, without the true Briatic consciousness, go beyond those limits.

In Briah the Ruach becomes accustomed to another kind of activity: not only *reasoning about* a matter, but having direct intuitive contact with that matter in its reality. This is through the working of the Intuitive Mind, of which the rational mind is the destined vehicle. It is this contact which brings the Ruach to its rightful development and which also brings the whole personality into the proportions of its true nature: human nature in its plenitude, no matter how far above the norms of human nature as generally conceived of.

Naturally, this immense development is not realized in its entirety as soon as the initiate enters the Gate of Tiphareth. While none can say that it could not, in ideal conditions, become manifest in a flash, there are other Sephiroth—Geburah and Chesed—to be entered in completing the experience of the Briatic World, and—as in all spiritual matters—the tasks to be accomplished grow immensely with the powers received for their achievement. But, it remains true that with the first simple experience of Tiphareth, that change is effected without which the rest would remain impossible: that entire certainty in *looking within* for Light which is a prime distinguishing characteristic of the adept. Even this change itself may take time to work through to the surface of consciousness and of daily life: but work through it will, like a growing seed or like the action of yeast in rising dough.

Here the psyche receives its first intimations of "divine intoxication": of the ability, and the need, to let go of the sense-data and acquired knowledge which have hitherto been its nourishment, so as to receive intimations from the Intuitive Mind whose source, as yet hidden, is higher still in the world of Atziluth.

The term "intoxication" should not mislead. Inadequate though it is, it has been used repeatedly in a number of languages through the centuries of the Western tradition, to express something which cannot otherwise be so succinctly named. As in earthly intoxication the outward appearance of things loses reality and importance, so in this intoxication the fascinations and fantasies of the imagination lose their hold over the will. Just as in earthly intoxication a person's words may fail through the non-functioning of the physical organs of speech, so here too a person may be from time to time inarticulate because of the failure of language, since only symbol and metaphor are available to express perceived truth. Indeed, these difficulties will be overcome and will pass until the initiate meets with them anew at a higher level: yet still in Briah there are perceptions, increasingly, of a reality which is more alluring than fantasy, of an inner illumination which is clearer and lovelier than any outward light, and of an unutterable sweetness at the center of being itself.

On the plan of the composite Tree there are two Spheres to be entered at the Briatic level: Geburah, which may be characterized as the Sephirah of Justice, and Chesed, which may be characterized as the Sephirah of Mercy. At the Yetziratic level some antithesis or opposition between justice and mercy is almost implicit in the very words, but in Briah the perfect balance and harmony between Geburah and Chesed is manifest. Each represents a State of Consciousness entirely distinct in nature from the other, yet the existence of each is complementary to the other. Justice in its perfection presupposes the existence of mercy: mercy in its perfection requires the existence of justice.

The Paths which, in this plan of the Composite Tree, are worked within the World of Briah, are the 23rd, 22nd, 21st, 20th, and 19th. They are governed by images of great brightness, beauty and evocative force: reflections of divine attributes humanly perceived.

Atziluth, the World of the divine, is represented on the Composite Tree by the three Supernal Sephiroth Binah, Chokmah, and Kether and the related Paths. Human ability to enter that World is sometimes contested, but is recognized in mystical theology and in Qabalistic thought, for the highest and inmost part of our nature is native to that World. The attainment of it is, however, supremely guarded by peril and obstacle. To enter the World of Yetzirah, the inertia of materiality must be overcome; to enter the World of Briah, the Gate of Tiphareth must be passed. To enter Atziluth, one must "cross the Abyss," a venture not easily to be undertaken even when the Paths and Sephiroth of Briah have been achieved.

Beyond the Abyss, attainment for its own sake is meaningless. The supernal Paths are traversed because the psyche yearns to realize the purpose of its being: if it is delayed therein, it is only because of the works, both outer and inner, which remain to be done for a more complete fulfillment of the Divine Plan.

This account of the composite Tree has gone far, although only in briefest outline, beyond the scope of the present book. It has in equal measure gone beyond the power of any human being to initiate another, properly speaking: for beyond Tiphareth the growing awareness of the Intuitive Mind can alone bring the adept into the realization of each stage of his or her further progress. Nevertheless an Order can, by conferring one of the higher grades, make acknowledgment of progress inwardly attained.

The purpose of this sketch is to show that the Paths of the Tree of Life, when understood in their relationship to the Four Worlds, or levels of consciousness, upon the Composite Tree, do indeed provide an effective system of inward initiation. Progress upwards in this manner likewise provides at each stage for the integration of those components in the psyche which have been brought into consciousness, so that all is kept in balance and develops in its rightful proportions. Thus (to bring in another Qabalistic concept) do we tread the coils of the Serpent Way of Return.

In the life of a magical Order, the Pathworkings are arranged so as to align with the course of ceremonial initiations and to assist their effectiveness. The manner of this alignment of programs can be easily perceived with regard to the ten-grade system used by various Orders of Rosicrucian and Golden Dawn origin. It applies equally to the three-grade system of Aurum Solis, for in this system each grade corresponds specifically to one the Gate Sephiroth. The first grade, "the sowing of the seed," relates to the awakening of the candidate's inner faculties as an individual, in the World of Assiah; the second grade relates to the aspiring magician's entrance into the corporate life of the Order, in the World of Yetzirah, and the third grade is the Gate of Briah and of adepthood.

The Paths themselves, however, belong to everyone including the independent beginner in Qabalah and the adept. They have not been invented, but discovered. The symbolism of the Paths up to Tiphareth is indicted in this book, but you will discover in your own Pathworking experience the realities underlying that symbolism. The texts in this book, and the Pathworking texts of any other Order, have been compiled, not to give meaning to the Paths but to bring their meanings into intelligible form.

That, as we have indicated, is why and how the Paths are initiatory. They do not have to be grafted into your soul or graven upon a blank-washed brain. Their beauty, life, and wonder is part of the beauty, life, and wonder of your own existence. Pathworking helps you awaken to your own self, explore the mystery of your own self.

That awakening, that exploration, is Initiation.

chapter 3

Computers and Castles

Pathworking has been with us for a long time, and we have learned a great deal about the ways a Pathworking should be given and received. However, we can at the present time look at it from a new angle, and understand more about the techniques we possess: we can see further into how Pathworking works, and thus, perhaps, how we (meaning you the reader as well as us the authors) can make it work better for more people.

In itself Pathworking has long been recognized as a powerful magical procedure, leading the mind through the successive influences upon each Path, through preliminary alterations of consciousness, and thus bringing it effectively to the climactic alteration which is the entry into the sphere. The plan of these necessary influences is based on the explorations of master thinkers in Qabalah who not only have been able to deduce (or to intuit) what *should* be effective, but also, by meditative introspection within themselves and by observation of their students, to observe what was effective. Nevertheless, everyone who has conducted Pathworkings has had the experience of finding a few participants who, on one or more occasions, have had difficulty with some particular Path.

Difficulties are not always a bad thing. So long as it does not happen too often, the experience of not "making" a particular Path the first time can be good for a person. With two Paths (26 and 24) not "making" them the first time is built into the system. We may also recall the examiner who, when a youthful candidate came through the driving test with a brilliant score at first attempt, said "I'm not going to give you your license this time, because I feel you should have a little more practical experience first." Meaning, "I feel you are doing all this with your very good intellect, but intellect won't help you in an emergency; and the deeper levels of your mind, which will help you, need time and practice to assimilate what you've learned."

In a Pathworking, too, the object is to engage the deeper levels of the mind, the so-called Unconscious, which has been given that name chiefly because the rational mind is unconscious of it and its activities. A tremendous amount of activity goes on incessantly beneath the relatively placid surface of the mind. Sometimes some of these hidden functions will force themselves upon the attention of a rational consciousness which is in some way maltreating them, and sometimes they have to be coaxed into daylight for therapeutic purposes; but much of what we are learning about the unconscious functions of the mind teaches us simply to replace the lid and "don't peek at the rice before it's cooked." The unconscious functions will produce their own results by methods which have to be respected, and the rational mind's understanding of them only helps insofar as it leads us to give them optimum supplies and conditions for doing their own thing. Instead of a pot of rice, a pot of honey would be a better image for the desired return gift to us.

In fact, a hive of bees is not a bad analogy for these "functions" of the unconscious. In understanding non-material processes, whether those we ascribe to Deity or those we ascribe to the psyche, it is a time-honored procedure to look for analagous processes in the material universe, and judiciously to draw conclusions from the comparison.

A striking threefold analogy can here be considered.

The physical body is made up of an incalculable number of cells, each living its own life without impinging on our main consciousness either physically, emotionally, or intellectually except by means of messages sent through the nervous system (which is made up of cells too).

If a healing process is going on in one part of the body we may be consciously aware of symptoms of intense activity, such as heat, swelling, etc. We may apply, or swallow, materials intended either to prevent interference with the healing process by micro-organisms, or else to supply the bloodstream with nutrients to aid the healing, but the real work seems to be a joint effort of the bodily cells acting in concert among themselves.

Supposing a "foreign body" such as a bullet becomes lodged in an inaccessible part of the anatomy, where it is not lethal, and where it may even remain undetected by the main consciousness? It is too large and deepseated for the cells to work to eject it as, in time, they would eject a thorn or a splinter; but it causes disruption to surrounding tissue and could in time do further harm if not isolated. Accordingly, the cells normally build around the bullet, in process of time, a complete enclosing wall of insensitive scar tissue, thus encapsuling the bullet so that it is no longer a threat to the functioning of the body as a whole.

Now let us consider our hive of bees. Supposing, as sometimes happens a slug gets into a beehive to break down the comb and consume the honey. It is too large for the bees to eject, and if they merely killed it its putrefying corpse would continue to be a nuisance to them. Therefore, the bees solve the problem by entombing the intruder in their wax (one of the most sterile and incorruptible substances in the natural world) which they deposit little by little until the slug is completely and permanently encapsuled.

This analogy of the body-cells and the bullet with the bees and the slug is already remarkable enough: but now comes the third point, the analogy with the human mind.

Supposing a person has to cope with a traumatic experience which can neither be thrown off nor, at the person's present stage of development, assimilated? Life, after all, must go on.

The traumatic memory (as the experience has now become) frequently passes from the conscious mind, which has no faculties to handle it, into the power of the unconscious. The unconscious usually deals with it very thoroughly, hedging it about with forgetfulness, with taboos which prevent any accidental approach to it, with a complete neurosis if that be necessary so that at no time is it likely to rise into consciousness while it might cause more damage to the personal life.

It is significant that in this type of happening, when the person has matured so as to be able to cope with the original cause of trauma: when it has lost relevance, or has become somewhat diminished in proportion to other experiences—or when the person is at least confronted with the stark fact of *having survived* what had once seemed lethal—then that which had been buried for so many years can come spontaneously to remembrance, to take its place among the happenings of the life. The mind finds within itself a power of growth and development which is, in fact, beyond that of any physical organism.

Nevertheless, when we think of the host of body-cells, and the hive of bees, dealing by similar means with their respective intruders, there is nothing here to prevent us from forming the image of a throng of "mind cells" dealing with the trauma.

In primitive life, whether human or other, the multiplicity of the unconscious mind is already to some extent in evidence. The conscious mind can, properly speaking, attend only to one matter at a time although the attention can move rapidly among several matters. An unconscious monitoring of the perceptions of each sense, however, needs to be constant, so that the attention of the conscious mind can be drawn to it if need be; while obviously the actions of heart, lungs, etc.— which, being instinctual, are also monitored by the unconscious mind— have to continue. There are circumstances, however, which suggest that in the primitive state the division of functions in the unconscious is kept as simple as possible: sleep or torpor during the digestion of a meal may not be only for the conservation of energy, since we know how anxiety, or even an entertaining television program, can impair digestion for some people.

When we turn to the unconscious mind of a human being of today, however—with the multiplicity of instinctual drives, inherited qualities, mimetic impulses, educational influences, personal experiences, collations of public opinion, dramatic moments gathered from the media, moods induced by bodily states, moods induced by the environment—

our personal transcription and interpretation of every influence which has impinged upon us from before birth, any part of which can be evoked by circumstance at any moment—we must conclude that the intensely complex cellular filing system of the brain is not only a necessary instrument, but also a representative image, of an equally "cellular" unconscious mind.

The question of the relationship of mind and brain should not sidetrack us. While it is worth pointing out that up-to-date researches are coming continually closer to the perception that brain is a product and instrument of mind (instead of mind being a mere product of brain, as the old view of materialist medicine has it), the question is barely relevant here as we are concerned entirely with living beings who use mind and brain together.

The "cell-mind" theory, which from many evidential viewpoints presents a model corresponding with reality, has been arrived at along avenues of inquiry other than ours, by experts Minsky and Papert who call their theory "The Society of Minds."[3] They call attention to groupings which we may term committees and sub-committees among the "small minds" of their system (which are the same as our "cell-minds"), and above all they point out the great amount of understanding we can gain of the workings of human thought, by exploration of the possibilities of the computer. We take up our own theme again from that point, whose value we heartily endorse. Seeing that the computer is an invention of the human mind, it is hardly surprising that the human mind can find something of itself mirrored therein and, gazing upon its own likeness, can find much which it had not consciously realized from its unaided inward cogitations.

A conclusion which follows clearly from these observations is that it is not the judgmental rational mind, but the unconscious, which bears the true likeness to the computer: to a computer which, before we begin deliberately to feed any data into it, is already pre-programmed with all the impulses, influences, and memories aforementioned.

---

3. "Of Two Minds" by Patrick Hughe, in *Psychology Today* (December 1983).

Here the question arises: *How, in such a situation, does the conscious, rational mind retain its supremacy and remain the decision-maker?*

The supremacy and the decision-making prerogative assumed by the rational mind to be its natural privileges are, in part, illusory; as, indeed, those privileges are when wielded by almost any human individual or group. The first privilege depends on the second, and the second depends upon what the mind, person or group knows and how it, he, she or they may have been conditioned to feel about that knowledge. It is not necessarily a question of whether it, he, she, or they think "logically." "Logic" has about as much to do with the matter as a food-processing machine has to do with the quality of the dinner: the machine can only process what is fed into it, and has no part in the selection of those materials. And for most people, the material offered to the conscious mind for judgment is pre-selected by the preprogrammed unconscious, even if external human agencies have no direct hand in the matter.

How do *you*, then, achieve true autonomy? The first and most important step is to realize that *you* are a complete person, not just a rational mind. Don't fight yourself. The unconscious mind is not "always right," but you as a complete person have it as a component just as you have your physical body and your rational mind as components. All this richness of identity is "you": not as something to deplore, but as a cause for rejoicing.

You do of course need to be in communication with your unconscious mind, and to train it. That is very frequently overlooked. To many people the idea of giving up the absolute overlordship of the rational mind is frightening: they can quote horrifying things which have happened when somebody's rational mind has failed to be in charge.

It is true that horrifying accidents do occasionally befall people who are certainly to be accounted sane and rational. Admittedly such accidents can be caused by a desperate bid for notice on the part of a badly repressed unconscious mind: but another and equally frequent cause is that the unconscious has no voice in the matter at all. If you muzzle your watchdog, you can hardly blame him for not warning you of trouble.

Here is an instance, with the harrowing details omitted. A scientist, highly qualified in inorganic chemistry, was alone in a laboratory with a colleague who was also a close friend, when an accident happened which neither man could either have caused or have foreseen. The colleague's life was in mortal jeopardy. Instant action was needed: but what? For a moment the scientist's mind was a complete blank: then, troubled by that delay, as soon as a line of reasoning came to his memory he acted on it. Chemically sound, it was biologically deadly, and it killed the man he was trying to save.

Of course every possible psychological theory was tested out, both at the inquest and by clever acquaintances, as to what might have gone on in the survivor's unconscious mind. Nobody could reach any plausible conclusion, for, quite certainly, nothing that went on in that region could possibly have surfaced in time to influence his actions. He had lived inside his intellect for years: his unconscious was totally unprepared to step in and take over, nor had the necessary information ever penetrated that deeply.

The intellect does not produce swift action: the unconscious mind can move like lightening in its own manner. In the days before everyone had a desk calculator, there were many people whose daily job entailed figure work, and who could tot up long columns of figures swiftly and accurately. They were not the people who could be heard saying, "Three and four is seven, and nine makes sixteen, and ..." Their unconscious minds recognized and leapt at certain groupings of figures, perhaps not adjacent in the column, and combined them in a flash. It takes a lot of practice, and, too, the unconscious likes to work (or play) with patterns; but, if there is only enough practice, it can make the patterns for itself.

Remember the driving examiner: "I feel you should have a little more practical experience." All these things considered, personal autonomy—being a truly responsible human being—has to be a result of being on communicating terms with your unconscious, going along with it. Certainly, rational consciousness can put in its own resolutions: these may be thrown out by the computer of the unconscious, but acceptance is (as with any computer) mostly a matter of the way the resolution is expressed. You have to know the code, the formula, the ritual. And—with this particular computer—you may have to keep repeating the action, or you may have to give the machine a jolt.

Another peculiarity, and this is a valuable one, of the human computer is the manifold valency of a single symbol. It is not only the standard type of "symbol" which is meant here, like "EGG means Easter, gift, springtime, new life, hope, future, treasure" or "RED means fire, heat, blood, love, anger, danger, Stop." That type of symbol belongs to a special language of symbol, and has a special value: but besides this there is the fact that every image, word or concept is a "symbol," and can mean to different people a good many things besides its direct significance.

The true domain of these associated ideas is in the unconscious, where any image, word or concept can be as a stone cast into a pool, sending the ringed ripples running outwards in every direction; but by natural aptitude, by practice (again) and by a certain knack of pattern-forming "mnemonics"—more and more of these associations can be called speedily into consciousness. Frequently, however, their presence in consciousness is not necessary and they will be most effective remaining below the surface. To quote *The Magical Philosophy*: "A good memory and a quick apprehension are valuable qualities in the mind which is to be trained, but the sure method for all is the ancient follow-my-leader dance of associated concepts. He who excels is he who, ahead of the rest, seizes and carries away the longest and most cluster-laden vine-trail of ideas; but the others are not left empty-handed either, and even the slowest finds his share.

"Let us pass to other likenesses. Symbolism is like a tuning-fork struck outside the personal mind, which sets ringing its corresponding bell or glass within. Once this has occurred, it is within the mind that the play continues, and the melody is developed from that first note ..."[4] Our computer becomes, in fact, a synthesizer.

All this gives us a practical subsidiary reason why Pathworking should be done: to intensify and strengthen communication between

---

4. The Magical Philosophy, Book I, Chapter VI: "The Work of the Mind."

levels of the psyche, to the benefit of our abilities in general. It is also very relevant to the way Pathworking is done.

Naturally the text of a Pathworking needs to be attractive to the conscious mind, because the conscious mind has to accept it and pass it through to the unconscious. Our only alternative would be to give Pathworkings only in subliminals or sleep-tapes, and the technical and other problems involved would be considerable. Besides, people really enjoy Pathworkings: not only Order members but all kinds of people love to participate whenever an opportunity is offered. And something which is good for you and can also be enjoyed, is even better for you.

So a Pathworking is presented as a fantasy adventure: fantasy because it involves the imagination to a high degree, and genuine adventure—not fiction—because the alterations which are involved in the states of consciousness are always an adventure. (That is, essentially, the experience for which people rush to Pathworkings.) This designation also gives the critical rational faculty a socially acceptable reason for relaxing and sitting back: the action of the narrative clearly takes place in a region to which earthly norms of probability don't apply.

Whether you are giving a Pathworking, then, or listening as a participant, you should be aware that the narrative is really addressed to the unconscious rather than the conscious minds of the listeners. Once below the threshold of consciousness of each listener, every word and phrase of the text is liable to trigger chain-reactions in a number of directions simultaneously. Even if some of these reactions do rise to the surface, the conscious mind can register only a few of them because it can only give attention to one at a time: whereas the cell-minds of the unconscious can not only at one time hold all the aspects among themselves, but can continue to multiply and combine them to their own satisfaction.

This may be more easily recognized if we point out that the participant is really in a *dream state*.

Clinical research on sleep (specifically) has established certain facts concerning the relationship of sleep and dream. During a period of sleep, the depth of sleep varies. Persons in very deep sleep are unconscious of dream or, indeed, of anything else. Coming into lighter sleep, they begin distinctive "rapid eye movements" and if awakened during that time will prove to have been consciously dreaming. Outside of research conditions, however, many people can recall that at some time or other they have awakened slowly and naturally from a vivid dream and, although "awake" in the sense that they would have known if anyone spoke to them, and perhaps they also knew whether it was yet morning, etc., yet the hallucination of the dream has still been strong enough for them to retain it and to follow its action with a part of their awareness before full wakefulness blotted it out.

This type of experience, with observation of the subject matter of dreams in renewed sleep, and also a consideration of passive imaginings on the part of children, leads strongly to the conclusion that *that part of the psyche which dreams, dreams continuously*, whether we are awake or asleep. We are not conscious of it when we are oblivious to all, nor when the activities of the conscious mind occupy our attention: but in a relaxed state of awareness, whether we are waking or sleeping, in proportion as our consciousness is free from its active occupations some part of the contents of the dream-mind can rise up into it.

For the multiple simultaneous activities of the dream-mind, waking rationality may sometimes be detected in its illicit task of trying to patch two simultaneous dream episodes into one, apparently in the mistaken certainty that they must have been one originally. "It seems to me I cut my leg, but then it seems to me at the same time I was doing something to the car. Maybe I was putting a plaster on the car, or getting a spanner to my leg—I don't remember clearly."

People who are sitting passively participating in a Pathworking, therefore, no matter how conscientiously they may be listening to the text, should not be troubled if some of the visual imagery, or the conceptual fantasy, which rises into their conscious mind is at odds with the words they hear. The only real danger is that if this discrepancy seriously disquiets them, this may in fact break the thread of continuity for them. If a change in consciousness is to occur, the continuity must be maintained, so it is a good thing always to warn participants beforehand not to be surprised or troubled if seemingly divergent ideas or visual imagery should arise. They will not necessarily find a place for every idea suggested by the text, and may find themselves bringing in ideas which are not in the text at all. They should give acceptance to these alternatives, then still go on listening to the text and following the narrative.

A difficulty is sometimes proposed concerning the order in which items of description are given in the text of a Pathworking. If the text has, for instance, "a castle with a square tower built all of red jasper," as soon as the word "castle" is uttered someone may visualize a castle with a round tower of gray granite. If the text has "A tall figure approaches us" and the figure proves to be a tall woman, someone is likely to have pictured it as a tall man. The visualized image has in such cases to be adjusted.

In the light of the foregoing paragraph on divergences in visualization, it may already be apparent that these changes are no such great matter as the questioners imagined. A visualized image can be so transformed unconsciously in the course of a Pathworking, that a few conscious changes will do no harm so long as they are made easily and naturally without any emotions such as dismay, anxiety, annoyance, which would be entirely out of place.

When for some specific purpose (which would not be a Pathworking) it is needful that a group of people should simultaneously visualize an exact image, the attention of the participants is first called to this and means are taken to clear their minds of any irrelevant image. The description of the desired visualization, couched in brief phrases and in the simplest possible language, is next read out to them in its entirety so that they can get the general picture. It is then given again, phrase by phrase, so that they can accurately build up the image.

That is quite a different procedure from the methods of Pathworking, and it is intended to serve a different purpose from the inner development of the participants. It is true that to inaugurate a Pathworking a clear break from extraneous matters is made, but the participants do not lay aside their identities; furthermore, when once the inner movement along the Path has commenced, the flow of thought and feeling, image and event should be continuous except where the text clearly proposes and creates a break. So you watch your castle walls blush from gray to red: or maybe you leave the gray one where it is, and a little further along the road you find the red one. Why not?—it's your adventure!

Remember, whether you are leader or listener, the keyword for success with the unconscious is "play," not "work."

It is in fact this incessant adding to and divergence from the text as the unconscious mind follows a Pathworking with the probability that different sections and cells of the unconscious will react in their own distinctive ways—which makes it a real, vital and deeply individual experience for each participant. As in Impressionist painting, the imagination's multicolored and imprecise brush-strokes produce an exciting, 3-D, stereoscopic effect. It is like a real journey in which uncertain objects appear in the distance, loom out of mist, or change color and outline with the fresh perspective of every few paces. If, afterwards, you show your friends snapshots or even slides of such a journey, they may find the scenes interesting, entertaining or even sublimely beautiful: but you yourself are still likely privately to wonder what became of all the magick the camera failed to capture, the magick which was born of change and movement and of inner response.

Some people who have been strongly impressed with the opportunities for self-discovery and self-development offered by the current style of adventure games—"Dungeons and Dragons" and the rest—have raised a criticism against traditional style Pathworkings that such opportunities do not exist therein: there are no moments of deliberate personal choice for the participants. An obvious reply would be that Pathworking is not that type of game: but to leave the question there would do less than justice to the type of "game" which Pathworking in fact is.

Although the text of each working certainly serves as a framework upon which the necessary symbols and correspondence are displayed, so to put it, this is not its only function. The narrative is in itself suited to the position of the Path upon the Tree, and its consequent spirit and nature: presenting situations and trials characteristic of the Path and of the philosophy associated therewith. The various hazards and dilemmas of the Path are admittedly resolved, often by the action of the Guide of the Path and without any direct reference to the individual participant: but, provided only that the narrative has held the attention, no matter what individual changes may have been wrought in the details, the archetypal nature of the situation ensures that the unconscious of the participant will live through each episode as a personal experience. While the "testing" function of the adventure game is largely absent, the "training" function is present and active, and brings with it the emotional exhilaration which is a vital characteristic of adventure games. It is not desired that a participant should "fail" any test, but sufficient of the moral possibility of failure is implied in the narrative to keep the unconscious attentive and eager to assimilate the teachings of the Path.

For the listeners, as we have seen, great breadth in interpreting the experiences of a Pathworking is valid. The reader needs none the less to give the text accurately and clearly, without making it a class-room lesson. A Pathworking text needs to be read slowly enough for those who may never have heard it before to formulate the images, but in a warm and lively enough manner to hold each person's interest and to stir the creative faculties. This is not too difficult, provided you yourself are thoroughly familiar with that particular text so as to be able to visualize, phrase by phrase, what it describes, and to live through it with the hearers. This permits the building up of *mind contact* between reader and listeners.

This mind contact, so difficult to describe, is a well known phenomenon in the worlds of teaching, of entertainment, of business management and many others. In general terms it consists in welding a number of receptive individuals, by means of seizing their attention, into a sufficient unity for a "group aura" to be formed: and at the same time establishing deeper communication with them through that aura. This means they will assimilate with greater ease, and fewer intellectual difficulties, whatever material the leader or teacher passes on to them: it also means—and this is a point of no small importance in Pathworking—that the leader is able to "feel," and sometimes with absolute precision, the location and extent of any dropping-out among the listeners, any failure to continue traveling the same route.

It might occasionally happen, from whatever cause, that most or all of the group discontinue this inward participation: in such a case the leader would have no choice but to discontinue the reading at some convenient point, and to close with a meditation in the Sphere of the Path's origin, or (at discretion) in the Earth Sphere, with suitable symbolism and correspondences introduced in either case. There should of course be no sense of "blame" attaching here, although a subsequent discussion as to the nature of the obstruction should take place later. If the leader feels that only one, or a minority, of the group has ceased to participate, then the Pathworking should be continued to its proper conclusion and the matter should be privately discussed afterwards with those who have seemed not to "make" the Path. (It should be recognized that emotional upset on the part of a participant, although not a standard occurrence, is much more likely to indicate success than the reverse.)

Some people may be simply unready for a particular Path, and should be advised to take it again at a future time, the interval to be a matter for discretion. Sometimes a participant may drift (so to speak) from a particular Path through having failed to discern its true inwardness: in such a case the mere alerting of the unconscious by the incident may be enough to correct the mistake for another occasion. One of the most frequent causes of "failure" is an inexperienced Pathworker's attempting to participate at the level of the rational consciousness alone, whether as a result of having a particularly competent intelligence or through mistrust of the deeper faculties, and some reassurance may be needed on that subject. Or, as a different kind of problem, some totally extraneous cause of emotional discord may prove to exist among the participants. The putting aside of all mundane concerns at the inauguration of a Pathworking needs to be no less than total.

It remains to be considered why the initial "failures" for all participants in the 24th and 26th Paths are, in fact, built into the workings.

The case stands thus. Every Sphere that we enter represents an alteration of consciousness. A Netzach (Venus) state of mind is quite different from a Yesod (Luna) or a Hod (Mercury) state of mind. But into all of these we can, and do, enter within the Astral World (Yetzirah). Entry into the Sun Sphere (Tiphareth), however, requires not only an altered *state* of consciousness but also an altered *level* of consciousness.

Certainly it is possible to enter into the Tiphareth of Yetzirah, the Sun Sphere of the purely astral level: but this as a life experience tends to be, for some people, Qliphothic (unbalanced) simply because the solar influence is so potent and intoxicating that we require a higher level of consciousness to control it. People who have entered upon the astral Sun Sphere have sometimes in fact become badly unbalanced, mad-drunk and blinded by the vision of their own glory, which is a true glory indeed but no greater than that of any other living soul. Some of the Roman emperors, and some geniuses of the creative arts who nevertheless lacked mystical insight, have been among that number.

In entering Tiphareth, therefore, as an initiatory experience, we need to be certain to pass the portal of the World of Briah. Briah, sometimes called the "Mental World," is the very high, wonderful and beautiful World which lies between the Astral and the World of the Divine: our Pathworkings will not give us more than a glimpse of it, but yet it is by these workings that we learn to be sure and confident on the ways between Sphere and Sphere, between World and World. To cross the boundary of Briah, and to know ourselves to have crossed it, is the most important thing in our Pathworkings now.

Three Paths lead into Tiphareth, but by only one of these can we gain our first admission, because to interpret the significance of the other two Paths aright you need to have the viewpoint of the Sun Sphere—the Sun Sphere of Briah already. It is like the matter of that famous utterance of Crowley's "Do what thou wilt shall be the whole of the Law." That is a saying of the Sun Sphere, and perceived in the light of that Sphere it is a great spiritual truth: but seen only in the light of the astral world, or of the material world, it can mislead utterly.

So it is with the Paths to Tiphareth. It is to be noted that these are not taken, as the other Paths have been, in descending numerical order—26, 25, 24—but 26, 24, 25. The 26th is the Path of Capricorn, the Goat. It leads to the heights, but only to the barren heights of the mountains. This Path shows us the goodness of all that has form, and the goodness of our own nature. If seen from the mystical viewpoint of the Sun Sphere, all this would be right and true and even sacred: but seen without this perception, it could lead only into materialism, narcissism, obsession. Therefore at this stage we are led safely back, not to the Sphere of the beginning of this Path—Hod—but to the Sphere of Earth.

The next Path taken, the 24th, leads in the opposite direction from Capricorn, down to the depths: it is the Path of Scorpio, whose Hebrew letter is Nun, the Fish. As children of Nature we should not see Death, the inevitable, as an evil. That is true: but to see it as final, or to desire it as final, is false and is to love falsehood. The philosophy of the Sun Sphere is that the descent is made only in order to rise again into life, refreshed and renewed. Thus without the true perception of the Sun Sphere, just as on the 26th Path we could not love Life aright, so on the 24th, we cannot love Death aright. Again we are led back to safety: but now, not to Malkuth but to Yesod. Even in these seeming failures, which are really important lessons, we are making progress upon the mystical Central Column of the Tree.

The 25th Path is the Path of the Archer. Again, as on the Path of Capricorn, we have the image of revelry, intoxication. But here is something different: we are lifted in vision beyond the self-seeking of that Path, and beyond the self-losing of the other Path: and without striving we follow where our high destiny leads us. If we had not learned, and practiced, how to entrust ourselves to that which is outside human reason—confidently, neither fearing nor desiring to cast ourselves away—how should we now trust ourselves to that which is above human reason? And only by that confidence and that trust, by that forgetfulness of self which comes of absorption in something greater, can we rise to that change in our level of consciousness which is entry into the Sphere of Tiphareth.

Having completed the 25th Path and made entry of the Sun Sphere, the 26th and 24th Paths are worked again: but now there is, for each of them, a true resolution in Tiphareth.

chapter 4

The Paths in Your Dreams

This chapter is for you as a person who is to experience Pathworking, so that you may not fail to realize and enjoy some special dimensions of adventure which Pathworking will bring you. If you are the leader of a group, the material in this chapter is important, not only for your own use and experience but also for you to pass on and maybe to discuss with your group. If you are going into Pathworking by yourself, this chapter also has particular value for you, because every dimension in which you can develop your experience of Pathworking will help reinforce for you the reality of what you do.

In the previous chapter we indicated how the dream activity of your psyche goes on and on, regardless of whether you are awake or asleep, conscious of it or otherwise. The happenings, words and actions which in any way impinge upon your waking life are fed into the computer/synthesizer of your deep mind. Some of them are accepted, others seem to be rejected or to have no effect. This selection, or at any rate grading, of materials, depends entirely upon the pre-programming of those hidden levels: and this pre-programming differs widely between one person and another.

Pathworking texts have for most people a high rate of immediate acceptance, partly because the eventful, colorful narratives are designed for swift assimilation, and partly because the hearers willingly place themselves in a passive and receptive state. The narrative, however, does not remain unadapted. Even while you are listening to it, as we have noted, it can undergo some modifictions: and certainly as the deeper levels of your psyche get to work on it, further adaptations will take place.

Not all of these adaptations will be changes. Many will consist in amplifying some of the components of a situation, or weaving a whole adventure around something which maybe was only briefly mentioned. These amplifications do not come into being as stories, or as abstract ideas. Your imagination dramatizes them, lives them. Then various episodes can be differently combined with one another, and the new forms, in several variations, can be tried out and experienced, even simultaneously, by groups of your "cell minds." The original text, and the correspondences given therein, will make the essential nature of the specific Path sufficiently clear to keep its identity *for you*: the ability to recognize wordlessly the point and significance of a correspondence, and to devise action in complete harmony with it and yet in personal freedom, is one of the important arts of Pathworking which the dream-levels of your psyche will speedily develop with practice. The material of the Path thus becomes "personalized" to you: to your life, your desires, your fears, your protests, your aspirations: but it is still the material of the same Path, with its particular influences conditioning the direction in which it takes you and the adventures you meet with on the way to the sphere of destination.

In considering the Path as the way to the magical state of consciousness of a Sphere, and the Path as a different, adventurous, and highly magical state of consciousness in its own right, these two aspects of Pathworking should never seem to contradict one another, although for various reasons we have sometimes to emphasize the one, sometimes the other.

To enter a Sphere—a Sephirah—is to enter a state of consciousness which enables you to attain specific very wonderful powers. Upon the Path which carries the influence of that Sephirah you are likely to experience something of those same powers, but they are not made available to you as in the sphere itself. For example: if a magician wanted to perform a work of magick relating to Fire, that work might very well be carried out within the ambience of, and with the power of, either Netzach or Geburah according to its precise nature and purpose. The magician would certainly not choose to perform it upon the 31st Path, although that Path is filled with the influence of pure elemental Fire. The Sephiroth can open up to us treauries of archetypal power far beyond our personal resources.

Certainly for this very reason, even if for no other, it would be understandable that the psyche should keep going over the experience of the Paths, to be assured of the means of going quickly and securely from one sephirothic state of consciousness to another. When once a Path has been successfully traveled, it becomes as it were a permanent bridge from the Sphere of its origin to that of its destination, and the deep mind accordingly strengthens and reinforces it continually.

However, that is by no means the only reason why the Paths are repeated, or partially repeated, so often by the deeper levels of the psyche, and by the dream level notably. It is an interesting fact that when people are working upon the Paths and the Sephiroth, although the workings of the Planetary Spheres can be intense and wonderful experiences, yet those do not show up in the dreams and waking fantasies of the practitioners nearly as often as do the experiences of the Paths.

To some extent, this can be explained at once. The Paths belong to us in a way that the Sephiroth never quite do. The archetypal images of the Spheres are woven into the very stuff of our lives, it is true: but the great archetypes, which cast the shadows which are those images, stand ever beyond the limits of any individual psyche.

Some Qabalists have dealt in a general way with this distinction, by saying that the Sephiroth are "objective," the Paths "subjective." This statement can be confusing, because the Paths in their general pattern, their directions and their significations, are the same for every person and are in that sense "objective": but the reality of the Paths is in the actual experience of them. As we have seen, even while you are listening to the narrative of a Pathworking your own "subjective" elements will begin to enter into it, and it is right that they should; while with the

Spheres the intention is always to enter as nearly as possible into their pristine purity.

The contrast between these two types of experience is to be found everywhere in human life. In religions both ancient and modern, all over the world, shrines have been established, with their special rites of worship: and then pilgrimages have been established to reach those shrines, and the traversing of rough ways and whatever adventures might befall the pilgrims have come to be regarded as a kind of spontaneous "rite" in themselves, with something of the merits which would attach to a rite.

Leaving aside any religious aspects of the matter, whether we look at the roads, the rivers, canals, oceans, or at any form of air travel, among the "serious travelers" whose only concern is to transfer themselves from Point A to Point B there are always a number of other people who, whatever the ostensible purpose of their journey, plainly are happy just to be on the move and going some place. Even the grimmest journeys have often been undertaken without real necessity. One of the most remarkable events of American history was the great Westward drive of the covered wagons. Who went? Not only seekers for a better life, for fortune: not only people who had nothing to lose and maybe much to gain by the desperate venture. Not only people who were deceived as to what lay ahead of them. There were men and women who left fortunes, estates, good careers and pleasant lives to go with the wagons, to be in the action, on the move, to see new things, to dare new perils. Human beings do such things.

Deeper than any single impulse in these matters is a curious fact of human nature, which many religions and philosophies in all ages have recognized, and have sought to interpret in their own terms. Man is a wanderer, whether it is said that he seeks a "heavenly home" or has arrived from another galaxy. Whether we conceive of it materially or metaphysically, we have each of us a Quest, and there is always something special to see and experience "over the next hill." Even those of us who care most for security, treasure it with an inner realization of its true fragility.

From the viewpoint of the Qabalah, none of these phenomena is astonishing. We know our Source, we know our Destiny: in this context the adjective "ultimate" would not be appropriate. We know the vast steeps of time and space which encompass our Way of Return: but we know, too, that the impulse of that journeying is recorded at every level of our psycho-physical composition and can be activated at any of those levels.

We are all "Travelers upon the Paths" by our very nature. But that does not destroy the adventure of the journeying, nor the wonder and delight which each one of us can find in it. In these chapters we have said much about our deep mind as if it were a machine. In a sense it is a machine, but it is also a living one. In its non-mechanical aspects we should do better to see it as a child. It responds to the idea of "play" rather than to that of "work," but it takes its "play" very seriously indeed. Like the child, the deep mind has an insatiable impulse to learn, to assimilate that which concerns it. A child learns and assimilates by repetition: often a listening adult will scream out in sheer torment of soul, "Sing something else!" before a child has half finished assimilating a popular hit. (Usually, but not always, the similar activities of our own deep mind are happily "soundproofed off" from consciousness. When they are not, we find the tune "running in our head.") A child also learns by selecting a given bit of experience, dramatizing it and acting it over and over: frequently with such additions or changes as may make the experience more complete, attractive or comprehensible. All this is very relevant to the developments of Pathworking which emerge in the dream state.

As complete persons, we are neither entitled, nor well advised to try to live without paying heed to what goes on in the nursery/computer room. For the right development of both conscious and unconscious, communication between the levels must be maintained: and one of the most effective mediums for this communication is through our dreaming. While this is true in any circumstances, it is not only true but of considerable importance when we consider how the greatest benefit can be derived from participation in Pathworking.

To be aware of what place Pathworking takes in our dreams, and to reflect upon it, is a sure way to gain much insight and understanding of the nature and reality of the Paths. It is also, as is any observation of dream experiences, a means of great and valuable extension of our self-knowledge. It is also a great deal of fun and interest, and an excellent relief from the stress and hassle of other occupations which propose themselves to us as "important."

Sharing the interests of younger members of the family helps us in this way. The company of animals helps us in this way. The company and the interests of our own deep mind are very good indeed for relaxation and refreshment. Besides, the deep mind always appreciates reassurance that its serious games are taken seriously, and that the rational mind enjoys its company and will even join in the fun.

There's another point, too. Besides being a computer/synthesizer and also a child, your deep mind is also the guardian of many marvelous things to which you should have access, and sometimes your deep mind may have something to tell you about those things.

When you are working with the Paths therefore, you can make for yourself a delightful and valuable supplement to this book by keeping a journal of your dreams. Don't make a chore of it, but keep it regularly: like most hobbies, it's more fun if you keep it up to date and well organized. Put in every dream or fragment of dream you can remember. Not all of them will relate to Pathworking, but in some cases the clues which link a dream to a Path may not be evident to you at first. Besides, if you carefully record them all, your deep mind will soon know you are interested in dreams and in Pathworking dreams particularly, and after a little while will begin to cooperate and will turn up some magnificent ones for you.

To keep your dream journal properly, the best thing for your permanent record is a loose-leaf book. This will enable you to illustrate a particularly vivid scene now and then, either with your own work in ink or paint or with clippings from magazines and so on which capture the feeling of a particular scene. You also need writing materials, or better still a tape recorder, near your bed to capture your immediate, waking recollections.

No matter how vivid a dream may have been, don't take for granted that you will be able to recall it all "later." A short delay can lose some details or even a whole episode for you. In that rough draft, try to down the main happenings with any details which strike you as special. Don't try to rationalize, or to make fragments fit together which may not belong; keep them just as you recall them. Make a note of any spoken words in the dream, any scenery or buildings of importance, and—this is one of the most important things—how you felt in the dream. If you had no emotions about the dream, make a note of that too. Make this rough draft as clear as possible.

Later, before putting together your final version, you may be able to review the dreams, perhaps to remember fragments which escaped you at first, perhaps to recognize where some of the imagery or the happenings in the dream came from. In your final version, give the dreams first, including all the details you have, and your feelings about them. Then, in a separate paragraph, give the "associations": that is, any source from which you can readily see that your deep mind has drawn the images or incidents to make up your dream.

Don't make too much of the "associations." They are not meant to explain the dreams away. A house, a tree, even a monster must have some kind of shape, and it is much easier for your deep mind to pull one out of the memory-bank than to create a new one. A person will quite likely wear the likeness of someone you know who is, in one way or another, the right sort of person. But if the association happens to be a reference to a Pathworking text, or one of the correspondences of a Path, make a particular note of that!

Part of the fun, and interest, in keeping a dream journal in connection with Pathworking, is deciding afterwards, if you can, which Path you were on. When you decide, make a note of it in the "associations." It can be a major factor in seeing the significance of some of your dream adventures.

For instance: a dreamer who was going through some strenuous experiences on a particularly austere and rocky 32nd Path found himself accompanied by a helpful fellow traveler who was clearly his "other self." These "friendly shadows" as they are called in the language of dream interpretation, are not infrequent characters in dream. Sometimes, when a person dreams often of such helpers taking the whole burden of a difficult situation off the dreamer's shoulders, the implication is that the dreamer underestimates his or her own abilities and looks to others to do what he or she could competently do alone. However, an outstanding characteristic of the 32nd Path is the psychic barrage of opposition, delay, and discouragement which it offers to the inexperienced traveler. To seek help from those of one's faculties which lie beyond the conscious range is therefore appropriate: and this view of the matter is confirmed, as we shall see from the ensuing development in the dream.

At one point in this harsh journey, the helpful friend reached a long arm down into a rift—an arm which grew very long indeed as it descended in the rocky depths—to bring out from the darkness a beautiful, flashing, Excalibur-type sword *which he handed to the dreamer.*

Here, we perceive, the dreamer is learning by his dream experience upon this Path to bring resources from the unconscious into consciousness, and to equip his conscious personality with them. The personal confidence is, in fact, being reinforced in this adventure by the realization *that the unconscious is a source of help.* Thus the 32nd Path gains a valuable new aspect for him.

Incidently this dream, of which we do not give the whole, manifests another feature which is quite frequently found in Pathworking dreams. In the course of it, the dreamer does not travel all the way from Malkuth to Yesod. He begins from a scene which is distinctly of Malkuth, and, his adventures done, is returned neatly to that same Sphere. The purpose of the dream is just what it appears to be: adventure, intensified experience of the Path and a deeper understanding of it. Certainly, instances occur of dreams in which a person travels a recognizable Path, with some of the symbols thereof, and gains the experience of the Sphere at the conclusion. Such dreams are exceptional and potent, and can change the dreamer's life: interestingly, they sometimes befall people who have never taken part in a Pathworking, who seem never to have heard of the Tree of Life. In such cases it becomes evident that the deep mind of the dreamer can no longer tolerate the conscious mind's oblivion to all that concerns it, and takes charge of the situation in order to remedy the matter. For the student of practical Qabalah who is beginning to know the Paths, and who moreover is establishing a good relationship with his or her deep mind, there is absolutely no need for this type of "initiatory dream" which compels acceptance through trauma.

One question remains to be answered in this chapter: If you begin your journal of dreams when you begin Pathworking, or thereabouts, when do you close it? In fact you need never close it, as Pathworking when once you have begun it will never be closed for you. When once the computer/synthesizer of your deep mind has assimilated the patterns of the Paths, no power can de-program it. New life-material, ideas and experiences will take their place in your deep mind, and will be illuminated by your understanding of the Paths as well as enriching their imagery for you. If you in your turn keep up your journal of dreams, your deep mind will be all the more encouraged in its play. And you may well do so, for in your dreams you have a never-failing source of interest, delight and surprise, with new vistas of understanding continually opening before you. You will know the heights and depths of the Paths: but both height and depth are endless vistas. Above all, never at any time—whether the most uneventful time or the most chaotic—will you be tempted to find the succession of your days, as some people say, "meaningless." For you will be recording the "inner history" of your life upon the Paths, the thrilling episodes of an epic. Your deep mind will be continually exploring, adventuring, questing upon the Paths, encountering strange and marvelous beings, learning the secrets of the inner worlds: and you—your conscious self—through your practiced and heightened dream awareness, will share those explorations and those secrets.

chapter 5

Preporotion ond Working

So you are going to explore the wonderful levels and states of consciousness which can be encountered in the inner worlds of your own being. Before giving the texts of the Pathworkings through which you will set out on this exploration, there are still several factors we need to consider. There is: I. some of the symbolism relating to the visualized temples of the Spheres; II. the furnishing and arrangement of the physical place of working; III. deep mind programming prior to the Pathworking; and IV. the method of opening and conducting a Pathworking.

I. Symbolism Relating to Visualized Temples

Some details of the Pathworkings given in this book are adapted specifically to Aurum Solis tradition and custom. However, the amount of Aurum Solis material employed in this way is minimal, and is confined entirely to some of the appurtenances of the temple of the Sphere of Destination in which each Path ends.

These appurtenances, as used in Pathworking, are here described with more particulars:

1. The Two Pillars, Machetes and Nomothetes

Other traditions have given them other names. These names are Greek, and signify Warrior and Lawgiver. The pillars represent the columns of Severity and Mercy of the Tree of Life, and in most of the Pathworkings they flank the interior of the temple entrance. In Aurum Solis tradition they are usually black with white capital and base and white with red capital and base respectively, and they should be considered so in these Pathworkings—that is, the black pillar on our left, the white on our right—unless stated otherwise.

The temples of the Sun Sphere, concluding the highest three Paths in this series, have each some variation regarding the pillars. On the 26th Path the pillars are a part of the megalithic structure, not additional to it, and are distinguished by being green and gold respectively. On the 24th Path the temple of the Sun Sphere consists of a pyramidal roof supported by four crystal pillars with no distinction of color, between two of which (the north-west and the south-west) we enter. On the 25th Path the pillars are the normal colors of Machetes and Nomothetes, and we find ourselves standing between them when the temple comes into manifestation around us; then we move forward into the temple, thus making our entrance in the normal manner.

In some traditions, notably the Medieval Guild mysteries, the pillars are white (Female—Severity) and red (Male—Mercy) respectively. An ancient pair found in Phoenicia were emerald and gold, comparably to those in our megalithic circle. A meaningful contrast is the essential.

The purpose of entering the temple of the sphere between the two pillars at the conclusion of our Pathworkings, is to confirm the influence of the Sphere, entrance to which has been made at an identifiable point a little previously, and to align our faculties with that influence.

2. The Bomos

This is an upright altar, traditionally proportioned as a double cube. As visualized in a Pathworking it is usually covered with drapery of a color suited to the Sphere, and may stand in the eastern end of the temple or centrally, as appropriate to a specific occasion.

3. The Banner of the New Life

The great symbol of Aurum Solis: the Eight-pointed Star in the form of an endless interlace, white upon a black ground. Within the center of the Star is a yellow octagon, "voided"—that is, consisting only of a perimetric strip—and having in its center, which is the center of the whole figure, a small equal-armed cross in red, solid upon the black ground. The endless renewal of the New Life is signified alike by these concentric figures as by the endless interlace of the Star itself.

4. The Mystical Tessera

This is the primal magical implement of Aurum Solis working, a talismanic focal point for the Inner Plane forces of the tradition. It consists of a small tablet of wood, about 2½ inches across. On this is represented another form of the Eight-pointed Star from that described above: two voided squares interlaced, one white and one red, the diagonals of one square being turned 45 degrees from the diagonals of the other upon a common centerpoint.

In these workings we visualize the Mystical Tessera as lying upon the Bomos.

When these objects are named in the text of a Pathworking, those who wish to follow Aurum Solis usage should visualize them as given above. When it is not desired to do this, symbols of another tradition may be substituted in visualization as found suitable. A Pentacle or the image of a Sphynx, for example, might replace the Mystical Tessera, or another emblem might replace the Banner of the New Life. The banner might show for instance the Hexagram, the red and white Alchemical Roses, or the Eye in the Triangle. What is essential here is that the symbolism of the banner should represent to those who visualize it the attainment of adepthood, the fulfillment of the Great Work, or the goal of their aspiration in whatever manner expressed.

Where the number Eight is used in connection with the symbolic imagery of the Sun Sphere, it should be recalled that this use of the number, together with its connotation of regeneration, has a venerable place in the Western Mystery Tradition generally and is by no means limited to Aurum Solis usage. However, if (as for example in the megalithic temple of the 26th Path) other groupings such as fives or twelves are preferred, that is fine too.

II. Furnishing and Arrangement of Place of Working

There should be no confusion between the symbolic contents of visualized temples and the requirements for the physical environment in which the Pathworking takes place. In the physical place of working, no matter which Path is being worked, the altar is always placed centrally and is always draped in black. Upon it is placed the Mystical Tessera (or other chosen device) and a single lighted lamp. Chairs for the participants are essential. These should be noiseless and comfortable enough not to distract the attention of the occupants and should be placed in a circle (or oval) around the altar. If only a few people are participating, so that they would be too isolated in a circle, an arc should be formed instead.

A reading desk or music stand should be placed for the use of the director of the working, who remains standing throughout. Near by should be a side table, with a bell or gavel for sounding the battery at the close of the working, and a thymiaterion (standing incense pot) with incense.

The wearing of a simple white robe, preferably hooded, is recommended for the participants but is optional.

At the conclusion of each Pathworking text will be found the direction, *Battery 3-5-3*. These indicate groupings of strokes of bell or gavel which are to be given in a steady, measured manner. It will be noticed that this battery conveys in a symmetrical pattern the great magical Number, 11: its purpose at the end of a working, after allowing the participants a moment to dwell inwardly upon the conclusion, is to re-center their consciousness in the material world.

The incense to be used for each Pathworking is associated with the Sphere of Destination. It is intended to attune the psyche to entry into the state of consciousness of that Sphere, and consequently in choosing the incense some consideration should also be made of the influences through which, upon this Path, approach has been effected. In each Pathworking text, indication is made of the point at which the incense should be placed upon the hot charcoal.

The traditional pure incenses for use for each Pathworking are as follows:

Working of Path No.	Incense
32	Galbanum, Jasmine
31	Yellow Sandalwood
30	Mastic
29	Young Amber
28	Red Sandalwood
27	Benzoin
26, 1st working	No incense
26, subsequent	Cinnamon
24, 1st working	No incense
24, subsequent	Rose
25	Heliotrope, Olibanum

If preferred, however, or should the traditional incenses not be obtainable, incense sticks may be used instead: regard being had, in choosing them, to one's personal feeling of their suitability to the Sphere of Destination and to the Path, as above mentioned.

III. Deep Mind Programming Prior to Pathworking

Preceding each Pathworking in the ensuing series (Chapter 7) there is a list of correspondences and a specially designed mandala.

The correspondences given include those of the Sphere in which the Path begins, of the Path itself, and of the Sphere of Destination. These lists are not meant to be exhaustive, but simply to give the symbols and representative materials which are introduced or expressed in the texts of the Pathworkings.

The symbolic design which is also to be found at the head of each Pathworking is termed by us a "mandala" for very specific reasons.

A mandala is by tradition usually circular, but not necessarily so. It is, essentially, a symbolic "statement" in visual form regarding the exterior cosmos, or an aspect or portion of it; or expressing an interior state. (The exterior and interior interpretations are not truly separable.) A circular mandala expresses a contemplation of these matters made in, and inducing, an inner ambience of non-stress, non-action. Other shapes, such as our rectangle, express and can create stresses in that aspect of being which is represented by the mandala as a whole. This is needed here: to initiate any psychic or magical action, the creation of stresses in the astral ambience is necessary, and much of the conduct and equipment of Art Magick generally are directed to pinpointing and activating the correct stresses for the desired outcome.

Here, the design of the mandalas and the guidelines about be to given for their use are directed solely to motivating action within the psyche of the individual in relation to the Path represented.

Besides incorporating a symbolic indication of the area of intended action, the mandala—any mandala—has another intensely significant feature: *its center.*

The center, in a typical mandala, is an image of that which is coming, or is to come, into being or manifestation.[5]

In each of our Pathworking mandalas, the center is represented by a carefully-chosen pattern which may remind you of a hypnotic device. It is not intended to throw you into deep trance, which is a relatively rare state and is not needed for most psychic purposes. The patterns at the

---

5. The "center" of the human body is the navel, which continues to represent the umbilical nexus with the astral matrix long after the umbilical cord to the physical mother has ceased to exist. The center of the symbolic Wheel of the Universe is the axle-hole, representing the "negative being" which is the perpetual source of all being. In the well-known representations of the Dance of Shiva, the deity represents the central cause and origin, which is also the end, of all. The center of the Rose Cross is the rose ever-becoming in an eternal blossoming. The center of the Banner of the New Life is the equal-armed cross which represents the new cycle of spiritual life forever springing forth. Each of these can be considered as a mandate, and each shows a special interpretation of "the center."

center of our mandalas are however sufficiently potent, when used as we direct, to induce in your deep mind the internal psychic action which they suggest. Each of these patterns, independently of your listening to the Pathworking text, sets up a "stress" relating to the particular Path of the Tree of Life. When one of the mandalas is employed as directed, your deep mind will be motivated to pass through the "doorway" of the mandala and to neutralize the stress by exploring the indicated Path.

A particularly effective way of combining the use of the mandala with the evocative power of the correspondences can be employed prior to a Pathworking to enhance and intensify it. One way of doing this on the occasion of the working is shown in the "Formula for Opening a Pathworking" given below. Here are two other methods, either of which would be used by participants privately and individually the evening before. Both are intended for participants with some experience of Pathworking: Method B is, additionally, more advanced than Method A. Preferably, either should be performed shortly before sleep.

Use of Mandala and Correspondences: Method A

First read the correspondences reflectively, not seeking to memorize them so much as to discover, through them, the character of the spiritual realities to which they relate. Go back over them if you wish, taking care not to confuse the sections to which they belong.

Put the list aside. Take the mandala, placing it at a normal reading distance from your eyes and central to your field of vision. Keeping it quite steady, rest your gaze upon it, not consciously concentrating upon any part. While you do this, mentally recall the correspondences as far as you can, and allow your mind to dwell especially upon any which you find particularly striking or appealing.

Half an hour is ample to allow for the whole of this practice. If it can be the last topic to occupy your mind before sleep, it will be particularly powerful in conditioning your deep mind for the next day's Pathworking.

Use of Mandala and Correspondences: Method B

As in Method A, read and reflect upon the correspondences. Then place the mandala at a normal reading distance from your eyes, taking particular care that it is central to your field of vision and is quite steady.

Gaze at the mandala: at first dwelling upon its symbolic design, then bringing your gaze to rest on the central pattern. Contemplate it passively: if it "plays tricks" with your sight, accept this without concern.

After a few minutes, when you should feel you can visualize the mandala—at least its main features—close your eyes and do so. (Don't look again to refresh your memory: you can be sure your deep mind is recalling more than your conscious mind can do!) With closed eyes, "see" as clearly as you can the surrounding design and the central pattern. *Then, in imagination, go right through the doorway, through the central pattern.* Imagine the pattern flowing all around you as lines of energy as you pass through it. Then allow the energy pattern to fade from consciousness, and, while you remain sitting with closed eyes, reflect upon the correspondences.

Make this practice if possible the last topic to occupy your mind before sleep. It is a powerful and advanced method of conditioning your deep mind for the next day's Pathworking.

IV. Opening and Conducting the Pathworking

We come now to the formula for opening a Pathworking, and to general observations on how a Pathworking should be given and received. The standard formula given here is effective and simple: the context of a Pathworking offers no place for elaborate preparatory rites. Provision is made within the formula for the inclusion of the practice with the correspondences and the mandala, if this practice has not been performed by the participants on the previous day.

Formula for Opening a Pathworking

All physical appurtenances being in readiness, the participants are assembled, standing in a circle around the altar.

1. A single stroke of bell or gavel is sounded.

2. The director states, "I proclaim a working of the _____ Path of the Tree of Life."

Uniting of Energy

3. *The director gives instructions step by step to guide participants through the following procedure:*

    i. Still standing in their circle, all link hands, right over left.

    ii. A single sphere of white light is visualized above the center of the circle.

    iii. This sphere grows brighter and more radiant, until the light from it encompasses all participants.

    iv. All participants feel energy flowing powerfully through them, *anti-clockwise* around the circle as their right hands give and left hands receive.

    v. Additionally to this, all participants visualize a wall of blue light enclosing their circle and revolving *clockwise*.

    vi. After a few moments, all visualizations and sensations are allowed to fade from consciousness.

    vii. The participants unlink hands and seat themselves.

Directives to the Deep Mind

4. The participants are reminded to sit in an easy posture, relaxed but not slumped, which they can maintain throughout the working. There should be no crossing of arms, legs or ankles. Breathing should be steady, even and quiet, and should be continued thus throughout the working.

5. *(This paragraph and the next should be omitted if the participants have performed the practices with the correspondences and the mandala the day before. In that case, proceed now to 7.)*

    The mandala of the Path is contemplated. If each person has a copy, the gaze should be kept upon this during the process of section 6 following. If there is but one copy, it should be looked at briefly but intently to fix its essentials in the memory, then it

63

should be passed to the next person. In the former case the eyes will naturally remain open until the end of 6. In the latter case, the eyes are to be closed as soon as they cease looking at the mandala, and the hood (if robes are worn) is to be drawn over them.

In the usage here described, no effort is made at this time to pass consciously through the "astral portal." Together with the material in 6 here following, this image becomes programmed into the working symbolism of the deep mind to give it direction and to enrich its resources.

6. The director reads aloud the list of correspondences which precedes the text of the Pathworking. The purpose of this is that the listeners may recognize, consciously or unconsciously, the significance of the references to those symbols or materials where they occur in the text. It is thus not necessary that the participants should try to memorize these items as they are read out, although some of them may easily remain distinct. It is important however that the reading should be done in an interesting manner, making sure the Hebrew letters are clearly identified for instance, adding perhaps a few words of explanation here or there. Above all, the three divisions of the correspondences (of the initial Sphere, of the Path itself, and of the Sphere of Destination) need to be plainly distinguished from one another.

Invocation of the Divine Names

7. After a suitable pause at the conclusion of this material, the Director makes the appropriate invocation for the Path. *The full texts of all the necessary invocations for the Pathworkings given in this book follow here:*

32ND PATH

May we be encompassed by the power of the name ADONAI MELEK and established in the Palace of Malkuth, the Kingdom. May the portal of the 32nd Path be opened to us, and may we journey thereon in the power of the names YAHVEH ELOHIM and AIMA to the gate of the Sphere of Yesod, the Foundation. And, in the name SHADDAI EL CHAI, may the gate of Yesod be opened to us and may we be firmly established in the wonders of that Sphere.

31ST PATH

May we be encompassed by the power of the name ADONAI MELEK and established in the palace of Malkuth, the Kingdom. May the portal of the 31st Path be opened to us, and may we journey thereon in the power of the name ELOHIM to the gate of the Sphere of Hod, Splendor. And, in the name ELOHIM TZABAOTH, may the gate of Hod be opened to us and may we be firmly established in the wonders of that Sphere.

30TH PATH

May we be encompassed by the power of the name SHADDAI EL CHAI and established in the palace of Yesod, the Foundation. May the portal of the 30th Path be opened to us, and may we journey thereon in the power of the name ELOAH V'DAATH to the gate of the Sphere of Hod, Splendor. And, in the name ELOHIM TZABAOTH, may the gate of Hod be opened to us and may we be firmly established in the wonders of that Sphere.

29TH PATH

May we be encompassed by the power of the name ADONAI MELEK and established in the palace of Malkuth, the Kingdom. May the portal of the 29th Path be opened to us, and may we journey thereon in the power of the name EL to the gate of the Sphere of Netzach, Victory. And, in the name YAHVEH TZABAOTH, may the gate of Netzach be opened to us and may we be firmly established in the wonders of that Sphere.

28TH PATH

May we be encompassed in the power of the name SHADDAI EL CHAI and established in the palace of Yesod, the Foundation. May the portal of the 28th Path be opened to us, and may we journey thereon in the power of the name YAHU to the gate of the Sphere of Netzach, Victory. And, in the name YAHVEH TZABAOTH, may the gate of Netzach be opened to us and may we be firmly established in the wonders of that Sphere.

27TH PATH

May we be encompassed in the power of the name ELOHIM TZA-BAOTH and established in the palace of Hod, Splendor. May the portal of the 27th Path be opened to us, and may we journey thereon in the power of the name ELOHIM GEBOR to the gate of the Sphere of Net-zach, Victory. And, in the name YAHVEH TZABAOTH, may the gate of Netzach be opened to us and may we be firmly established in the wonders of that Sphere.

26TH PATH (FIRST WORKING)

May we be encompassed by the power of the name ELOHIM TZA-BAOTH and established in the palace of Hod, Splendor. May the por-tal of the 26th Path be opened to us, and may we journey thereon in the power of the name YAHVEH ELOHIM. And, having tasted of the adventures of that Path, in the name ADONAI MELEK may we be received and established in the Sphere of Malkuth, the Kingdom.

26TH PATH (SUBSEQUENT WORKINGS)

May we be encompassed by the power of the name ELOHIM TZA-BAOTH and established in the palace of Hod, Splendor. May the portal of the 26th Path be opened to us, and may we journey thereon in the power of the name YAHVEH ELOHIM to the gate of the Sphere of Tiphareth, Beauty. And, in the name YAHVEH ELOAH V'DAATH, may the gate of Tiphareth be opened to us and may we be firmly established in the wonders of that Sphere.

24TH PATH (FIRST WORKING)

May we be encompassed by the power of the name YAHVEH TZA-BAOTH and established in the Sphere of Netzach, Victory. May the portal of the 24th Path be opened to us, and may we journey thereon in the power of the name ELOHIM GEBOR. And, having tasted of the adventures of that Path, in the name SHADDAI EL CHAI may we be received and established in the Sphere of Yesod, the Foundation.

24TH PATH (SUBSEQUENT WORKINGS)

May we be encompassed by the power of the name YAHVEH TZA-BAOTH and established in the palace of Netzach, Victory. May the portal of the 24th Path be opened to us, and may we journey thereon in the power of the name ELOHIM GEBOR to the gate of the Sphere of Tiphareth, Beauty. And, in the name YAHVEH ELOAH V'DAATH, may the gate of Tiphareth be opened to us and may we be firmly established in the wonders of that Sphere.

25TH PATH

May we be encompassed by the power of the name SHADDAI EL CHAI and established in the palace of Yesod, the Foundation. May the portal of the 25th Path be opened to us, and may we journey thereon in the power of the name EL to the gate of the Sphere of Tiphareth, Beauty. And, in the name YAHVEH ELOAH V'DAATH, may the gate of Tiphareth be opened to us and may we be firmly established in the wonders of that Sphere.

The Pathworking proper

8. The director now proceeds to the reading of the relevant Pathworking text, as given in Chapter 7.

Reading and Receiving the Pathworking

The art of reading a Pathworking has some features in common with the traditional art of storytelling. There is a certain intimacy about it, a feeling that the reader is speaking to each participant. The reader should speak loudly enough to be distinctly heard, but without any needless declaiming the general effect should be pleasant and soothing, but the highlights in the text should be given as much dramatic emphasis and staccato rendering as the subject matter warrants.

To be able to read in this manner, we would repeat that the reader should be thoroughly familiar with the text, so as to deliver it in naturally meaningful tones and phrases. The mind of the reader should all the time be on the meaning rather than on the words: besides helping expressiveness, this approach also helps the reader to avoid stumbling. The reader of a Pathworking should practice visualizing the images in the text while reading. If the initial linking of energies has been potent, this visualization will ensure that the Pathworking is a profound and vital experience for reader and recipients alike. Even if the initial linking has seemed to lack something (as is sometimes the case when a number of the participants are meeting for the first time) the quality of the working itself, and above all the psychically shared experiences of the visualizations, can completely transform the feeling of the meeting.

(Here a note may be interposed for the attention of leaders of Pathworking groups. The stronger the bond of fellowship which develops among the members of your group, the more intense and valuable will be their experiences of Pathworking: also, the easier it will be for any newcomer to discover, and identify with, the special feeling of the group and of the working. One reason for this is that the unconscious of each person will feel more secure within the group aura which will be generated. So why not have the members of our group regard themselves as a kind of Astral Exploration Club, or Pathworkers' Guild, or whatever? Remember, the unconscious loves a game, and the best games are the kind which the secret self can play seriously. The concept might be developed according to the ideas of your group, perhaps with tokens of membership, perhaps with a clubroom with annotated "maps" of the Paths, anything which helps make the project real for all participants.)

The participants—those who sit listening to the text of a Pathworking as it is read to them—have also their share to contribute towards its success. A Pathworking is, after all, a *working*, passive though the listeners' part in it may seem to be.

This is not a work of the intellect: but while the intellect stands aside, the other faculties of the psyche will be as busy as the colony of bees referred to in an earlier chapter. Attention needs to be kept upon the text as it is read out, whether one is hearing it for the first or the tenth time. It can always be a new experience, for one is never quite the same person receiving it. Besides being engaged in maintaining this attention (which, at the most, can in reality be only approximately continuous) the will has also to maintain the process of visualization until this becomes spontaneous. Visualization should comprise at least the main scenes and symbols of the narrative, and will most probably include much more.

As has been indicated, this visualization is not a matter of the exact reproduction of images. This is where the deep mind most noticeably begins to play its part. Attention should be given also to its contributions, which are likely to build their own patterns around the main theme: the conscious mind should in this be receptive and not censorious.

It should be remembered here that (1) not every part of the deep mind need be working along the particular line of fantasy which now impinges upon the consciousness: quite other material is probably being produced at more hidden levels; (2) that which is unconscious is not lost, but remains in the "memory bank" for future recall and even for future unconscious development; (3) as a result of the claims of this intense inward activity upon the conscious attention and also upon the unconscious focus, an altered state of consciousness will almost certainly be entered. (Some altered states of consciousness are so tenuous as frequently to escape detection, but they are none the less real for that, and prepare the way for easy entry into a deeper state.) The alteration will be further developed by entry into the Sphere of Destination. Even though the final battery with bell or gavel will be recognized as a signal for return to normal consciousness, this return may take a few seconds to accomplish satisfactorily. You have journeyed upon the Path and have entered into a Magical State of Consciousness: and you may be assured that your deep mind will take care not to lose, at your return to normal consciousness, the treasures of achievement and experience which it has garnered in the working.

chapter 6

Individual Working

If you don't belong to a Pathworking group and if you see no prospect of joining one which already exists, the ideal answer is to form your own. Even if you plan to do that, however, maybe you have no experience of Pathworking and want to get the feel of it in a practical way before asking others to join you.

Whatever your plans, this chapter is specially for you if you are on your own *now*, to show you how best to succeed in your Pathworking program as an individual unit.

In reading through this book, you will have perceived that even for people who are Pathworking as members of a group, the main action is essentially inward and individual. It is also a fact, however, that this inwardness is by no means isolation. Whether physically we are alone or in the company of others, we are all part of an immense psychic network which extends at all levels of being: the unity of all life, the unity of the human race, special psychic contacts with friends known and unknown, the deep mind's contact with the archetypal powers, and the unique link between the individual and his or her Higher Self. Nor is that all: for the Divine Flame which is the source and center of your individual being is itself a part of the divine mind, and thus (no matter what divisions among people you may see or experience in the outer world) is in direct and loving contact endlessly with the Divine Flame of each and every other person soever.

People sharing an activity can keep one another "up to the mark," can stir up one another's enthusiasm and sense of commitment to a project. In planning any "lone" activity, decision and organization are of great importance.

The simple white robe, preferably hooded, which is recommended for members of Pathworking groups, is more emphatically recommended for "solitary" Pathworkers. To put on a special garment regularly for an activity carries your sense of the high worth of that activity right through all levels of your being. Your body and your deep mind are as much involved as your conscious emotions and your higher faculties. Besides that, it helps again to remind you that *you are not really alone*. You are one of the great number of explorers of the inner worlds who, whether in groups or singly, sit down and cut out distractions for a span of time while they gather spiritual strength, perception and illumination.

In setting up your place of working, you will need but one chair: this is required as, unlike the director of a group, you will be seated while reading the text of the Pathworking. In all other particulars, have your place of working as nearly as you can in accordance with the directives in Chapter 5, adapting according to your own needs.

In the *formula for Opening a Pathworking* which is given in Chapter 5, instead of the *Uniting of Energy* you will use the *circulation of Energy* which is given below: the subsections iv., v., and vi. differ most notably from the one technique to the other.

For the Use of *Mandala and Correspondences* you can employ either Method A or Method B on the day before, just as is suggested for members of a group: or else, on the occasion of the Pathworking itself, you can use Method A in place of the procedure outline in sections 4, 5 and 6 of the *formula for Opening a Pathworking*.

Circulation of Energy

i. Stand facing your altar, in an upright and balanced posture, but not "to attention."

ii. Visualize, at a little distance directly above your head, a sphere of white light.

iii. Visualize the sphere growing brighter and more radiant.

iv. Visualize a continuous *anti-clockwise* spiral of white light descending from the sphere: it whirls rapidly downwards around you, and its lower end can be imagined as disappearing at your feet.

v. In addition to this continuous descending spiral of white light, visualize, just within the limits of your place of working, a wall of blue light, strong and steady, revolving slowly in a *clockwise* direction.

vi. After a few moments, allow all visualizations to fade from your consciousness.

vii. Seat yourself in a balanced, easy posture, relaxed but not slumped, which you can maintain, or easily resume, throughout the working. There should be no crossing of arms, legs or ankles. Breathing should be steady and even, and such as you can comfortably maintain whenever you are not reading aloud.

Do not read the text of the Pathworking silently unless this is really necessary: to read aloud will keep your attention better fixed upon the complete succession of ideas. Read slowly, allowing yourself time to visualize each scene and to assimilate each succession of ideas. At the end of the Pathworking, allow yourself a period of reflection before sounding the battery.

Another activity which can help intensify and extend the experience of Pathworking for the "lone" Pathworker particularly, is the keeping of the Dream Journal. You should read Chapter 4 with special attention to see how much you can make of this. Your Journal of Dreams can become a real log-book of exploration and discovery.

Through reflection upon the Pathworkings and upon your dreams, you will develop a great understanding, and the initiations of the Paths will be yours. The day may come sooner than you think, when you will feel ready and resolved to call others together, to find with your guidance their own inner adventures and initiations upon the Paths which you will have come to know so deeply, and to love.

chapter 7

Pathworking Texts and Preliminary Materials

The Paths should first be worked in order of ascent, from 32 thru 24. Remember, however, that Paths 26 and 24 are not completed until after Path 25 is achieved. They are given here with subsequent completions, for use after the 25th Path of the Tree has been worked. In the initial order of working, the Paths are 32, 31, 30, 29, 28, 27, 26 (resolving in Malkuth), 24 (resolving in Yesod), 25, 26 and 24 (resolving in Tiphareth).

After the initial series of workings in order of ascent, the subsequent Tipharic completions (which are actually the norm) should be employed for Paths 26 and 24.

Continued working of the Paths, after adventuring them in ascending order, need not involve strict ascent on the Tree of Life, but may be adapted to preference and magical need: in this regard, see Chapter 8.

If, after the initial series of workings, further series are undertaken in order of ascent, the sequence 32, 31, 30, 29, 28, 27, 26, 24, 25 should be maintained.

Where the symbol ★ occurs in any Pathworking text, the appropriate incense is at that point to be used.

The Working of the 32nd Path

(Correspondences)

SPHERE OF COMMENCEMENT: Malkuth (Kingdom)

Hebrew Divine Name: Adonai Melek

Planetary correspondence: The Earth

Element: Earth

Symbol: The gateway; the cavern entrance

Colors: Shadowed natural hues

PATH OF THE TREE OF LIFE: 32

Intelligence: The 32nd Path is the Governing Intelligence, so named because it governs and co-ordinates the seven planets singly and collectively, each and all in their proper orbits.[6]

Hebrew Divine Name: Yahveh Elohim; Aima

Influence on Path: Saturn

Hebrew Letter: Tau (The sign)

Path Stanza: Thine is the Sign of the End, Being fulfilled
Sum of existences:
Thine is the ultimate Door opened on Night's
unuttered mystery:
Thine, the first hesitant step into the dark
of those but latterly
Born to the Labyrinth![7]

Tarot arcanum: The Universe (21)

Element of the Path: Earth

Symbols: The labyrinth, darkness, the well-head, the white cypress, the Fish-goat.

Living Creatures: Saurian monsters, Elementals, the Guardians of the Gates of Night.

---

6. The text quoted here, and every other text under the head *Intelligence* in these lists of correspondences, is from the Aurum Solis translation of *The Thirty-two Paths of Wisdom* by Johannes Stephanus Rittangelius (1642).

7. The *Path Stanzas* quoted throughout these lists of correspondences are from *The Song of Praises*, an Aurum Solis text given in full in Book III of *The Magical Philosophy*, Llewellyn, 1975.

Magical phenomena: The Watcher at the Threshold, passing the portals of Night, re-entry into the womb and starry rebirth, vision of destiny in the magick mirror of the unconsious.

SPHERE OF DESTINATION: Yesod (Foundation)

Hebrew Divine Name: Shaddai El Chai

Planetary correspondence: The Moon

Planetary number: 9

Element: Air

Symbols: The sickle, the garden

Minerals: Crystal, silver, porphyry

Colors: Violet, white

Living being: The stag

Magical phenomenon: The experience of primal and changeless reality amid ever-changing illusion.

Comments

This Path takes the traveler not only from Malkuth to Yesod, but also (by virtue of the principle of the Composite Tree) from the World of Assiah, the material plane, to the world of Yetzirah, the astral plane, of which Yesod is the Gate-Sephirah. When the Paths are worked in series, therefore, it is necessary that the 32nd should be worked the first.

Here, then, ends our course of involution—increasing involvement in the material world—and begins our course of evolution, progress upwards towards the world of spirit. Is matter, then, evil? Certainly not: but this turnaround has to be made, for two reasons. First, this stage of our development which is represented by the 32nd Path does not suppose us to be able to discern clearly wherein the excellence of the material universe consists, and without that discernment we cannot appreciate it aright. Second, a harmonious pattern of relationships has to be set up, stage by stage, among the parts or functions of the psyche: and for this, a definite direction of the will has to be affirmed at several crucial points in our journey. In Malkuth we are born into material life, on the 32nd Path we are born into our Way of Return. Hence *The Song of Praises* refers to "the first hesitant step into the dark of those but latterly Born to the Labyrinth."

The 32nd Path is called a labyrinth not only because it is dark, mysterious and monster-haunted, but also because, through the influence of Saturn, it is under the dominance—as yet dark and remote—of the Supernal Mother. Upon this Path the traveler is beset by the so-called "malefic" side of the planetary influence, which burdens the imagination with suggestions of fear and despondency, and with temptations to a misplaced nostalgia for the past or sense of loyalty to it. Some foretaste is here, too, of the "Dark Night of the Soul" which belongs to Binah. The traveler strives, however, to escape from the pull of elemental Earth and to rise into the emotive and changeful atmosphere of elemental Air, the element of the Moon sphere. Over this "birth" presides the Mother, whose work is to bring all things to their true level of being: the "Governing Intelligence" of the verse from *The 32 Paths of Wisdom*.

The reward of this Path is thus the psyche's consciousness of liberation from the weight of material existence, as in the Orphic mysteries, and the perpetual adventure of the Nephesh (the astral level of the psyche) in its native world.

The Working of the 32nd Path

We stand in a wild, ancient forest on a hillside, where rocky bluffs rise amid the trees. It is early evening, and the stillness is broken only by an occasional bird song. There is a pleasant odor from the many tall, cone-bearing trees which surround us, and from the fragrant mosses which grow thickly in the moist shade. Here we feel a deep awareness of peace, of belonging, of unity with our Mother Earth.

Our attention is caught by a darker shadow in the face of an irregular natural wall of rock which stands before us. Surely it looks like the entrance to a cave? It is as though a magical door had opened for us in the hillside. With a feeling of being invited to exploration, to adventure, we go to examine the shadowy archway.

We are not disappointed. There is a cave; not a large one, but at the back of it is a second natural arch giving us access to an inner chamber. This even more mysterious entrance offers a further invitation,

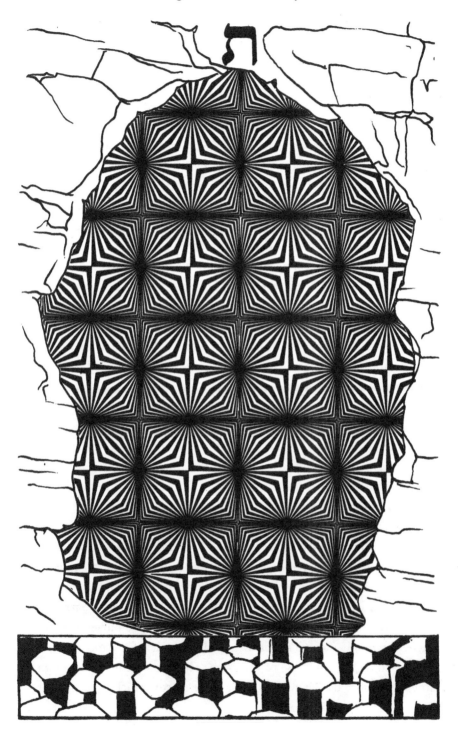

and we go in. The rays of the sinking sun, shining level with the cave mouth, penetrate here with an intensity which fills the area with warm golden light, reflecting from the rocky walls and roof. Here is a feeling of unmeasured time. We look about us in awe.

On one of the walls the rays of the sun throw into relief a group of faint spiral markings. We examine them, without being sure of their significance. Are they the result of some irregularity in the composition of the rock?—some fossil form, perhaps, of which the original material has long since disappeared?—or are we looking at one of those mysterious glyphs left in hidden places by the humanity of an earlier age, perhaps to show the way to a shrine, perhaps to express some inner truth? We cannot be sure, and this cave contains no other visible sign to help us.

There is, however, an aperture leading into yet a third chamber. In that further recess, we feel, there may be some clue to those enigmatic markings; some further evidence as to their nature, or as to the meaning of their message.

Why do the traces of time past hold so much fascination for us? No matter how full our lives may be, or how rationally planned, there is always in the depths of the human soul a quest for cause and purpose, a restless desire to seek outside the circle of what is known and familiar for something which has been forgotten, or for something unexplained. Whether the mystery we have found here concerns the earlier ages of the Earth itself, or whether it relates to the non-material levels of human experience, we feel impelled to seek it out if that is possible to us. We go through the opening into the third cave.

The soft sand beneath our feet gives back no sound. Instantly it is as if a curtain had fallen between us and the outer world, as if we were enveloped in a coccoon of silence. Even while we stand still, waiting for our eyes to become accustomed to the dimmer light of this enclosure, in the outer world the sun sinks lower in the sky. We are left in darkness.

Already unsure of our way back, and afraid to lose ourselves completely by hastily moving about, we stand motionless for some minutes, hoping to regain our sense of direction. The darkness feels as though it would absorb us. Then, slowly, for some reason which we cannot at once comprehend, there appears before us a faint area of less intense blackness. We fix our attention upon it in wonder.

The patch of luminosity increases. As it does so, we see there is movement in it: a faint spiralling of pale light up from the ground, gradually forming itself into a whirling ovoid of light suspended in the air before us. It spins more and more rapidly. In this whirling light there grows a central region of stillness and of greater brightness. This increases, until finally this center occupies the whole of the ovoid. The whirling ceases. For a moment the shape hangs motionless; then, suddenly, it is transformed into a beautiful and radiant figure, surrounded by an aura of white light.

Before us stands the tall and commanding form of a woman. Upon her dark hair is a cone-shaped silver helmet, adorned at each side with wings of the same gleaming metal. A long cloak of metallic black rests upon her shoulders; beneath it she wears a white robe with a broad border of gold, and a golden girdle is about her waist. In her right hand she carries a silver sickle. Within her aura of light, her form is wholly luminous.

We look at her in amazement and admiration, while she looks at us with understanding. Then, with a gesture, she bids us follow her.

We watch as she turns and moves along the opposite wall of the cave. We resolve to follow, although it seems evident she will not lead us back along the way we entered. So bright is the radiance which emanates from her aura that by it we can see clearly the rocky walls of the cave, and even the floor upon which we walk.

As this luminous being glides forward, we are able to perceive several further openings in the mass of rock confronting us. At one of these openings our guide pauses, raising her sickle so that it flashes like a miniature crescent moon; clearly she wishes to ensure that we follow closely, and take exactly the path she shows us. Through the opening, she turns to one side and once more signals to us to remain prudently on the path.

It is evident that she is leading us deeper into the earth. We are descending by a track which appears to be a sloping ridge on the edge of a great abyss. On one side of us is the rugged vertical wall of the cavern; on the other side, beyond our path is the huge cavity, dark save for the gleaming reflections from the aura of our Guide, revealing the glistening shafts of mighty stalactites, like the columns of a cathedral, descending into the blackness. Nothing breaks the stillness save the distant sounds of water: a continual gentle dripping, and, even more remotely, the rushing of a torrent in the depths. The descending ridge which forms our path may itself have been formed by the action of water, for it is smooth and gleaming, and is slightly channeled towards its center. The place is awesome, and we cannot but wonder how our journey will end.

Gradually as we continue our descent we realize that our path is taking on a progressively steeper slope. This does not at first occasion us any real difficulty, but it increases our apprehension considerably. Still in the dark void beside us we see only the shafts of the stalactites; there are no answering domes or points of stalagmites such as we should expect to find growing up from the floor of the great cavern, if floor there be. To return to the upper air by the way we have descended would already be a most difficult task. Our path now slopes downward even more steeply, as if it were approaching some shoulder of rock from which in ages past the bygone flow of water had plunged into the abyss. How can we continue to trust the mysterious figure which glides ahead of us, luminous and enigmatic?

What choice have we but to trust her?

Instinctively we slow our pace as the steeper slope of the path now ominously throws us forward. Just at that moment, however, our Guide who is some five paces ahead of us pauses and raises her flashing sickle as a sign to us, then turns towards the solid rock, moves forward into it and disappears. It does not seem to us, however, that she has altogether abandoned us. At the point where she was lost to our sight, the luminosity of her aura still lingers.

We pause, considering what we should do. We have taken this beautiful and luminous being as our guide; surely we should at least venture upon this other few paces?

Cautiously we make our way down the smooth and disturbingly sloping path to the point where our Guide disappeared. There, invisible from above, we find a narrow fissure running into the rock at right angles to the sloping ledge. A little way in, a burst of radiance reveals to us the waiting figure of our Guide. This fissure has an uneven but solid rocky floor, forming a kind of passage way between the rocky masses.

To one side of us the layers of different hue and structure, which indicate successive epochs in the rock's formation, run parallel to the floor of the passage; but on the other side these layers are inclined at a sharp angle, giving evidence of a violent fracture and piling together of the masses of rock at some remote time. This, doubtless, was the origin of the rifts through which we move.

The path is almost horizontal now as the black-cloaked but luminous figure again leads us forward. The narrow way branches, then branches again through the fissures of the rock; only our Guide can know which way we should take.

Without warning the path opens into a cave of considerable extent, although of no great height, its roof, about fifteen feet from the floor at one side, slopes down to some four feet at the other. At the lower side, an inclined shaft leads down into this cave from above. We consider the shaft, but it runs up into total blackness, and no breath of air comes from it; doubtless its upper opening, by whatever accident, has long been blocked.

The cave in which we stand holds much to draw our attention. In places, narrow cracks in the roof give admission to a slight intermittent flow of water which, falling to the uneven floor of the cave, flows over the surface before running away in little vein-like channels at one side. From above and below, there has thus been built up during long ages a considerable formation of stalactites and stalagmites, for whose strange and beautiful forms our imagination tries to find names: pillars, javelins, the strings of a musical instrument, elfin domes and spires, festive pennants, all glistening with white crystals and with the delicate mineral tints of Earth. Not the whole of the cave is thus adorned, however. The higher part of the roof is unbroken; no mineral-laden water has made its way through, and below this, in its lair of millennia past, still lie some of the bones, and the skull, of one of the huge carnivores who evidently inhabited this cave while the outer shaft was open.

Passing through this cave, we follow our guide into a further narrow passage in the rock. Now again there is a gentle downward slope. We move silently, almost as if a sound from us might attract danger. The darkness is complete but for the radiant aura of our Guide, who now again moves some distance ahead of us; the lack of vision, and the sense of being enclosed in the depths of the earth, is oppressive. Besides this, an increasing awareness troubles us, that some other Presence besides that of our guide is near to us in this obscurity. Without knowing what this other Presence may be, we fear it. We long for light, yet we dread what light might show us.

All movement, and breathing itself, becomes difficult as the awareness of this other Presence increases. When we move, it moves. It seems to be all around us. We feel it hovering before us, like dark wings beating to deafen us from hearing any warning sound, and yet it breathes at the back of our neck to impel us forward. It seems to be clinging about our feet as if to entangle them, and we withdraw in involuntary horror; it moves near our hands, as if about to grasp them with a moist and reptillian touch. It comprises every horror belonging to life and to death, to the material and non-material worlds. We know not what it is nor whence it comes, but with every step we advance it seems more imminently about to seize upon us from every direction. At the same time, a strange lethargy seems to take possession of us. We move more and more slowly; our feet feel as if made of lead.

Our Guide turns, for we are following her no longer. She raises her gleaming sickle, and we wait, expecting her to drive off whatever unseen Power it is that so besets us with horror.

Once more, however, she does but make a sign to urge us forward, then she turns and continues on the path. She would have us know that here is nothing to fear. For a moment we still hesitate. Our Guide has brought us safely through the perils of our entry into these regions; but plainly she herself is more than mortal, and where for her there is in truth nothing to fear we poor humans might be less confident. The strange lethargy of body and soul which afflicts us is still in operation, and we cannot at once decide what to do.

As we stand doubting, the horror grows more intense. We see the shining form of our Guide recede as she continues upon her way, and the darkness grows thicker about us. We cannot remain here without her, for we should be altogether lost! Whatever effort it costs us to go forward, go forward we must.

With all the force of our will we compel our reluctant feet to move, and after the first steps we can go more freely. Now as we walk we begin to understand. It is the Guardian of the Threshold whose presence we have been experiencing; a presence which has been so full of horror for us, but is not in truth evil. It is a reflection, here in this Lower Astral darkness, of our own faithful Divine Guardian: a reflection distorted by our own fears and misgivings, since at this time we could relate to it no true image of its own sublime beauty and power. Even thus, Psyche in the ancient story was persuaded that her invisible divine lover, Eros, must be a hideous monster. There is, in truth, nothing in this part of our journey that can harm us except our own fears, and these we are to put away from us. We hasten to rejoin our Guide, and as she turns to welcome us her eyes shine beneath her silver helmet with joy and encouragement. Moving her sickle so that it flashes in the radiance of her aura, she scatters the shadows which have seemed so menacing and beckons us onward.

The gentle downward slope continues. We follow our Guide through a maze of dividing and crossing passages, narrow fissures and sudden changes of direction. The sense of oppression is gone, but we feel a deeper awareness of mystery, an increasing involvement in experiences which are no longer wholly those of Earth. From time to time our Guide raises her sickle to reassure us that this is indeed the path we are to follow; and the radiance surrounding her lights us safely through every difficult place.

Now the path levels out and becomes wider. Another cave lies before us; but as soon as we enter, we perceive that this is no simple natural cavity. It is a rectangular hall of immeasurable extent, hewn in the solid rock.

Our Guide moves forward into this space. By the brilliant light emanating from her aura we observe that around the sides of this hall have been gathered together, since the earliest ages of humanity, treasures of every description.

Here are weapons of war, of stone and bronze, iron and steel, heaped together, eaten away with stains of green and of rust-red. Here is statuary representing mysterious divine and heroic beings, the ideals and aspirations of mankind through countless centuries. Some of these images are carved in stark plain stone or bone; some are of exquisite artistry, of precious metals and priceless gems. All have represented beings of power; but here we have only the burden of the past, and none of these images are of deities that we can recognize. Many appear to have been wrought in high civilizations differing from any of which history now has any trace. Here are ikons and effigies representing lost myths, forgotten victories, men and women who were at one time renowned; now even these unnamed images are faded, flaking into dust. Here are numberless tablets of clay and wax, painstakingly impressed with closely-packed characters. Here too are paper, parchment, papyrus, scrolls and stacked sheets written and sometimes written over again, now crumbling mutely away. Here and there a burst of splendor gleams where chests of wood or metal have spilled their massive contents: the barbaric crowns and scepters of kings and queens, intricate jeweled vessels and ornaments whose purpose is outside our knowledge, tumbled piles of gold and silver coins bearing proud but remote countenances.

A profound sadness takes possession of us as we gaze upon these relics and reminders of wisdom, power and riches, treasured and lost ages before we were born. We feel impelled to linger here, to make this the goal of our journey; for surely, it seems to us, nothing in the outer world can equal in beauty, in significance, and in inexpressible appeal, the treasures of the past.

While we are reflecting upon these things, a deep sound quivers through the air of the vast hall. It is like the reverberation of a heavy gong, heard or rather felt from a great distance. We feel disturbed, and in our perlexity we look to our Guide for some indication of what we should do. The light of her aura flashes with a sudden intense radiance, which floods into our consciousness and awakens our inner perception to a higher pitch. We understand, now, the reason why the past history of humanity, and of the world, holds so deep an appeal for us; for it is our own past history. None of this for which we feel so much yearning, so much nostalgia, is lost. Like calls to like, and that which we have found again in this place is, in its spiritual reality, a part of our own being. We may indeed venerate the past, we may feel a deep gratitude because we are indeed its heirs, we may seek out its mysteries and love it for the beauty and wonder it holds; but we must not be bound to the past, neither to possess it nor to be possessed by it. To be bound to the past would be to miss our present destiny; and did that occur, we should fail, even in our trust to the past itself. It is in our own lives lived aright that the past finds its fulfilment.

Resolutely we turn from the heaped repository of time past, and our Guide leads us on our way.

With renewed energy we follow our Guide through the dark caverns beyond the treasure house, led by her luminous aura and by the sickle which, when she raises it, shines like a crescent moon. Now through our experience in the treasure house and through our resolution in leaving it, we have loosened the grip of many ancestral and personal formative influences which have held us to the limitations of material existence. This new freedom of soul has brought us a greater understanding and a keener perception; one result of which is that we are now aware of some of the more subtle modes of existence which previously were hidden from us.

At first this perception comes to us in strange and undirected glimpses. With our Guide leading some distance ahead of us, again our path is descending gradually to deeper levels. Now and again, elemental beings appear; sometimes crossing our path with the speed of lightning, sometimes lingering and moving with us for a short distance. Sometimes, too, for a moment, a fragment of wild melody reaches us, and then is gone.

Now, ahead of us, our Guide signals to us to be watchful. Again we are approaching a place of rifts and fissures in the rock. One such rift, about five feet wide, forms a chasm across our path and is bridged only by a narrow splinter of rock which lies across it. Our Guide glides across this fearsome place, then turns to await us at the far side. She holds up her sickle so that each person, while crossing the slender and insecure bridge, can do so with eyes fixed steadily upon that gleaming emblem. We feel our fingers and the soles of our feet tingle with apprehension as we come to the rift, and we know we must shut out of our consciousness the impenetrable blackness of the awesome abyss, and the sound of falling water which rises, echoing, from its incalculable depths. We must keep our gaze upon the silver sickle held before us by our Guide, and go steadily forward in confidence.

The elemental beings again appear, however; and to them the chasm is a place to dance. Involuntarily we glimpse them, now whirling in a wild pirouette above the void as on a solid surface, now linking in a chain or following each other closely to sweep across to the midst of our bridge, swerving aside and, with a shrill chant of joy, gliding down to the depths and with the same flowing rhythm rising again. We can scarcely help turning to make sure of what we have seen, to follow the course of a trail of sound or of movement.

But no. Innocent, certainly, is the delight of those carefree children of elemental Earth, but our way does not lie with them. When our new-found power of vision is not a help to us but a hindrance, we must discover how to turn our attention from it as simply and naturally as we could close our bodily eyes. We set foot firmly upon the narrow bridge of rock, and, fixing our entire attention on the gleaming sickle on the far side, swiftly and surely we make the crossing.

Once we have crossed the bridge, our path runs into a broad, rugged tunnel running amid the rifts and cavities of the rock. The sense of mystery and wonder remains with us, even more strongly than before. We move in earthly fashion because thus we feel secure, but we are aware that even here, in the depths of elemental Earth, this is no mundane quest that we pursue. Now our path descends in a wide clockwise spiral; we are conscious of the slight but continuous turning to the right, the slight forward impetus which indicates our descent. Our Guide, moving somewhat ahead of us, remains in sight, her luminous aura lighting our path.

Gradually, however, the curve of the spiral becomes smaller, the angle of descent steeper. Our progress is almost like the movement of a circular dance, still turning, turning, turning. The walls of rock between which our Guide moves are torn in places by deep fissures, which frequently encroach upon the floor of the passage also. As long as our Guide remains in sight, we can easily avoid these pitfalls; but when the path turns in a smaller curve, at the same time sloping downward more steeply, we can no longer keep within sight of her and only the lingering gleam reflected from her bright aura remains to light our way. We move more rapidly, partly impelled by the increasing slope and partly to avoid being left in darkness.

Now from the black crevasses which gape beside our path, new horrors threaten us: bestial demonic forms having their own pale greenish phosphorescence, their small deep-set eyes glowing with a red fire of malevolence. All are of monstrous size, all of squat saurian form; but the other attributes of these hideous assailants are as varied as Chaos itself.

To one side of our path a long flexible snout snuffs the ground, then rears out of the shadows with curved gleaming tusks to quest after us; to the other side, a torpid seeming head suddenly lances towards us with serpent fangs dripping venom. As we still continue the spiral descent, the scaly, powerful tail of another monster ceases to lash from side to side and is arched overhead, displaying in its tip a menacing dart like a scorpion's. Among the shadows behind us, we are aware of powerful gaping jaws, and webbed, legless feet dragging a broad belly over the ground with relentless purpose in pursuit of us.

The spiral in which we descend is now so acute that our pace makes us dizzy. We fear to collapse, to fall; that would be to be instantly seized by the monsters, to be devoured instantly or to be dragged off to drown in the deeps. Even the gleam from our Guide's bright aura is now beyond our sight; in darkness save for the corrupt luminescence of our pursuers, we impel ourselves desperately down that vertiginous spiral, our senses reeling.

The descent ends abruptly. We stagger forward into light, not at once conscious that both the spiral course and the pursuit are over.

Before us stands our Guide, looking at us, beautiful, calm and luminous. She raises her shining sickle, and as we gaze we seem to be drinking its light like pure, refreshing water. No benighted offspring of primal Chaos will brave that radiant emblem, nor venture to look upon the pure light of our Guide's aura.

With a gesture, she bids us to advance. We take a few steps, and gaze in wonder at the scene before us.

We have come to a mighty portal closed with doors of dark bronze. Upon the doors, many massive panels are framed in rectangular borders of the same metal; these borders being adorned with plant forms in low relief, with fruits, seedpods and ears of grain. The panels themselves, sculptured in higher relief, show the histories of Night, of Sleep and of the domain of Saturn. In one of these scenes, in a barren mountain land we behold a monstrous giant who devours his own children: for the giant is Time, which devours all it produces. In another panel, a delicate and graceful Moon Maiden kisses the brow of a beautiful sleeping youth. Only while he sleeps is he hers, while he sleeps he is immortal, while he sleeps he is ever happy and beautiful; so, although thus he can see her only in dreams, she bids him sleep for ever. Here, in another panel, the young daughter of the Earth Mother, gathering flowers, has left her companions in order to pluck a single, perfect narcissus which grows by a pool. Unseen by her, from a wide fissure in the earth rises the Lord of the Underworld in his chariot, managing the fierce horses with one hand while in the other he holds a jeweled crown to place on the head of the maiden he intends to carry off as his bride. In yet another panel, we see represented a place at the fork of a road which runs through open country. There stands a tall pillar surmounted by a crowned and veiled head with three faces, looking in three directions: the face of a young woman, that of a mature woman and that of a woman advanced in years. Before this tall pillar are several human figures: some are holding torches, signifying that the time is at night, some are placing offerings, while some are raising their hands in prayer to the Invincible Queen. In the background, some dogs with raised heads are baying at the disc of the full moon, and beyond are the waves of the sea; these things signifying that the whole world of nature pays the same homage in its own manner.

There are many other panels in these mighty doors, but whenever we look from one panel to another we realize there are others surrounding it on which we have not yet fixed our gaze. Indeed, the images seem to be continually changing so as to be truly without limit. They are but images of images; and, worthy of study and reflection though they are, they must not detain us from the further experiences which lie before us. At each side of the portal stands a massive column of black stone; and by each of these columns stands a wondrous Being which is not at once clearly visible to us.

This portal before which we stand is one of the lower entrances to the Palace of Night; those who guard it are of the higher spiritual levels of the Astral World. To us they appear like colossal figures hewn of crystal: figures of men of mighty strength, nude, and each having upon his shoulders the head of a bull. Each wields a powerful sword, with a blade that looks like frozen fire.

As we approach, these Guardians make a gesture of salutation to our Guide, then clash their swords together so that the blades cross before the doors. In a voice like the roar of thunder echoing in a mountain pass, the Guardian to the left of the portal asks "Who are you?" Our Guide replies, without haste but in a high clear ringing tone, "We are travelers upon our lawful path."

Then in a harsh whisper, like a cold wind from the stars, the Guardian to the right of the portal asks, "Why need you to pass the Doors of Night?" Again our Guide replies, calmly and as one affirming assured truths, "We seek honey to taste, and milk to drink, and a mirror wherein to see."

The Guardians raise their swords. As they do so, a ripple of flame runs gloriously through the blades, and a deep musical sound vibrates in the air; it grows louder, then dies away. These mighty spiritual beings give no further sign, but the ponderous doors slowly open. Led by our Guide, we enter.

At first nothing meets our eyes save the changeful glitter of gems. Our Guide pauses: by the light of her aura we see that we are in an enclosed chamber or cavern, which is regularly ovoid in shape. The floor on which we stand is concave, and continuous in curve with the rest of the enclosure. No opening is anywhere visible. We have entered, we realize, at one end of this womblike chamber; as we advance towards the other, it is evident that there is indeed no means of egress. And now we hear the resonant crash of the great doors of bronze closing behind us.

Disturbing though this is, however, we cannot but yield our attention to the marvelous crystalline brilliance of the rock surface. From above and around us, points of light flash insistently from myriad gems of every color and size, incomparable in their magnificence.

But now, the luminous image of our Guide shines less and less brightly. It no longer illumines the rock surface, which swiftly disappears into blackness, although from this blackness, the radiance of the many-hued gems still shines out. Now we see our Guide no longer, she has vanished from our sight. We gaze at the place where she has been, but in vain; she has assuredly left us.

The pulsating brilliance of the gems, however, remains: it is born of their own luminosity. Now their beauty seems to mock us. Bereft of the aid of our Guide, we are prisoners of the unearthly bull-headed giants; we know not even in what region of the worlds, or between worlds, we are held captive.

We wait, expecting perhaps some voice or sign of guidance, but nothing stirs. Only the quivering light of the gems is blazing forth, even more brightly than before.

Still more brightly do they shine, so that their colors lose depth as they gain in radiance. In many areas, too, above and around us, innumerable clustered facets of light become newly visible, forming glimmering clouds around gems which before had seemed isolated. Our feet have not stirred from the place where we have been standing, but a cool wind strikes us.

We are enclosed no longer in the womblike rocky chamber: we are standing on a hill top, with the dome of heaven all about us filled with its radiant gems, the stars, and with the wide-spreading and unsearchable luminance of the Milky Way.

We stand there in silence and amazement, poised between earth and air, gazing. The august beauty of the Night stirs us to the depth of our being.

We seem to grow in stature, taller and taller, as though we would reach to the stars themselves, and an ecstasy fills us. Here upon this hill top, high above any horizon, we feel suspended in space. The stars seem closer to us; even the planet Saturn, which we see at the highest point in the skies, appears less remote than usual. Each of the other planets of our Solar System also, from where we stand at this point in our journey, is to be seen shining clear and perfect in its due orbit.

The light of the Milky Way is a living glory, more dazzling than in the clearest earthly night. Looking up into it, we raise our arms in the form of a Tau cross and breathe in its downpouring radiance. We rejoice as we drink deep of it, the light of million upon million suns: we are steeped in it, permeated with its whiteness and its power.

We lower our arms, and are again aware of ourselves standing upon the hill top under the stars. And now a sound of singing meets our ears, an austere chant whose slow, lilting rhythms and unfamiliar harmonies suggest the high, vast perspectives of space.

It is the song of Night and the Stars, and its haunting theme and cosmic harmonies seem to hold a message for us, a key to our own experience.

We cannot seek counsel from our Guide; she is not with us, and evidently we must decide our own future course. For a little while longer we pause, listening to the sublime and ecstatic chanting which seems to call to us, then we make our way down from the hill top, in the direction of that compelling song.

We descend some distance before we find a path; and then, beyond a cluster of pine trees, we catch sight of the sparkle of fire.

From that same direction comes the sound of the chanting.

Into a gently rising slope, seemingly from long ago, a wide horizontal track has been cut and paved: so that as we advance upon it the enclosing grassy banks rise higher on both sides of it, until the paved way ends in a series of eight wide stone steps ascending to a naturally level place beyond.

To left and right upon each of the first seven steps stand white robed figures, facing inward and leaving a clear space in the center. Each has a white band encircling the brow, and each is singing ecstatically: these are the initiates who are uttering the chant of Night and the Stars.

Upon the topmost step are two heavy metal bowls. From each bowl water overflows to run down the steps before the feet of the initiates and to descend into a stream that flows directly across the path before the lowest step. And, marvelously, from each of the bowls bright flames continually rise proudly upward.

Between the bowls of flowing water and rising flame, facing us at the top of the steps, stands our Guide.

As we approach the steps, we come to the stream of clear water, and without hesitation we wade across it. The water moves swiftly but is not very deep.

Slowly we ascend the steps, passing between the two lines of chanting initiates and the water flowing down from the bowls of flame.

We near the top of the steps.

Assuredly we are about to enter upon some primal mystery.

Our Guide raises both her arms towards the starry sky, her sickle gleaming and flashing in flamelight and starlight; then she turns and goes ahead to lead us.

As we follow her, passing between the two bowls on the topmost step, we see that the flames rise from the surface of the water which fills the bowls. We rejoice that we are no longer beneath the earth. It is deep night, but the glorious stars are over us and the chanting of the initiates accompanies us.

Led by our Guide and by the clear light of her aura, we traverse in silence the dark level expanse which forms the summit of this area of the Mysteries. The chanting of the initiates sounds more softly as we progress, then we begin to lose it as a gentle breeze carries the sound away from us.

Now, a little distance ahead of us we see a solitary tree, a white cypress, tall and slender: the only one of its kind. We draw near to it, and in its shadow we find a circular well-head of stonework elaborately carved, before which we pause. The well-head seems to have been wrought in ancient times; it shows an intricate pattern of continuous spirals, coiled around medallions depicting the "Fish-Goat," the horned goat whose body ends in the tail of a fish. That strange hybrid, we know, in these times is associated with the zodiacal sign of Capricorn; but in the ancient world it was the symbol for the planet Saturn.

We look down into the well. Deep in its shadows, far down, we catch the sparkle of water. Our bodies lean relaxed upon the stone of the well-head, while our minds seek the further shadows of mystery; then, as our eyes become accustomed to the darkness, we see our own reflection gazing back at us, the head surrounded by a silver radiance of light from the starlit sky above us.

But that is not all we see. As we continue to gaze, our sight penetrates by degrees into the very depths of the well. There, in that dark and timeless water, a primitive, fish-like creature moves. We cannot see it clearly because its shape is almost entirely obscured by the superimposed reflection, but none the less we realize what the well is showing us. The truth we see here is not single, but a double truth, for it shows us what we are: we are that which has descended from the luminous heights to this depth, and we are that which is now rising up from that depth towards the heights.

Before leaving the well-head, we look again at the sculpture which adorns it. We are treading at this time in reality that labyrinthine Path which carries us in the endless spirals of life's progression, and upon us in truth is the influence of Saturn, symbolized by the Fish Goat. For our involutionary descent into Matter is ended, and upon this Path begins our evolutionary return journey towards the spiritual heights. But here is only a beginning of that long ascent, and the Fish of the depths and the Goat of the mountain peaks are still in our consciousness.

Again our Guide leads us. We descend by a gentle slope from the area of the Mysteries, and follow a path leading into a sheltered valley.

Without our noticing it, a light veil of cloud has covered the sky, so that the stars are no longer to be seen; and although the full Moon has now arisen, her orb is concealed and only her diffused light reaches us. It fills the whole sky with misty brilliance.

We pass beneath a dark arch, and fmd ourselves walking in a garden. Benches and paved paths of gleaming marble stand out amid the luxuriant abundance of living things. The air is rich with the fragrance of jasmine and of lilies, mingled only slightly with resinous and bitter odor from the dark cypresses and spreading yew-trees which stand as landmarks in the garden and form its background. Beyond is a wood of gnarled and venerable ash trees, from whose branches sound the call of birds: now and then the mournful cry of an owl, and with a wild music that for a moment stops the heart-beat—the song of a nightingale. It is as if a sparkling cascade of cool water had been endowed with a singing voice, and given also the quality of individual consciousness. The song utters all that the human heart has forgotten how to utter; it tells, again and again, the rapture which is the central principle of emotional-instinctual nature, the life of the natural soul. It is limitless question, and limitless answer: it is the fire of action, and the tranquil water of being. As we listen, we feel that every moment of horror or distress which assailed us on our way here, every deep care which may be buried in our hearts, is lifted and assuaged with melodious sound.

From a marble urn which surmounts a pedestal beside the path, a large fern is growing. Its long, plumelike fronds rise up, and curve over, and sweep downwards almost to the ground. We pause to admire it, when our attention is caught by a multitude of flashing emerald particles, brilliant and iridescent as tiny bubbles, which dance in the air above and around the fern. Some of these tiny sparkles, evidently more charged with energy than the others, fly off altogether so that at first we know not where they go. This sight surprises us, until we remember the special power of vision which has been given us in this journey; we are seeing more than would correspond to the outer nature of things. Looking again over the varied herbs and flowering plants of the garden, we see that every leaf and blossom, bud and fruit, is surrounded by a similar dance of particles of light: green, fiery red, gold, intense blue or pearly white according to their nature. Over the shadowy corners and serene expanses of the garden, besides, those particles of light which have flown far from their own environment meet and mingle in a shimmering rainbow of changeful colors until, caught and concentrated in a stray moonbeam, they form a vortex and stream upwards, still dancing and shimmering towards its unseen source.

We stand looking to that shining immensity as if we ourselves would be drawn up into it. But all at once, look! What is that which seems to be returning, descending out of that luminous vortex? Are the shimmering particles changing their course?

It is not those particles which now seep downward across the sky, turning and gliding into the garden. The new manifestation is a swarm of silvery bees with delicate rainbow wings; softly humming bees which disperse in every direction seeking the nectar of the fragrant blossoms which have opened in the misty light. Their drowsy humming 'becomes part of the spell of this enchanted region.

As we turn to move on, some of the silver bees leave the blossoms and fly directly towards us. Our Guide makes a sign that there is no cause for alarm, so we stand still and let the gentle little creatures approach. Their rainbow wings briefly fan our skin; then they are gone, having left a drop of sweet honey on the lips of each of us.

As we taste it, we become aware of a new discernment awakening within us: a perception of spiritual order, which will enable our minds to reject any confusion in what is put before them, and to see the elements which compose the matter in their true likeness.

We find too, that now we have the key to other things which were previously obscure to us.

As beings reborn we have passed through the Doors of Night, seeking, as our Guide said, "honey to taste, and milk to drink, and a mirror wherein to see." We have bathed in the milk of the stars, we have drunk the milk of heaven. We have looked into the Well, and in its mirror have seen the course of our destiny. And we have tasted one drop of honey from the Garden of the Moon: one sweet drop of that liberation of the spirit whose plenitude is a supernal prize still far distant.

We continue along the marble-paved path, delighting in the visible beauty, the sounds and perfumes of the garden. The song of the nightingale is carried to us on a fitful breeze, like a nostalgic memory. Then we cross the bridge over a little stream, and once more we are out of the garden, in the open country.

The cloud is thinner now, and in the misty moonlight the scene before us is clear. We are on a grassy slope; below us, further down in the valley, is a thick forest.

Here our Guide bids us farewell; we have no further need of her now, she tells us. "On this journey," she says, "the only obstacles come from within. There is naught of evil but human fear and malice. Be free of these, and you are free in all the worlds." She makes a sign of salutation to us, then raises her silver sickle high and makes the diffused moonlight flash upon its blade, as if giving a sign to another beyond our awareness; then, gathering her black cloak around herself, she blends into the night and is gone from us. This time, we know, we are not to look for her return.

None the less, we stand bewildered. We ponder her words; they are like an echo of something we have known long ago. Our spirit knows its home in the world of Spirit. We can look up to the inaccessible heavens and feel a relatedness, a deep peace in contemplating those high emblems of our supreme destiny. *We have bathed in the milk of the stars.* But the life which we share with the material and astral worlds—the life of the emotions, of the instincts, of the body—this it is which needs to be strengthened and purified, nurtured and guided on the Way of Return. When our inner nature is truly whole, the higher with the lower, then truly we shall be able to live without fear and without heartache. Now, however, we can but continue our journey.

We look about us, considering what to do. Approaching us from the valley, we see shining among the trees a small patch of gleaming light with, behind it, a dim shape. We stand still, watching it. Out from the deeper shadows it comes, with calm and majestic pace: a noble antlered stag, upon whose tawny brow shines a single moon-spot. That silvery gleam it was which first made his approach known to us. For the space of a breath he stands regarding us, then he turns and moves slowly away. After a few paces he turns his head towards us; we are to follow. He moves along the path he is showing us.

The stag continues to lead us. Sometimes trees hide him from us; but then in the dark shadows he turns his head again, and we catch the gleam of the mark upon his brow. It does not seem strange to us to be guided by a stag, for he came in response to the signal of our other Guide, and in the high spiritual unity in which she abides, all beings of the natural world act together when there is need. We follow the stag on and on, down long slopes which lie quiet and colorless in the diffused moonlight, and up hillsides where dark pinetrees, like living emblems of aspiration, stand in clusters to mark the turns of the path.

Now a sharp wind rises, bringing heavy clouds to send across the skies to engulf us for long intervals in deep blackness. We can only discern our Guide the Stag by the shining moon-spot on his brow when, frequently, he turns his head to await us. But we have made good progress in the favorable time, and now, although the difficulties we encounter may impede us, they can put no insuperable barrier in our way. We recall the words of our former Guide, that the only real obstacles upon this path could come from within ourselves; and although the wind snatches and tugs at our garments, the stag goes onward and we know we have to follow. We press on, while the wind becomes even stronger and makes our progress yet more difficult.

At last it seems as if we are trying to push our way through a solid wall of air. This invisible and, usually, most flexible element has become a supreme test of our resolution.

Leaning forward, we struggle with all our strength and with all our will.

Now, suddenly, we are through the barrier. ★

The wind dies away, the clouds are gone. And, look! High in the dark sky before us shines the moon in splendor, her silver orb surrounded by a ring of intense violet light.

Beneath the moon, on the shoulder of a hill, stands a massive circular building surmounted by a dome. Walls and dome are of purple porphyry, highly polished. The edge of the dome projects beyond the wall, forming a colonnade around the building, supported by nine columns of crystal. Within this colonnade, facing us, is the entrance to the building: a door of silver, which stands slightly ajar.

The stag goes before us to where the roof overhangs the door of the building: there he stands aside, looking at us as if inviting us to enter. As we approach, he tosses his magnificent head with its crown of antlers, and bounds away towards the hills.

We pass through the door into the building. So thick is the wall, that we seem at first to have entered a tunnel; the stillness we have felt since the cessation of the wind is in a marvelous way redoubled, and as we emerge into the interior of the building we have a sense of having unmistakeably entered a place set apart, a place of great and vibrant power.

Before us, to left and right, stand the two pillars Machetes and Nomothetes. Reverently we pass between them, and stop to salute the

East; then we contemplate that which lies within the spacious circle of the building.

The interior of the enclosing wall is covered with moonstone, translucent and milky white, mingled with subtle veins of gold which gleam upon and beneath its surface. The floor on which we stand is likewise translucent, smooth and hard; but this floor gives a strange suggestion of continual movement, for as we look at it, the hues of blue and silver radiance deep within it seem to shift and change, to swirl and spread and to take new origin one from another like an iridescent lake of violet-blue, turquoise, silver-grey and flashing white. In the center of this solid lake of changeful color, a circle some fifteen feet in diameter is defined by a band of silver set into the floor: and within this band there rises a squat mass of unpolished natural crystal, forming a steep-sided truncated cone about five feet high; grey and translucent, its surface rough with projections and hollows, and only its top smoothed into a level circular platform.

This rock is like an intrusion of primitive awareness, stark and uncompromising, into a world of delicate fantasy.

Hewn into this mass of rough crystal, on the side facing us, are nine steps; and on the flat summit, beneath the central Lamp of the Mysteries, stands the Bomos. The Bomos, is draped with deep blue-violet, and upon it rests the Mystical Tessera. Beyond the Bomos, in the East, we see the Banner of the New Life.

From the Bomos, and from the crystal rock upon which it stands, emanates a calm stability, an enduring strength which not only surmounts, but governs, the variable energies of astral power. However erratic and unpredictable the manifestations of that power may appear, there are immutable laws to which they are subject; laws of causality, of reciprocity and of harmony. These laws are not imposed arbirarily upon the astral world from without, but are intrinsic to its own nature. Let us but keep faith with those laws within ourselves, acknowledging the interdependence of the inner with the outer at all levels of being, and in that harmony the astral powers will be to us a source not of weakness and disunity but of strength and integrity.

From the many roads and experiences of the outer world, we have met together and have traveled the first Path on the Way of the Mysteries, and we have arrived in this place. In considering what we have won from our journey, it is well to ask what we sought when we set out upon it.

When we look into our hearts, each of us might return a different answer: there is the quest for self-knowledge, the quest for an understanding of the forces of the Universe, the quest for spiritual power, the quest for life in greater fullness, the desire to hasten our evolution. In all these quests and aspirations there is a common factor: the will to look beyond the irrelevant, the non-significant, the ephemeral, to find that which endures and that which carries the great indicators of life's purposes. To know those purposes so as to be able to work in harmony with them, is the key to spiritual power. To live with spiritual perception is to live more fully and to advance our evolution; and to understand what we are to do is the most needful part of knowledge of what we are.

The Moon is known as Mistress of Illusion; but illusion is the nurse of true vision. From the changeful floor which stretches before our feet in this temple like a sea of dreams and fantasies, emotions and impulses, there rises the rock of crystal, upon which is the Bomos. The crystal rock is a symbol in a special way of the Sphere of the Moon, the Foundation; for even so amid the changeful imagery of our emotional-instinctual nature must stand the clear perception upon which our directing faculties are to be based.

Let us contemplate anew, therefore, the translucency and stability of the rock of crystal; let us seek its like within ourselves as the foundation of our work, and, finding it, let us rejoice.

Battery 3-5-3

The Working of the 31st Path

SPHERE OF COMMENCEMENT: Malkuth (Kingdom)

Hebrew Divine Name: Adonai Melek

Planetary correspondence: The Earth Symbol: The primitive arch

Minerals: Flint, granite

PATH OF THE TREE OF LIFE: 31

Intelligence: The 31st Path is called the Unresting Intelligence, and why? Because it controls the movement of Sun and Moon, each by its rightful laws and in its due orbit.

Hebrew Divine Name: Elohim

Influence on Path: Fire (the Element)

Hebrew Letter: Shin (Tooth)

Path Stanza: Shining O Fire in thy strength, laughing
in flames rushing to heavenward, Sharp is thy tooth to
devour all things of
earth, all things transmutable, Winning them into
thine own force incor-
rupt, turning them hiddenly
Back to their principles!

Tarot arcanum: Judgment (20)

Symbol: Ram's horns

Colors: Every flame color from yellow into deep red, with flashes of bright blue and green; also white

Mineral: Steel

Living beings: The Winged Watchers

Magical phenomena: Visions of transformation and renewal

Philosophy of the Path: Stoicism: the will to endure, the knowledge that seeming destruction is but transformation

SPHERE OF DESTINATION: Hod (Splendor)

Hebrew Divine Name: Elohim Tzabaoth

Planetary correspondence: Mercury

Planetary Number: 8

Element: Water

Symbols: The shimmering curtain, the Caduceus

Minerals: Carnelian, "living" silver

Colors: Orange, black, white

Magical phenomenon: The balance of opposed forces whose outcome is repose

Comments

This Path takes us from the Earth Sphere, Malkuth, to Hod in Yetzirah: the astral level of the Sphere of Mercury.

"Trial by Fire" is an ancient and harsh concept, whether the material to be tried is mineral or human. Significantly therefore we encounter this element in the course of our first movement to the column of Severity of the Tree of Life.

Only that which is immutable—the spirit itself—can withstand the power of Fire to produce change. If Fire represents energy in its most dynamic form which is within our apprehension, then truly we can say with the stoic, Heraclitus, that the whole dynamism of the universe is of the nature of Fire. This elucidates the verse from *The 32 Paths of Wisdom*. With the Stoic, too, we have to acknowledge that "all things transmutable" (as *The Song of Praises* puts it) are, through this endless surging of fiery energy, on their way "back to their principles."

Having overcome the trials of this Path, we arrive in Hod, the Sphere of magick and of science. It is notable that the very name of Magick comes from the Magians who were worshipers of the powers of Fire. Those who rule the unresting energies of the universe are not those who refuse to acknowledge those energies but those who work with them, "producing change in accordance with will." We, with all else that is, are on our way back to our glorious Source: but by virtue of the spirit within us we can so will and direct our course as to make our Way of Return a triumphal progress.

The Working of the 31st Path

We stand in the warm light of a summer day, beneath a sky of intense blue. No living thing can be seen save the thorn-bushes which grow amid the harsh rocks. This is no friendly region, here is neither shade of

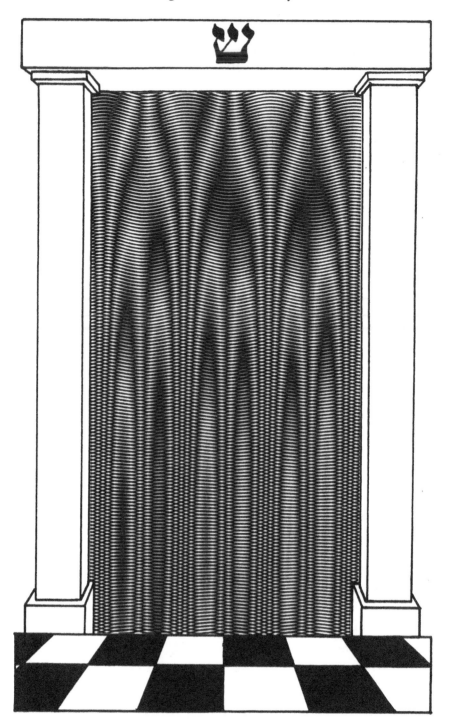

tree nor sound of grazing herd; yet in this place, in its austerity, we may the better find that which today we seek.

Some little distance ahead of us there stands a solitary arch, built of flints by men in some past age. The keystone of the arch is of pale granite, sparkling with a myriad points of transient white fire; and carved deeply into this keystone is an emblem, the curling horns of a ram.

Why has this single arch been thus left in a wilderness of rocks and thorns? What means this mysterious emblem upon the keystone? We go forward and pass through the arch, feeling for a moment its shadow upon us.

Now we have come into an even more desolate region, a bare stony expanse; and from what cause we cannot say, the sky above us is darkened.

As we look about us, a plume of smoke arises from a fissure in the ground, to be swiftly followed by a leaping flame. Immediately, to the other side, a second flame leaps up; then several in rapid succession burst forth some distance before us. These flames grow to a great height, filling the sky: free and immense are they, the unshorn tresses of Fire. We look to the way by which we have come: but no retreat is possible, for flames have sprung up in that direction also.

New flames now arise, and struggle to ascend; but it seems there is not air enough to support them, and with a great sound like the beating of wings the lesser flames writhe and vanish. The tall flames also seem to strive together: they bend and entwine, they divide into tongues which blaze with yellow light, they spring up again in renewed strength and unity. Continually they roar and hiss and crackle, and seem to drum upon the air. We are caught in the midst of this fury of fire; we feel its scorching breath and are oppressed by the lack of air, but no way of escape is evident.

Now the flames commence a new movement: they bend sidelong, with a tumult of sound as if they shouted and shrieked their protest against the sudden wind that lashes them. Even above this we hear the menacing voice of storm, the majestic command of the thunder. Now the fire of the heavens replies to the fire of earth: lightning quivers and dances above the leaping flames.

The air detonates; the flames are dimmed by a brilliance which seems to tear the skies; a shaft of lightning descends directly before us, throwing the fire itself momentarily into a disregarded blackness. Even in that moment, we are aware of a change in the atmosphere about us: as the lightning fades, we see that we are indeed in the presence of one whose very gaze separates us at once from the seared and exhausted air of the material region. He is tall, of dominating appearance, with glowing countenance and with bright discerning eyes. His head is crowned with large curling ram's horns, ivory-white and adorned with bands of steel; he wears a robe of brilliant white girdled with red gold. His aspect expresses limitless energy.

With a commanding gesture he bids us to follow him, and when he ascends swiftly into the air we find it easy to do likewise. We know that we are being taken from the domain of earthly fire, not merely to save us from it, but so that we may be shown something of its cosmic meaning.

We rise into a region which seems to be filled with cool, pure air, for we are at once refreshed; but in fact these are no longer the material elements which we experience, for led by our guide we have crossed the boundary from the material world to the astral: with the perception of the astral world we now behold that which occurs behind the veil of material phenomena. Now there flows around and before us a stream of other hues, red-orange, blood-crimson, golden-green, sky-blue, which appear briefly, to be reabsorbed or to pass to other modes of being.

As we watch this vision of living light which swirls and undulates ceaselessly, we become aware of fleeting and phantasmal forms, flashing likewise within that tide of supramundane Flame. Shapes of tall trees shimmer awhile in the changeful vision, trees vast of trunk or strangely plumed of leafage; animal forms appear too, semblances of armored fish, fanged and flightless birds, dragon-like reptiles. Here appears a noble stag with slender limbs and towering antlers, challenging and dominant until a wave of the flashing stream brightens and swirls, and the shape vanishes; there is the supple shape of a lion which crouches as if to stalk its prey, seemingly invincible, a marvel of lithe muscle armed with steely claws and with elongated canine teeth like downward-stabbing tusks. Again the current shifts and flashes, and the lion disappears. Human forms, too, are seen, massive or refined of limb and feature: some bear the aspect of the warrior, some of the thinker, some of the craftsman; women maternal, amazonian or metetricious. All appear but briefly, to be swiftly engulfed in the tide of astral fire.

We are saddened with an irresistible melancholy by this showing of the transitory nature of all life-forms!—nothing flourishes for ever, nothing endures!—but then, in other parts of the current, we behold new and different forms emerging, in like measure as the old disappeared. We see new animal forms, but fewer; new human forms, and more numerous. We see the new briefly prospering in their particular modes, until they in their turn are consumed by the stream: but now, instead of being merely saddened, we watch to see where they shall reappear and in what changed aspects. Furthermore, among these many fleeting forms we glimpse some few which are strangely familiar to us, whose life-experience we seem to have known from within. For each one of us the tale of this succession of lives will be different, but slowly its pattern will become clear to us: we also who watch this changing tide of shinning flame which is the current of natural life, we also are part of it; we likewise shall pass and be reabsorbed; yet elsewhere, changed but not destroyed, we shall reappear to continue our course. There is strength in this knowledge—strength, and the will to endure.

Led by our stately and indomitable guide, we move forward through the scintillating current which surrounds us. The astral fire still swirls and darts forth from time to time its long pulsing flashes of radiance, and as we become more closely united to its subtle nature we detect in it not only movement and color, but also sound: scarcely perceptible but wholly harmonious chords, answering to the coruscations of the light, impinge upon our consciousness. Those vibrations which at first only manifested to us as color, now make themselves known as sound also; but whereas the colors had appeared to be sometimes discordant in their brightness, yet now that the vibrations manifest in some measure as sound, our spiritual perception begins to grasp their essential harmony, the intellectual significance beyond the simply astral.

The musical quality of the rhythm increases. It does not at first give the impression of an actual melody, so much as a series of harmonies, drifting cadences, broken lilting snatches, brought into unity by a grand and sonorous descant; then an undertone of melody becomes distinguishable and gradually develops, swelling into an austere and measured chorus of sound which answers, meets, interweaves with the descant, then fitfully sinks to a near-silence while huge chords take its place. Then the sublime melody is resumed.

This music is not altogether that of the human voice, nor of any recognisable instrument for it is the direct effect of that which every voice and instrument attempts, that is, a simultaneous stress wrought in the atmosphere and in the sphere of mind: here we have the audible rush and leap and pulsating radiance of the essential nature of fire, that fire which visibly still courses around us. But not yet have we come to the heart of it.

Fire shining and quivering, fire flashing with life and running its course through the universe! Vital, ever-changing fire: coruscating, singing, triumphant fire!

We have risen above the surface of the flowing astral fire, and the choiring flame-voices sound ever more clearly and jubilantly; we are ascending into the realm of spiritual fire, which the astral but mirrors. This is ecstasy, stark and yet glorious. This is the life of fire, assimilating all things to itself yet totally denuded, even of material form. Thus live the Gods! Are we then as they, we who are thus uplifted? We look to our guide. He, who has proceeded ahead of us, shines altogether as a flame of whiteness; we behold neither the ram's horns with which he is crowned, nor the bright robe which envelops him. Higher yet we arise: that which seems like air around us is filled with bright and rippling sparkles, and holds an intensely dry heat. We become aware of a throng of beings therein, a throng scarcely perceptible even to our new consciousness, beings of a nature more entirely spiritual than we have previously encountered. The united gaze of great brilliant eyes is fixed silently upon us as we pass through their ranks We are to be in some unknown manner put to the test, proved by the fire.

We ascend still higher. Hotter and brighter, more scintillating is the atmosphere in which we move. A sensation like thirst assails us, but it is not a thirst for water: it is a craving for shade, for the least vestige of shadow to which to direct our movement. There is none. We are encompassed by a world composed entirely of sparkling radiance; if we advance further we must also go further into it. There is no other possibility. And still the eyes await the outcome.

That which must be endured, let it be accepted with a good will; for we cannot avoid the pain, but by reluctance we might fail to assimilate the potential of the experience.

A ripple of heat, like a breath from a furnace, flashes scarlet and silver as it runs onward across and through us without hindrance; then another and another wave of fire follows it. We feel strangely lightened, emotionless and liberated from fear by the touch of this spiritual flame, even though its fiery nature oppresses all our powers of sensation and leaves us arid, unutterably void of every opposite quality. The intellectual vision however, is intensified. We comprehend why this purgation of every emotion is at this time needful, since we are to behold something of the eternal ordering of things, and emotion is in its very essence turbulent and chaotic. We are upon the verge of many perceptions; and still we are surveyed by the high pure eyes of the winged watchers. A burst of sheet-lightning expands around the luminous form of our guide who still goes star-like before us. He turns: in the fading of the flash we see his arms raised in benediction and farewell; then he is gone from us.

Another wave of fire meets us: this time, of blazing whiteness sparkling into flame-orange. We are absorbed into it, we are transformed to very flame; we feel and behold only that intense radiance until we reach the essential heart of it—

Blackness: icy, intense cold and blackness.

It strikes and benumbs.

There is nothing, nothing even to endure. We wait passively, until at last, released from the ice-heart of the flame, we find a dewy mist drawn down upon us. We move forward upon our path, but we now behold only shadowy shapes veiled by the moist and gentle vapor. The mist thickens to actual drops: we are walking through falling water, through water that swirls about our feet. Now before us a waterfall crashes and cascades in the dim uncertain light. We pass through the force of the torrent to find ourselves standing on the rocky floor of a large cavern. ★ A faint luminescence filters through the waterfall behind us; the smooth stone of the cavern walls is variegated, translucent white and orange with veinings of black. We proceed into the depths of the cave: as we go, the sound of the waterfall which at first is loud in our ears, gradually recedes until we hear it only as a faint murmur.

As we reach the end of the cavern, where a shaft of light shines from above, we see worn steps ascending, cut into the living rock. We climb the steps; eight are they in number, and when we have reached the topmost we find ourselves on the threshold of a sacred place: we are about to enter a temple which now opens before us.

As we enter and walk across the expanse of the black lustrous floor, our eyes are drawn to the far end of the chamber. We pass between the two pillars, Machetes and Nomothetes, into the very center of this temple whose walls are of translucent stone, of the appearance of carnelian. Before us is that which first drew our gaze: a great curtain, silvery and iridescent, with the gentle play of unnumbered colors upon its surface. It moves and shimmers, magnifying every least stirring, and seeming almost alive in its ceaseless quivering. Upon it is depicted the Caduceus, the staff of Hermes entwined with the twin Serpents, the White and the Black. Before the curtain stands the Bomos, draped in glowing flame-orange, and upon it a smoking censer and the mystical Tessara. To the south of the Bomos is the Banner of the New Life; above us, suspended from the high ceiling, burns a single lamp, symbol of the Eternal Flame. We salute the East.

Stillness pervades the temple, with a sense of calm expectancy. We have come through ascending flame and through falling water, and we have arrived at this quietness. We comprehend that where all is ordered in just measure, there is balance and stillness; nor is this the stillness of an inert mass, but rather it is a vibrant and living quality, the equipoise of force against force. As a man stands upright, he appears to be balanced without effort; yet the interplay of tendon and muscle is continuous to maintain him thus. So does the Caduceus, which is in one sense an image of Man, show us Serpent entwined with Serpent, pinion balancing pinion, and symmetry ruling all. Thus in the realm of Mind are opposites to be balanced, for in their balance do the multiplicity of qualities compose a true unity, even as the man with all his diversity of corporeal parts and qualities of mind and of spirit, is yet one individual. Again: not only the final totality is one, but the initial totality is one. In the material world all things are intricately wrought of one fundamental Energy; likewise the astral stream of life-forces continues through phases of change and of becoming, while upon the spiritual level all has come from one unity and shall return thither. Knowing this, we can regard no extreme as ultimate, for all shall be balanced and counterpoised in the totality. This also do we acknowledge in the sign of the Caduceus: for these truths are of the dominion of Reason, which is of Mercury.

Battery 3-5-3

The Working of the 30th Path

(Correspondences)

SPHERE OF COMMENCEMENT: Yesod (Foundation)

Hebrew Divine Name: Shaddai El Chai

Planetary correspondence: The Moon

Element: Air

Deific Forces: God and Goddess of Nature, Triple Goddess

Symbols: Circle, crescent, fountain, the crescent boat Plants: Lily, jasmine, rosemary, hazel, willow, yellow poppies, fern, ivy

Colors: Lavender, silver, white, ivory, pale yellow

PATH OF THE TREE OF LIFE: 30

Intelligence: The 30th Path is the Collating Intelligence, so named because by means of it the astrologers judge the verdict of the stars and of other heavenly portents, refining their decisions in accordance with the principles of their art.

Hebrew Divine Name: Eloah V'Daath

Influence on Path: The Sun

Planetary number: 6

Hebrew Letter: Resh (Head)

Path Stanza: Rise in thy splendor, O King!—glorious
brow, gaze on thy governance
Gladdening all who behold! Soaring as
song, rule and illuminate:
Crysoleth gleaming thy crown, rise and
inspire, Lion-gold, Falcon-flight,
Joyous, ambrosial!

Tarot arcanum: The Sun (19)

Element of the Path: Air

Symbols: The wheel, the lamen or breastplate Plant: Rose

Colors: All golden shades, into red

Minerals: Gold, sulphur, all sparkling and shining materials

Living beings: Children, griffins (eagle-lions), dragon

Optical effects: Dazzling golden brightness, mirage

Magical phenomena: Awakening to new realization of powers, the Elixir of Life

Philosophy of the Path: Alchemy

SPHERE OF DESTINATION: Hod (Splendor)

Hebrew Divine Name: Elohim Tzabaoth

Planetary correspondence: Mercury

Planetary number: 8

Element: Water

Symbols: The Silver Sea, Unicorn, Winged Horse, the Red Flower

Plants: All medicinal and magical herbs

Minerals: Quicksilver, carnelian

Colors: All shades of orange, countercharged black and white, variegated and iridescent hues as the "Peacock's Tail" of alchemy

Magical phenomena: Swiftness of movement, duality resolved by balance of forces, magical regeneration as foreshadowing mystical regeneration

Comments

The imaginative and fertile influence of Yesod in which this Path begins is made truly creative by the power of the Sun upon the Path itself. Here there is no heavy influence of Earth to be countered: both Moon and Sun have Air as their element. Furthermore the destination of the Path is Hod, the Sphere of Mercury: and although the element corresponding to that Sephirah is Water, the symbolism of Mercury-Hermes the Messenger of the Gods with his winged caduceus has evident aerial affinities. The arts of science and magick which belong to our goal are thus, as we approach by this Path, winged with visionary inspiration.

One of the significant themes which contribute to that inspiration is the relationship between the male and female sexuality of Yesod to the unity-in-duality of Hod. The two children, typical figures of alchemical symbolism, express this theme.

The Red Flower is an alchemical symbol for the Red Elixir, which in turn signifies the Philosophers' Stone in its healing and regenerative aspects. "Red" in medieval naming of colors included the hues of gold and of flame. In this Pathworking the Red Flower has eight petals. The number 8 has a threefold significance: (1) it relates to the formative influence of Saturn as "octave" of Planet Earth and manifestor of the formative power of Binah, in wisdom, in artistic creativity, and in every expression of an inspired idea by material means; (2) it relates to the regenerative powers of the Sun Sphere as symbolized by the Eight-pointed Star; (3) it relates to Hod, the 8th Sephirah. Hod does indeed govern forces of regeneration, through alchemical transmutation, through magick, and through every art of healing.

It is in this relationship to Hod that the eight-petaled Red Flower is introduced as the culminating symbol in this working, but there are echoes from the other correspondences of the number. The strong influence of the Sun upon the Path casts upon us a reflected gleam from Tiphareth; while the recurrent glimpses of the two young lovers, with their hints of the salt-sulphur-mercury theory of the Philosophers' Stone, carry a suggestion of the romantic and inspirational force of Binah as Triune Neshamah.

Two aspects of the matter are referred to in our quoted texts: *The Song of Praises* celebrates the soaring inspiration of the Path, while *The 32 Paths of Wisdom* typifies "the Collating Intelligence" by the astrological art of interpreting celestial influences in terms of earthly effects.

The Working of the 30th Path

In stillness of mind, in freedom from the cares and from the reasonings of every day, we are aware of ourselves afloat in peaceful yet vibrant darkness. A feeling of mystery fills us: a feeling which is not the passive and aimless questioning which arises from mere bewilderment, but a sense of wonderment and of reverence. Here we have true mystery, the living, creative darkness of the Sphere of the Moon.

While we remain aware of this wonderment, the obscurity gradually lightens to a blue astral mist. The mist in its turn completely encompasses us; it moves and swirls into the suggestion of uncounted shapes, of which nothing appears clearly or remains fixed. Then the mist itself disperses, and we stand in clear moonlight; a cool, bright radiance which allows us to see as clearly as by the light of the Sun, but to enjoy also the

strong contrast of deep velvet shadows belonging to the Moon Sphere. Above us, the sky is suffused with an intense pale lavender, blotting out the stars. Before us, surrounded by a delicate balcony of ivory-colored stone, is a sunken garden. An opening in the balcony shows where a flight of steps, of the same ivory stone, descends into the garden. The rhythmic plashing music of a fountain sounds from below, and a rich fragrance of flowers and fruit rises to greet us. We make our way down the steps.

Large gentle moths, with bodies soft as down and wings like enameled steel, brush us in their silent flight, their eyes shining like sparks as they glide to sip the juices of ripe fruits and the alluring nectar of the pale flowers which open in the shadows.

Around us are lilies and yellow poppies, starry jasmine and clustering bushes of fragrant rosemary, hazel trees and willows; but in truth every plant—fruit-trees and gourds, roses and vines and conifers and all the others—whatever their nature, all in some measure own the dominion of the Moon and flourish as she bids them. Manifold and wonderful is the beauty of this garden in the Sphere of the Moon!

In the center of the garden the water of the fountain arches high, its descending drops flashing in a rainbow of emeralds and rubies, sapphires and pearls as they disperse to fall, wide of the circular pool below. A multitude of delicate ferns and ivies, nourished by this moisture, veil the brink; and they, and the taller plants beyond, wear the flashing drops proudly upon their leaves like jeweled trophies.

We move through the garden, conscious of its intensely living and vibrant quality. Here are plants such as we have never before seen. All is a riot of beauty and vitality: delicate cups of frosted rose spread wide to reveal a center of metallic violet seeds, flame-red tendrils spring from the tips of deep azure leaves, while some mysterious clumps of slender trees prove to be gigantic grasses bearing at their summit huge iridescent plumes of blossom.

From time to time, breaking through the voice of the fountain and the fitful rustling of the higher branches of the trees as a wandering breeze moves them, distant sounds reach our ears: now voices raised in melodious song, now laughter and cries of joy. Evidently we hear the sounds of some distant festival; but when we try to listen the voices are lost to us and we hear only the plashing fountain and the rustling breeze.

However, the garden has another secret to disclose. As we continue to explore its intricate paths we find a kind of arbor formed by loosely interwoven supports over which a magnificent vine is growing. The leaves of this vine are glossy scarlet, and from the sinuous branches hang heavy clusters of grapes, deep purple strewn over with glittering gold-dust. Within the arbor is a stone platform on which stand two sculptured human figures. These figures are ancient representations of the male and female tutelary deities of the garden, both nude as befits their dignity. The male figure, expressive of energy and muscular force, is represented with the horns of a bull, with erect phallus and with arms raised in a gesture of blessing; the maternal proportions of the female figure are no less expressive of directing power in and over the forces of nature, and this figure bears a basket filled with the good fruits of the earth.

As we look at these figures, we realize they seem to be sculptured from a very translucent, almost transparent form of alabaster, so that in part we see through them the leaves and branches of the vine. Far from making them seem less real, this translucency adds to the power of their appearance: we seem almost to be gazing at veritable beings of an order more removed from the material world than is the garden wherein we see them. We make salutation to them in veneration to the beneficent Powers which they represent.

But now a clearer burst of singing arises unexpectedly from near at hand: the singing of many voices, interspersed with the sound of stringed instruments and of flutes, and accompanied by drums and cymbals. The gladness and sweetness of the music is intoxicating, and the rhythm of the drums takes possession of our feet. We leave the garden and mount the steps; the singers remain unseen to us, but we whirl into a dance that answers their voices. The music grows even louder and more insistent: as we circle to its cadence we are lifted from the ground. We stream up and up into the brilliant lavender sky.

The music is out of our hearing now, and the garden is lost in the shadows far beneath us; but still we float in the height, hovering and looking about us in the luminous expanse.

Far off from us to one side, and as it were down from us a little, the bright lavender sky is divided by a wide river of intense blue light that flows across it. The blue is darkened by huge shadows which move in it, but we cannot discern their form. Upon this river of blue there floats a little white crescent. Fixing our attention upon it, we see that it is a boat; and in it, upon pillows of pink pearl, sits a woman. She rests her arms on the side of the boat, and her chin upon her arms, and gazes long upon the moving shadows in the blue river, as if she could read them. Her unbound hair covers her shoulders, and a lock of it trails in the river: she is a maiden, and the youngest of three sisters. She sees our reflection, and raises her eyes to find us. Then, smiling, she lifts an arm flashing with silver bangles in a brief gesture of greeting and dismissal.

Evidently she had seen what we could not:, for, on the instant, a great wind comes and lifts us, carrying us to even greater heights. The sky over us changes from lavender to electric green, and from green to white. Not even a wisp of cloud accompanies us in our swift flight; and, if we glance downwards, any object which might exist in that direction is hidden by a pale haze of illimitable remoteness.

We feel no fear, for here nothing to fear is visible, and in our hearts there remains the joyous memory of the ecstatic song which bore us up to this height. Now another great gust of cosmic wind catches us and bears us onward, we know not whither.

As we glide forward we perceive at last, in front of us and a measureless space below, rising up out of the misty distances what appears to be part of the upper curve of an immense wheel, the rest of which remains hidden from us. The rim of this wheel gleams in the light and appears to be of pure gold. Evidently, too, it exerts some degree of gravitational force, for, almost imperceptibly at first, we begin a long, gliding descent towards it.

We are traveling at a great velocity, but our progress seems slow because of the immensity of the space through which we are moving. As the distance between ourselves and our destination gradually becomes less vast, we begin to see that the golden surface, at first apparently quite smooth, is made up of a myriad of separate fragments like grains of sand, gleaming and flashing. Then, as we continue to glide swiftly onwards and downwards towards them and these fragments become less remote, we form a clearer idea of their size until each of these seeming sand-gains has the dimensions of a planet. At the same time, their collective gravitational pull increasingly counteracts our forward motion.

As we continue to approach, we seem to be hovering above these whirling worlds. We perceive that each of them has its own individual character; but, now we are close enough to see them in their true dimensions, our progress is so slow that our choice of a landing place is limited.

We find ourselves as if suspended above a large fragment whose form we cannot discern; it is hidden from us by a mantle of dense vapor, from which rising currents of hot air, mounting in gusty billows, seem deliberately to impede our descent. A variation in these currents, as the fragment world tumbles upon its axis, allows us to sink again to some extent, but we see nothing of what is below us before we are flung violently upwards again. However, we are caught in the heavy atmosphere and the gravitational field of this particular fragment, and as we slowly sink again we are still drawn towards its surface. Once again the opaque vapors hold us aloft in their turbulent web, now tossed upwards, now allowed to fall, but unable to choose our direction or to see any reason for a choice.

Suddenly, by some unknown and unforeseen combination of forces, as we are again sinking slowly the cloudy vapors are parted asunder. There comes into sight a wide lake whose surface works and froths strangely, with spurts of vapor of varying colors arising from it. As these billowing vapors in turn separate for a moment, we catch sight of an intense fiery glow beneath. We are hovering over a vast volcanic crater. The lake is an entire mineral ferment, the prelude to a structured world. Involuntarily we draw back, even at our considerable height above it, from its menacing heat and noxious fumes. As we do so, the turbulent currents of rising vapor catch us with redoubled force, and send us to an even great altitude away from the molten minerals.

Even as we are borne away, however, a strange vision of a happening in that world comes to us with the force of an inner knowledge. Around the edges of the crater, among the wierd pinnacles and deeply fissured masses of brown rock which have solidified from that burning lake, there appear gleaming deposits of metals and other minerals that have separated out from the rest in cooling. In that inert and perilous land-scape, we are astonished and shocked to see a small boy, who appears to be about five years of age, clambering about the harsh rocks. He is quite alone, and has the air of searching intently for some specific object. He is wearing a belted tunic of scarlet over long hose of the same color; and in his hand he carries a small wooden box, exquisitely fashioned and intended to hold something of great value.

The boy finds what he seeks: a cluster of large crystals of sulphur, their pure pale yellow gleaming in the bright light, stands out at the very lip of the fiery lake. We hold our breath as we see him making his way by uncertain footholds to gain his objective, but he himself goes fear-lessly to achieve his purpose. Carefully he breaks off smaller crystals from the mass of sulphur, and fills the box which he carries; then, hold-ing fast to his treasure, he turns away from the hazardous brink.

The clouds of vapor swirl over the whole area, and that volcanic world with its powerful upward air-currents is lost to us. We soar aloft, we hover, and again we descend, becoming caught in the pull of another of these fragment worlds. Here we are sure no volcano awaits us; the gleaming expanse beneath us suggests a smooth, peaceful terrain, veiled by nothing more than the shimmer of reflected light.

While it spins evenly, the planet at which we gaze seems all at once to rush to meet us. We are very willing to descend to try the hospitality of this shining world; and here nothing hinders us.

Suddenly we are moving over the ground of the planet. We are no longer gliding but walking: walking in the desert of tawny, gleaming sand which extends in every direction as far as we can see. The sun is just rising, and such a blaze of color fills the air with shining reds, golden yellows and a scorching, ardent blue, that the horizon disappears at once in the dazzle of concentrated brilliance. If we walk by blind faith, all is well; if we try to see where we tread, the surface of the sand disappears in a third and fourth dimension of diamond light, amid which the luminous colors dance in elusive rainbows.

We have no reason to remain where we are, and every reason to discover what lies ahead; so we continue to advance. With no measure of time or distance, it soon seems to us that we have been walking onward for an age.

Even though the sun is not very high, the hot rays reflected back by the dazzling sand begin to be oppresive to us. We look for any rock which might throw a vestige of shade, but there is none. We cannot tell if we are moving in a straight line, but we keep up the best pace we can in the hope that at some time a limit or at least a variation in the desert will show itself. Our mouths are dry from thirst.

We walk mechanically, for even our feet seem lost in the changing and dazzling radiance through which we go, and if we were to look down we should stumble and fall. The light itself has an arid, parching quality, so that our eyes weary of it and feel as parched as our lips. How welcome would be a cool spring or a stream of flowing, sweet water!

As we scan the distance ahead, our anxiety turns to surprise and then to delight. The long, level waves of a clear lake, cool and limpid, throw pearly shadows upon the sand as they course over it. We hasten forward and stoop to gather the precious water in our hands, but as we change our posture it vanishes: it is a mirage.

Deeply disappointed, we go forward again. The mirage accompanies us, changing only the form of its illusory images: we cannot tell if these images are creations of the elements, heightened perhaps by our imagination, or whether they are true pictures of phenomena really existing at some other intersection of time and space, and by a trick of refraction flung before us as if upon a screen. In this way we see gleaming lakes, waterfalls, swift rivers and wild sea coasts—always water, water, water—but we try to close our minds to them as we keep advancing.

Now, however, we see something which grips our attention. Amid the floating lines of shimmering light which form these illusory scenes, a detailed landscape builds up. In the distance we can recognize the long rolling breakers of a sea shore; in the foreground is an area of sun-scorched grassy land, with shallow depressions in which pools of sea water have dried out to form glistening white deposits of salt. Into this scene moves a small figure clothed in bright red; we recognize the same little boy whom we saw previously by the crater in that other fragmentary world, and we observe that he is still carrying the casket into which he gathered the sulphur.

Now he draws near to the salt pans. As he does so, however, we realize another child is there before him. A little girl of about the same age as the boy, and wearing a long white dress, is kneeling beside one of the dried-out pools and is gathering the pure, sparkling granules of salt into a crystal cup. As the boy approaches she fills the cup with salt, places a lid upon it and stands up, holding the cup carefully. She extends her free hand to the boy; he takes it, and the two children without exchanging a word walk away together. Even as they do so, the visionary landscape loses its clarity for us and again we see only the brilliant sunlight blazing on and above the sand.

The heat and the dazzling light seem to hold us as in a trap; we feel we must rest, no matter what may come of it. We stop, but remain standing: only in final exhaustion, surely, could we sink down upon these burning sands! The Sun, mounting gradually in the sky, is scarcely distinguishable in the white-hot blaze of that entire quarter. For a moment we turn our gaze to it, incredulous that the same light which sustains our life can be so hostile. Then we close our eyes, completely dazzled. A flight of rose-colored flecks, the aftermath of extreme brightness, drifts before our eyelids.

We open and close our eyes several times in order to banish the drifting spots. We seem to have succeeded; but when we open our eyes again, a new series of flecks and flakes of rose-color appear, floating in the air from the direction of the Sun. Some of these flecks fade away and disappear, but a few of the largest of them, despite all our efforts, continue to drift towards us and increase in size as they do so. They are like petals, petals from an immense rose; and standing upright upon the largest of them, looking towards us with a calm and benign expression, is a tall and dignified figure.

This is a man, apparently of middle age, with hair and beard dark and considerably silvered; he wears a long sleeveless surcoat of spectrum blue over an ample gown of deep yellow. About his neck is a heavy golden chain supporting a large circular lamen, also of gold: this lamen bears cryptic words and emblems in finely engraved lines. In his right hand this personage carries a staff, which could be used for walking: now, he points it towards us, as if to guide his course or to declare his concern. By his attire, and by the golden lamen about his neck, we recognize that he is an Alchemist: a Master Alchemist, to whom the inner secrets of the natural forces lie open. His entire form is surrounded by a bright radiance of transparent golden light, like mild sunshine; this radiance is concentrated with particular brilliance about his head, around which it seems to form a globe of pulsating rays. From his whole being emanates an assurance of measureless generosity and wise counsel.

As the great rose-petal upon which he stands touches the ground, it loses substance and rapidly disappears. The other petals which accompanied him would seem to be the vehicles of other beings, not visible to us; for now, without touching the ground, they hover for a moment, then rise higher and glide off again in the direction from which they had come.

The Alchemist raises his staff and, with the tip of it, gently touches each of us upon the brow. Instantly all our weariness and sense of oppression is gone. Not only do we feel refreshed and joyful; we have as it were awakened from an inward sleep, into a new consciousness of our powers. We have no need to tread step by step through this desert place! Nor has our august helper any need of a vehicle, although it was through the rose-petals of the Sun that he first made contact with us. In like manner he could have awakened us without the touch of his staff. But, we perceive, it is often good to use material means, either while oneself is learning or in order to teach another, to achieve something which will later be done without those means because the true doer of the action is the inner spirit. When this powerful and benevolent being turns away and, in the same movement, rises almost vertically into the air, he scarcely needs bid us to follow him.

We step forward and rise up, without effort soaring higher and higher. The burning desert falls away beneath us, then the tumbling fragmentary worlds merge into the smooth curve of the gleaming rim. Finally, as we and our Guide the Alchemist soar onwards, the arc of the vast wheel fades away below and behind us in space.

On and on we glide into an immense nacreous void, the luminous distance shimmering upon all sides of us with the luster of pearl. Gradually, from different regions of this unbounded space, there come to our hearing the sounds of distant but mighty voices, calling to each other with resonant musical cries. The sounds grow louder as the creatures who cause them, six in number, converge on us, soaring upon their powerful wings.

When we can begin to distinguish their appearance it is terrible to us; but our Guide reassures us with a smiling look, and without pausing we continue to glide steadily forward. These are Griffins, marvelous winged quadrupeds which dwell high in the light of the Sun. They have golden-hued eagle pinions spreading wider than those of a condor, and the noble head of an eagle; but the neck and breast, over the whole ribcage, are covered with large overlapping scales which flash like gilded mail. Their forelegs are similarly armored, and end in mighty talons shaped like those of an eagle. From the end of the ribs, the body is covered in glossy tawny hair; the belly, tail and hind limbs are those of a lion, although the claws are fully as powerful as those of the forelimbs.

As they fly, the eagle-taloned forelegs are drawn up under the body, while hind legs and the long fexible tail are extended behind; the whole muscular frame seems wrought of gold, and of brass, and of golden bronze. Repeatedly they circle around us, they soar above us and below, while, ever and anon, one or another of them opens its beak and utters their majestic, ringing call.

Escorted by these magnificent solar beasts who seem to delight in our presence, we continue our flight into unknown regions. The Sun is still mounting in the sky. Gradually, however, in the luminous expanse about the Sun, we become aware of a shadow upon the pearly hues which fill the boundless void. As we sweep onward, this shadow takes on a vast phantasmal form. The griffins perceive it even before we do.

From the throat of each of them there issues a deep, harsh, menacing sound, while at the same time the scaly plates upon the neck of each rise up to form a warlike crest. Unerringly they have recognized an ancient enemy.

Now the phantasmal form appears more solid, and its contours become more clearly defined. We see it to be an immense dragon, coiled upon itself in the heavens. Its reptilian shape and folded bat-wings are a dead green color, the hue of verdigris, but the monster is visibly full of malevolent life. The greater part of the dragon's body is coiled below and level with the Sun, but the long neck rears and arches upwards so that the widely gaping, slavering jaws are spread just above the point the Sun must inevitably reach in a few moments.

With our Guide, we hover motionless, watching. The one thing unthinkable, we realize, is that the Sun should swerve in its course. But to continue that course is to fall into the jaws of the embodiment of cosmic evil and negation. Already the upper portion of the Sun's glorious orb is shorn of its rays, and there a dull coppery sheen shows where the venom diipping from the monster's jaws has obscured its radiance.

The griffins, however, make no delay. With a piercing scream of rage they speed across the airy gulf and hurl themselves upon the dragon. They have no easy victory. The first griffin to arrive receives a lashing blow from the dragon's tail which sends the golden creature skimming like a great fireball across the heavens. Of the other griffins, three seize where they can upon the dragon's body and limbs; they hold fast with their eagle talons, while with beak and with lion claws they tear at the green scaly skin; but more they cannot do. Another griffin secures a fast hold on the monster's tail and is flung from side to side ceaselessly, but will not let go; at least the attention of the great reptile is somewhat distracted thereby. Yet still the hideous jaws gape over the Sun, and the Sun mounts inevitably into their poisonous depths. A shadow darkens all the vault of the sky, and a great stillness awaits the outcome of the contest.

The sixth griffin, which has been circling around the dragon, soars high now and drops sheer upon the arching neck, digging claws and talons deep, flapping great wing-tips around to baffle the small red eyes in the green head. The dragon rears upward very slightly under this attack.

But, just at this moment, back like a golden javelin hurled by a god comes the first griffin, that was flung out of the combat by the dragon's tail in the initial encounter. Straight for the lifted and unprotected throat of the dragon darts this griffin, and clings there where the fangs cannot reach, only to be dislodged if the dragon moves away-from the Sun.

Effulgent light streams forth in all its perfection as the dragon twists all its length suddenly away from the Sun. Violently the green monster shakes off its assailants and, with another sudden movement, sweeps downward, bellowing, to disappear in 'the lower vapors. The griffins, calling to each other in triumph at having put their ancient enemy to flight, circle several times above the region where the dragon disappeared and then themselves make off, we know not whither.

We look to our Guide. He turns to the direction in which we had been advancing before the appearance of the dragon, and extends his staff so that it points horizontally before him; then he lowers the tip so that it inclines slightly downwards. In response to this gesture, he, and we, begin to glide forward and to descend gradually along the line he is thus indicating. After some time, the snowy summits of a high mountain range appear far before and below us, sparkling in the sunlight. We descend steadily at the same rate as before, but we seem to be dropping far more rapidly as the side of the mountain rises to meet us. Now the windswept trees below the snow line become visible, and our Guide directs us to survey the approaching landscape.

Somewhat apart from the highest peaks of the range, we see a tall cone-shaped mount which is covered with trees almost to its summit. Towards the foot of this hill our Guide directs his flight; and we wonder at the strange power which resides in his staff, or rather in him, the Alchemist, so that as he indicates the direction he wills to take, so our direction is determined likewise. We cannot feel that this is any contravention of our will, since it is we who choose to take him as our Guide; rather we see it as another example of the way in which whatever materials come to hand, and one's own magical instruments in particular, should be used to accord with their nature for the fulfillment on one's inner spiritual purpose.

Our Guide comes to earth at the base of the cone-shaped mount, and within a moment we too feel the ground beneath our feet. From where we stand, a path leads up the mount. To judge by its low incline, it must take a spiral course, but from the beginning it is so overgrown with dense leafage that we can distinguish no feature of the mount save for the small platform of bare and craggy rock at the summit. A heady, almost intoxicating odor of spice-bearing trees comes to our nostrils.

Using his staff to aid his steps, our Guide begins the ascent of the mount and we follow. The winding path is narrow and uneven, and, on the far side of the mount from the commencement of the path, we find a clear stream falling in cascades from the summit. As we climb, we drop behind our Guide a little way; yet still we take care to keep him in sight, for here and there the path divides. Now it offers a less steep ascent on the outer edge of the mount, now it shows us a shorter route by means of steps cut vertically into the face of the slope. Although for the most part the Alchemist prefers the well-worn middle course, on occasion he does not despise an alternative and evidently he chooses his route entirely by his own understanding and judgment.

However, for us the matter is not quite so simple, even though we have but to follow our Guide. From our first few upward steps, when the branches of the trees of the mount began to close in upon us, we have become more and more aware of the insistent rustling and murmuring in their leaves. Now the murmuring forms itself into patterns of speech:

"What do they seek?"

"The Red Flower of the Sun."

"Then must they cross the silvery sea."

"But this is not the way."

"They do not know the way."

"Take care! Take care!"

"Come and learn the way!"

"Turn aside to this path!"

"Here is the path to fortune!"

"You do not know the way."

Do the voices really come from the odorous leaves, we wonder, or do they come from within our own minds, expressing our own hidden thoughts? Either way, they are full of warning and perhaps we should heed them.

"They do not know the way."

"Take care! Take care!"

"Come and learn the way!"

Several times we pause, irresolute, and the Alchemist goes on further ahead of us. At other times we try to shut the quiet voices out of our consciousness, but they persist in their murmuring attempts to lead us aside from our path.

"Turn aside to this path!"

"Here is the path to fortune!"

"You do not know the way!"

Suddenly from the tree-cloaked slopes above us there ring out the cries of youthful voices in fear and in desperate appeal for aid. Despite a last warning rustle from the leaves, we spring up the slope by the nearest way; none the less, so far had we fallen behind our Guide, that his luminous form is on the spot before us.

The green dragon, thwarted in its attempt to swallow the Sun, has sought out easier prey. Above us in the side of the mount gapes a dark cavern, in which the monster has been lurking; from this lair it has now sprung, its long neck undulating, its bat-like wings raised, to gloat over two children who stand helpless on the path before it.

These children, a girl and a boy, their first moment of terror over, are trying by attitude and gesture each to encourage and comfort the other. We recognize them as the same two children of whom we caught visionary glimpses earlier, although now they both seem to be somewhat older: he is still dressed in red, she in white, he still carries the box in which he placed the sulphur, she still carries the crystal cup in which she placed the salt. In that shadowy place both shine with youth and life; but there is nothing they can do to escape from the monster which threatens them.

We stand below them, gazing immobile as in a dream at the scene before us. It is the Alchemist who takes action. Resting his staff against a tree, he raises his hands skyward and calls in a resounding voice six splendid and ambrosial names. We realize he is calling the six griffins, each by its own name. Almost instantly, high above us, the mighty Sun-creatures appear. They circle once above the mount, then with raised wings plummet down to combat.

The green dragon, however, has also heard the powerful summoning of the golden beasts, and has no desire to meet with them in the open. Raising its head of the cold, baleful color of verdigris, it makes a swift lunge to seize the two children in its jaws; but a griffin, hovering over them, with hooked eagle beak menaces the monster's eyes. Snarling in fury the dragon backs into the dark cavern. There it brings into play the most potentially terrible of its weapons: darting its head forward and back, to one side and the other, above and below, from open jaws it breathes forth fire to fill the whole opening of the cavern. Nor is it pure elemental fire. Some of the flames issuing from that venomous maw turn into living fire-serpents which writhe and hiss, forked tongues flickering, and strike viciously into the air before disappearing from our vision.

The griffins are not daunted. The great plates of their neck-mail lifting in an embattled crest, with a concerted shriek they swoop in on low-planing wings. The fire itself cannot touch their fiery nature, and they are through the barrier before even its venomous fumes can harm them. In the relatively cramped area of the cavern's throat, where the clawed, webbed feet of the dragon cannot twist around to strike a blow, nor can the massive scaly tail find room to lash, the griffins tear with beak and claws at the flanks of their foe.

Bellowing in rage and pain, the dragon rushes forth from the cave; then it turns about and, with the griffins still clinging to its sides or hovering above its back, it hurtles into the depths of the cavern. From that black pit the sounds of violent combat come to us; the ceaseless implacable screaming of the griffins mingled with the hoarse roaring of the dragon and the reverberation of crashing blows. For a long time we are unable to determine anything of the progress of the fight; then at last the furious tones of the dragon take on a shrill desperate note. This high-pitched bellowing becomes fainter, and seems to die away into the depths of the mount to which the dragon has fled; and after a short interval the six griffins emerge into the light of day.

As we can see, the great eagle-cats are nearly exhausted: not so much from exertion or from wounds, as from having had to struggle so long and violently in the darkness of the cavern, in the noxious fumes breathed forth by the monster, and away from the Sun's rays which are life to them. Our Guide, while the combat was taking place in the cavern, had led the two chidren away and set them upon their road; now he has returned, and the weary griffins welcome him as a friend.

We are not far from the rocky summit of the mount, and to that point our Guide now directs us. Again we follow him up the winding path; the griffins, seeing whither we are bound, with slow flapping wing-strokes make their way there before us. While we walk, we consider a matter which had seemed strange to us; why the warlike griffins, even on this second occasion when they had the advantage of the green dragon, did not slay so malevolent an enemy but once more simply put it to flight? We arrive at a realization that the green dragon, like many other powerful and noxious entities, can neither be destroyed nor laid to rest, at least not within the term of this evolution; they can be put to flight, they can by a powerful champion of the Light be held in check for long ages, but they do not die.

Now we approach the summit of the mount. The trees and fragrant bushes end, and for a short distance we climb by footholds cut in the bare rock. Soon we reach the top, and stand with the Alchemist and the couching griffins on a natural, almost flat rocky platform. From a crevice in the rock near the center of this platform issues the clear and copious spring whose waters, cascading down the mount, we have encountered during our ascent.

The Alchemist contemplates this spring, and looks to the Sun which has now arisen almost to its noonday height. Having laid his staff down gently upon the rock, from beneath the ample folds of his blue surcoat he carefully lifts a pouch made of softly padded and quilted silk; he opens this pouch, and from it he takes, with care, an ancient drinking vessel.

It is of glass; but so old is it, its like would be hard to find. The cup is deep and bell-shaped, and a short stem unites it to a small base. The rim of the cup is turned completely outward so as to close upon itself and to hold, all round, a fine thread of imprisoned air. So old is this cup that the swirling lines of its making show in the glass like the water about a whirlpool; it is transparent no longer, but gleams with dusky blue and green, and flashes with strange metallic sparkles.

The Alchemist takes this wonderful vessel to the spring, rinses it, then fills it with fresh water. Holding this in his left hand, in his right he lifts his massive golden lamen without removing the chain from his neck. He turns the lamen and catches the rays of the Sun upon the bright gold, so that as they reflect back the metal seems to blaze with their effulgence; and, just at the moment when the Sun mounts to its zenith, he speaks something in a quiet voice, holding the cup and lamen so that the full force of the noonday Sun is deflected into the limpid water. The water flashes and sparkles with a myriad tiny bubbles; the Alchemist, watching this intently, silently replaces the lamen upon his breast.

He calls to the griffins, and in a circle around the cup the six dip their beaks to drink of this marvelous water charged with the power of the Sun. At once their weakness and weariness are gone. Again they stand proudly, shining like images of burning metal; again their eyes flash with fiery light. Stepping back, they utter in chorus their ringing, musical cries. They spread their wings and, still calling to one another, with powerful strokes they rise in the air, wheel several times above the summit of the mount, then soar up towards the Sun and vanish from our sight in their native region. The Alchemist, having watched their departure, again puts away the venerable vessel of ancient glass.

Now as we look towards the high snowy peaks which on one side break our horizon, a strong vigorous wind arises at our back. Our Guide indicates that we shall travel with it. He takes up his staff and extends it; lightly and easily then we allow the wind to lift us from the top of the mount, and to carry us high once more into the shining sky.

The snowy peaks sink out of sight as we rise, and, our Guide leading, we fly rapidly onwards. Now we behold only the shimmering vapors of this astral region, under a remote sky whose luminous pale hue changes continually as if it were the vault of an immense sea-shell containing us. Caught in this variable illumination, opaline columns suddenly flash into being, extending from the depths to the height above us; then, just as suddenly, they vanish as we speed away. Delicate webs of emerald and amethystine light seem spread to entrap us, then are left far behind in our flight.

As the luminous vapors coil and surge into strange shapes, during the brief time that we see them they suggest strange images to our consciousness. Here a tree laden with starry fruit grows from the top of a fantastic fortified tower, a dream castle; a flight of birds with extravagantly streaming plumes come to eat of the shining globes. Now the scene is gone, and geat fan-shapes of light, scarlet and intense blue, well up across the heavens and disperse. Through the succeeding blackness a white chariot advances, drawn by horses of flashing brightness; in the chariot sits a woman crowned as a queen. One of the plumed birds appears again and, gliding down past the chariot, places a star-fruit in the woman's lap where it glows like a ruby. The image is snatched away from us and the sky blazes like a rainbow curtain. Scenes and countenances of an-intense visionary quality flash upon us as we journey long and far.

Now the voice of the wind itself takes on a new, melodious tone. We hear a succession of notes, sonorous, slow, majestic, as from an Aeolian harp; and now, after a pause, the same succession of notes again. We look all about us, but in vain, for any visible manifestation which might be related to this sound. Our Guide, the Alchemist, does not look about. Without pausing in his advance, he looks upwards, and raises his right hand in acknowledgment and salutation to the sound. And now again we hear the same sonorous majestic tone, but this time in a different succession of slowly changing notes, like an equinoctial gale singing in the branches of a gigantic tree.

Now the air is full of shining rosy flecks. The intense light irradiates them, creating a hue almost of dawn or of sunset. In every direction, the atmosphere is thronged with little semi-transparent particles, some transmitting and some reflecting the light but all pervading it with the same radiant color. The sight calls to mind the drift of rose-petals which brought our Guide to us.

Indeed, just when these diminutive flecks of rose color, becoming less distinct, have merged into a soft luminous tint in the air, there comes floating down from the illimitable height of the skies just such a drift of immense rose petals as we witnessed in the desert. He, and we, cease to go forward. A few of the largest petals draw near, and hover in the air before our Guide. Without hesitation he steps on to the central petal, then as they begin to ascend he turns to face us. He raises his arms as in blessing to us, and his wise and benevolent gaze is fixed on us. The brightness of the light which encompasses him, and of the rose petals which surround him, grows more and more intense; but the glowing light about his head increases beyond the rest, so that it first is lost to our sight in the effulgence. Then all merges in a glaze of rose-colored light. It fades from our perception, and we are hovering in the airy vastness without our Guide.

By an effort of will we begin to go onward again, and our flight continues. We have no knowledge of what direction we should take, so we go straight forward.

At length, looking down, we see a gleam as of the ocean. We remember the words of the talking trees on the mount, that we must cross the silvery sea. Perhaps, then, we shall also find the Red Flower of the Sun.

We resolve to cross the bright ocean before us, even though at present we can see no further shore. As we gaze at it, we realize we are losing height. It is a marvelous silvery sea which confronts us, with shining billows which, as they rise and fall, weave a pulsating web of light. As we gaze fascinated we find we are drawing still nearer to the bright expanse.

Surely, even so, we have no need to be greatly concerned! We have learned much by watching the Alchemist, our Guide. We have no wand, as he had, but it seems to us that the correct motion of hand and arm should suffice.

We extend right hand and arm before us as we glide along, in a gesture to indicate rising; but the immediate result is that we drop suddenly lower. Now we are almost skimming the waves. We do not have the deep knowledge, or the power, to direct our course aright; neither do we know the depth, or the extent, of this strange silvery ocean. We make one more attempt, and the waves splash us. They do not feel wet, however.

Now two slender, luminous figures come flying across the waves. They are the two children, dressed in the same colors as before—he in red, she in white—but now they are grown almost to man and woman. Between them they carry a two-handled jar of yellowish red clay, with two bands of geometrical pattern countercharged in black and white. In their other hands they each hold the vessels they carried previously. Both the children are laughing.

They bid us to descend willingly into the silvery sea. "This is water, but no common water! This is mercury, but not mercury of the material world!" they tell us.

We have faith in these two beautiful and radiant beings, and we allow ourselves to slip into the welcoming waves. For an instant we are immersed; then we float to the surface, and the waves support us. As we gently rise and fall with their rhythmic motion, we feel we are renewed and vitalized by our contact with the pulsating web of light we observed previously. In this sea is a magically creative force which, we realize, is derived from, although not the same as, the mystical power of that great Ocean which is the Mother of all that has form. Here we must learn by rule and measure, but still we must use the magical energies to think and act creatively for ourselves.

Now the children call out, and, laughing again, begin running across the waves away from us. Spontaneously we rise up, and speed also over the silvery waters, under a pale saffron sky. ★

At last we reach a grey rocky shore. Here the children stop, and we linger also to watch as they fill their jar with the silvery liquid of the waves which break on the rocks. As they complete this task and gather up their treasures of salt, sulphur and mercury, we ask them how it is that they who are so young have such deep knowledge.

Suddenly as they formulate the answer to our question they are entirely man and woman. Their smile is wonderful as they reply, "We have no deep knowledge: we love each other." In their luminance they blaze together like twin stars. We see that the polarity between them is a power which otherwise might be achieved only by much skill. We look at the path which leads from the shore, and we ask the young lovers if they will accompany us. "Ours is a different way," they say, and, with their treasures of salt, sulphur and the mysterious mercury, their forms are absorbed into their own radiance which in turn slowly fades from our sight. As we watch the fading light, we hear their voices bidding us go and prosper in our quest. "Knowledge without love avails little," they add; "love, even without knowledge, has great power; but knowledge gained and used with love is the greatest force there is."

As we ponder these words, we recall the wise and benign countenance of the Alchemist, and we understand why he has been our Guide on the path which lies behind us.

Beyond the shore we find a low stone wall, a gap in which is closed by a pair of swinging gates. The path leads through these gates and we willingly enter because of the mingled fragrance of sweet flowers and aromatic leaves which greets us.

The greenery, and the atmosphere, are full of moisture; but here we have neither the fantastic and riotous life of the garden in the Sphere of the Moon, nor the contradictory, baffling voices of the talking leaves through which the Alchemist guided us safely to the summit of the mount. We are now passing through a garden laid out in neat, well-tended beds, intersected by paved paths and filled with plants of many kinds. Each plant, whether large or small, has an inscribed clay tablet accompanying it, giving not only its name but also its curative scientific properties as well as its association in myth and folklore. Here also are small citruses and a number of taller trees which give shade as well as fragrance.

It is evening. The heat and brilliance of the Sun have now considerably declined, and it would be both pleasant and instructive to linger in this curious garden; but we must continue on our way. Beyond the garden we see a large octagonal building, which seems built of carnelian. We walk towrds it.

The sky above this building is filled with splendor. The sinking Sun suffuses it with gold and blue and green, shimmering with lines and waves of shining brightness. The effect is of the wide spreading fan of a peacock's tail.

At each side of the entrance to the building is sculptured a symbolic beast; to the left side a unicorn, representing singleness of purpose, and to the right a winged horse, signifying inspiration.

We enter into this sanctuary, where the air is cool and still, and pass between the two columns, Machetes and Nomothetes. We pause, and salute the East.

The Lamp of the Mysteries hangs from the center of the roof and beyond it, before the far wall, in the East, stands the Bomos. The Bomos is draped in glowing flame-orange, and upon it is the Mystical Tessera. Beneath our feet extends a checkered floor in which squares of almost luminous whiteness, as of marble, alternate with squares of metallic mirror-like blackness. The interior of the roof is similarly adorned. The eight walls have a luster of dark pearl, with iridescent gleams of brilliant colors playing swiftly and changefully over the surface. With the fitful gleaming of these colors and the complex play of reflections between floor and roof, the whole temple seems to be quivering with movement.

To the south-east, to the right of the Bomos, is the Banner of the New Life. Directly behind the Bomos, between two narrow open portals, hangs a curtain rich with mingled colors in the embroidered design of a Phoenix rising gloriously from the ashes of its former self. The passage from an old life to a new one, like the transmutation sought by the alchemists, can take place in many ways and at many levels of being.

We cross the floor and, taking the left hand portal, we pass into a small chamber behind the Phoenix curtain.

We enter with a great sense of reverence; it is evident that some great wonder is here to be seen.

The floor, the walls and roof are of the same materials and colors as the temple itself; but in the middle of this chamber is a low plinth of stone, on top of which stands a brazier of glowing fire. Upon this fire rests a crucible, itself glowing to red heat; and within the crucible is some black substance which we cannot identify, but which gives forth a hot, sweet smell. The greatest marvel, however, is a small plant with leaves that shine like golden lace, a plant which seems to be growing from the burning material within the crucible. From the center of this plant arises a tall, slender stem, surmounted by a single bud.

We stand admiring this golden plant, uncertain what art has produced this strange and beautiful sight; when, as we watch, the bud slowly opens, and a living flower spreads its eight petals, each petal red and glowing as a fire opal. And the heart of the flower is of yellow light.

We cannot touch this marvel because of the heat of the fire. We can but contemplate it, and that which it signifies. We have come by the Path of the Sun and crossed the silvery sea to find it; its eight petals represent the regenerative and healing power which is of this Sphere of Mercury, yet which bears the light of the Sun in its center. It is the regenerative and healing power of knowledge; yet everything of this Sphere is dual in nature, and, as the two children told us, the completion of Knowledge is with Love.

We have come from the Sphere of Luna, the place of dreams, to the Sphere of Mercury, the place of magical knowledge. We have traveled by way of the Path of the Sun, for the transition from dream to knowledge must be by way of Illumination, in which neither the creativity of dreaming is lost nor the effectiveness of knowledge impaired.

The Path we travel governs the fruition we win in the Sphere at which we arrive; none the less, the fruition is truly won from the Sphere itself. The treasure we have attained in this Temple of Mercury is the Red Flower, which is a traditional manifestation of the alchemical Elixir of Regeneration: itself a form of the Philosophers' Stone. We have found it springing up in the crucible, which is a symbol of the mind. This is truly the magical work of the Sphere of Mercury; but beneath the crucible glows the fire, which is a ray from the splendor of the Sun and is of the heart. For each Sphere contains every other Sphere after its own manner; and to attain to the Sphere of Mercury, the Sphere of Magick, is not a limitation therein but a limitless treasure to be brought into realization of knowledge, power, and inspiration in the New Life.

Battery 3-5-3

The Working of the 29th Path
(Correspondences)

SPHERE OF COMMENCEMENT: Malkuth (Kingdom)

Hebrew Divine Name: Adonai Melek

Planetary correspondence: The Earth

Element: Earth

Deific forces: The Rustic Gods

Symbols: The Gateway

Plants: Ferns, ancient trees, forms recalling the Carboniferous Age

Colors: Soft browns and greens

PATH OF THE TREE OF LIFE: 29

Intelligence: The 29th Path is the Bodily Intelligence, so called because it gives materiality to every shape which is brought to being in the lowest of the Worlds, and by the influence of all the Worlds.

Hebrew Divine Name: El

Influence on Path: Pisces (the Fishes)

Planetary correspondence: Jupiter

Hebrew Letter: Qoph (Back of the Head)

Path Stanza: Quietly under the Moon vanishes Day's
vaunted autonomy:
Softly the voices of Night sound at our gates,
stir from oblivion
Calling for sacrifice! Lo, children are we
all of one parentage:
Go we with thanksgiving!

Tarot arcanum: The Moon (18)

Element of Path: Water

Symbol: The cup

Colors: Dark brown rayed yellow, lilac, deep blue Plant: Oak

Minerals: Earth, water and air in various co-minglings

Living beings: All amphibious and aquatic creatures

Optical effects: Confusion and obscurity, illusions of fear

Magical phenomena: Spiritual progress in fellowship with aspirants of all eras and with other living beings

Philosophy of the Path: Epicurean: "terrors flee when we learn to see only what is ... without the additions and inter-pretations of an ungoverned imagination."

SPHERE OF DESTINATION: Netzach (Victory)

Hebrew Divine Name: Yahveh Tzabaoth

Planetary correspondence: Venus

Planetary number: 7

Element: Fire

Symbols: The pyramid or ziggurat of 7 stages, the aniconic (not shaped) meteorite

Minerals: Malachite, blue crystal

Colors: Green, blue, black

Magical phenomena: Manifestation of the cosmic power of the Mother: realization of our spiritual birthright within the natural order.

Comments

Once again on this Path we set out from the Earth Sphere, Malkuth, and have something of its influence to overcome. This time our destination is Netzach in Yetzirah, the astral level of the Sphere of Venus.

We might expect to encounter a feminine force upon this Path, but this is not the case. Here we travel under the zodiacal sign of Pisces, whose ruling planet is Jupiter, and whose element is Water. We take this Path as children of Zeus, the All-Father, giver of the rains, rivers and oceans which are necessary to all forms of life. (Neptune or Poseidon, in mythology the brother of Jupiter-Zeus, is Qabalistically regarded as his other self, his aquatic manifestation.)

Civilized people build up many arificial concepts to shield them-selves from having to see the natural realities of their life. Epicurus, whose philosophy is taken as characteristic of this Path, perceived that through these artificial concepts and through the distorted imagination they engender, we create for ourselves many phantasmal and needless causes of grief and fear. An essential condition, if we are to rediscover the rightful happiness of our being, is to recognize ourselves as a part of all life, so as to live simply, fearlessly, and with the natural dignity of all creatures.

The 32 Paths of Wisdom calls the guiding influence of this Path the "Bodily Intelligence," but at the same time draws attention to the fact that every form in Nature comes into being "by the influence of all the Worlds." We can trace the patterns of the Divine Plan and of the World of Mind in all that exists: we therefore need neither fear nor scorn to own our fellowship therewith. "Lo, children are we all of one parentage: Go we with thanksgiving!" says *The Song of Praises*.

The Goddess image which we find at the culmination of this journey is in keeping with this ancient wisdom. Some of the earliest and most revered objects relating to the Mother have in fact been shapeless meteoric rocks. The people of old were not deterred by the lack of likeness to human shape in these rocks literally "fallen from heaven," nor by any idea that they came from an alien region of space. There is but one Universe, and the same Powers govern all.

There is but one Universe, and we are part of it. Reviewing our petty dissensions beneath the sublimity of the Cosmos, it is good for our sanity to regain this understanding.

The Working of the 29th Path

It is evening in summer-time; the air is moist and warm. We are in a strange place. In centuries past it has been the site of a monastery, built in the Gothic style. Now, fully-grown trees, birch and ash, spread their branches in spaces which once were covered by a roof, and thick grass grows where once there were paved floors. A bird flies from bough to bough; a squirrel scampers across the ground, disappearing into the leafy shadows. Only a few ruined walls of grey stone remain to show what once has been. There is no sorrow here, but peace: the peace of a harmony and equilibrium that with the passage of time is being restored.

Yet there are mysterious stresses in time and space which, once established, do not easily pass away but become portals between sphere and sphere. Before us is a section of broken wall containing a gateway, which had once consisted of an arch with a square tower at each side:

now the arch is gone, but the towers remain. Through this opening the further landscape appears remote and dreamlike. An air of extraordinary invitation reaches us from that partly-perceived distance. Such an evening as this calls strongly to us to go forth, in our bodies or out of them, to seek reunion with the forces of Nature. We walk over to the gateway, and pass through it.

Now, truly, we are walking through another region. Here also is grassland, a clearing with clusters of trees and with a denser wood behind it; but of these trees, some are gnarled, twisted and ancient-looking, while others have the exotic appearance of other climates and elder growth. The woodland is full of blue mist, which makes the distances questionable and eerie. A smell of aromatic bushes and of humid ferns hangs upon the air. No moving creature is in sight. The branches do not stir, the whole scene is watchfully silent: yet it does not seem to be uninhabited. So remote is it from time and place, so truly pagan in its elemental serenity, this might be a region of the Eastern Mediterranean as it was over two thousand years ago, plane-trees and terebinths meeting with cypresses and palms: and we would suppose some joyful troop of humans, celebrating the gods with song and with ringing cymbals, to have passed through but now, or to be about to appear, accompanied perhaps by graceful and garlanded leopards. The breath of such mysteries clings to the clustered trees, it broods in the veiled distances. We walk on until we reach the woodland.

A faint sound of running water invites us to find its origin. We wander among trees of different kinds, over slopes of soft earth and of projecting rock, the sound of water, plashing and rippling, becoming continually louder. Then we see where, from the higher part of a steep tree-covered slope, a small spring falls into a rocky basin to which human hands have given the shape of a true cup. We stop and look into this cup, where the water shows deep blue with swirling white bubbles. The cascade is overshadowed by a great and primeval oak, and in the rock above the pool we can trace the outline of a venerable bearded head. We acknowledge that this dedicated fountain is a symbol of the benevolent Sky-Father who provides for the need of all living beings; with cupped hands we take this cold water, and from cupped hands we drink of it in acceptance of this provision and in recognition of the underlying unity of all life-forms.

As we drink, a faint peal of thunder sounds from high overhead, and the leaves of the oak rustle as if in recognition of our pledge.

We see that the overflow from the basin runs away in a dark stream, which is concealed, and at the outset almost swallowed up, by ferns and by water-loving plants with starry flowers. In the deepening twilight, we follow the course of the stream as it gradually becomes wider. Tall grass moves in a pleasant breeze, and a fine rain begins to fall. So gentle and warm is the rain that we scarcely feel it, but soon we are drenched in its moisture. We might almost be immersed in the stream which we are following, except that we can walk and breathe without effort. Nevertheless, the boundaries which mark off the world of waters are lost, and from time to time we are conscious of the presence of amphibious creatures, both mammals and reptiles, traveling in the same direction as ourselves, some climbing from the water to move for a while on land, some leaving the bank suddenly to swim in the stream. It makes no difference how they choose to travel, nor whether we find their forms beautiful or grotesque. We are all making the same journey at this time, and we and they are to some degree kindred—the human organism is, at one stage of its embryonic existence, typically an aquatic creature.

Now the stream which we have been following cascades into a river, and we walk on beside the river, only now we are not moving in the direction of the current, we are following the river towards its source.

Night has fallen, and in the darkness the water shows deep brown, carrying upon its rain-starred surface the yellow rays of the moon. Slowly we make our way along the bank, but it is irregular and eroded. We are eager to press forward but at the same time we are fearful of stumbling, afraid of putting down a foot in shadows which seem solid but which will fall away into a watery blackness beneath us. Gradually a chill takes, possession of our hands and feet, coldness and trembling and uncertainty seize upon us. We stand still; we feel drained of strength, powerless to move. With a strange sense of horror and bewilderment, we begin to wonder if we are not lost indeed. But lost where? How can we be lost? For we are part of the Universe, participating in all the conditions and qualities within it, and all these conditions and qualities are part of ourselves. That which we experience cannot be altogether alien to us. We compel ourselves to breathe steadily and to look ahead into the night.

Suddenly a gleam of brilliant lilac light shines before us. It increases rapidly in size, suffusing with blue, until it becomes a large ovoid of blue light. This dims slightly, and we see standing within it an august and majestic form. He is clad in a ample and undulating cloak of a deeper blue, and beneath this is a flowing robe of blood-red. His hair, deep green in color, descends to his shoulders, long and curling at the ends: his beard is similar. From his head two vertical horns arise, slender and tapering, each with a spiral marking channeled from base to tip. His face is calm and benevolent, with broad forehead, heavy brows, and with luminous eyes filled with wisdom, although deep-set and almost hypnotic in their intensity. Having raised his arms in a gesture of welcome and blessing, he turns and leads the way forward. Our path is now illuminated by the blue radiance which emanates from him, and we follow with renewed confidence and strength.

As we advance in this watery atmosphere, with the swift river beside us and the fine rain falling, the light shining about our Guide enables us to see other human forms proceeding on the same path as ourselves. We recognize these as people of many varied cultures, in garments of different periods of past time and of the present, and some which we can discern to be of the future. We see united families, forming centres of peace and harmony in their shared lives and willing an equal peace and harmony to others. We see monastic communities, Buddhist, Essene, Christian, some of men, some of women; we see Quakers and Dervishes; hermits and recluses of every faith, dedicated people of every kind. On and on we follow, together with these other companions. The rain becomes stronger and heavier. The river, which has been rising almost imperceptibly for some time, now floods over the path. Unable to discern where the river-channel lies, we can only keep our eyes upon the form of our Guide, with the surrounding blue luminosity which shines in the darkness even through the falling torrent. The voices of the rain and of the flooding river have become a choir, with a wild hissing and rushing and the broken warbling of small currents of water passing an obstacle, sounding shrilly and intermittently above the incessant central song, the almost melodious chanting and calling of the main body of water; and far below that again, heard from time to time in tones of menace and warning, the deep booming and roaring of the flood.

The water becomes deeper over the path until we are wading waist-deep in the flood: but our Guide, proceeding ahead of us, is mighty in the world of waters, and moves forward upon the surface. We struggle forward, following him, but uneven and slippery rocks are beneath our feet, and the strong current pulls at our garments, now,to one side, now to the other, until we feel we must fall.

Our Guide turns to face us, and at his gesture we all pause. Instinctively, we know what we are to do. Stripping off all our clothes, we abandon them to the dark river; quickly they are swirled away, and now we can move with more freedom since the currents have less hold upon us.

Our Guide, ever shining in blue radiance, now beckons us to continue following him, and the whole company does so. We advance slowly through the wilderness of waters, until at last he leads us up a series of footholds to a trackway which is clear of the flood. We are still aware, in the dim light, of the presence of all the people we saw previously, of whatever sort, walking with us, completely unclothed as we are. There is no distinction here. For upon this Path which we are now treading it is not the formal code of a man's or a woman's belief that signifies, but the perception of certain natural values and a resolution to live by them in whatever time and place we find ourselves. Whether in hope to attain a better birth or to escape altogether from births; whether for desire of a future paradise or for no reward save a life well-lived here and now; whether for love of Deity or for love of Humanity or for pure love of the the goodness of Being, upon this Path it matters not, for all these loves and purpose alike manifest a love of the forces of Life.

Slowly the tumultuous sound of the rain becomes less, until it is a gentle pattering. The voice of the river becomes lighter and softer. Our Guide leads us continually onward.

We walk beside the river for some time, then we come to a place where a sharp bend in the course of the river turns it away from our path. The ground underfoot is grass-covered, with here and there tall clumps of rushes; and by these, and by the way our feet sink slightly into the wet earth, we can tell that it is in places marshy. We tread with careful and unhurried steps, watching the blue light which surrounds our Guide, until at last he pauses, as the moon shines brightly out from the slowly dispersing clouds. We stand overlooking a wide morass partially covered with slowly-drifting mist, upon which the variable moonbeams play strangely. For a time we see only the vague abstract shapes of the mist, drifting and breaking and re-forming itself in the cold light: now plainly visible, now indistinct and uncertain. Slowly a feeling comes to us that there is a living presence out there beyond the mist, hidden, alien, perhaps hostile. What its visible form might be, we do not know, but its silent brooding impresses itself upon us so that we wait apprehensively, with a coldness in the hands and a prickling in the scalp.

About a hundred yards from us there stands a small group of birch-trees, their white trunks gleaming. Near to them, close above the ground, wavering and restless shadow-forms go back and forth, back and forth like beasts of prey; then little by little we lose sight of them as the mist thickens in that place and drifts gradually nearer to us. We cannot tell whether they have remained by the trees or whether they have moved elsewhere. Something seems to be standing far over to the right, rather closer to us, but we cannot discern it well enough to be certain whether it is another tree or perhaps a human figure. Suddenly the moon disappears behind a mass of cloud, and the scene before us vanishes in blackness. We stand motionless, straining our ears to hear and our eyes to see, but only our hearts beat in the chill oppressive silence while we wonder what has become of the ghostly forms we had been watching—have they ceased to exist now that the light has gone, or are they moving stealthily in the dark, gaining positions from which to spring upon us? Try as we may, we can descry nothing clearly, although from time to time an indefinable greyness seems to move in the gloom and then to disappear again. Slowly the moonlight begins to return, showing us the white birch-trees and indistinct patches of mist. Now a cold breeze has arisen, carrying the strange unwelcoming smell of the marshes: the areas of mist move and re-shape themselves more rapidly. Do we catch sight of low-gliding, menacing forms which are whirled about or rear themselves up in the grey vapor? Is that an aim outstretched, pointing towards us, or is it a broken and leafless bough which was previously unnoticed? Surely the whole scene has changed in some way, is more alive with sinister suggestion? Still there is no sound, and the formless clouds extend themselves, break, and are re-shaped as they move towards us. Now the breeze catches them again, and with a sudden twist it whirls them behind us! We turn sharply to see how we may be beset, but the moon is covered by cloud again, and whatever may be present crouches in black shadow. A thin high-pitched cry strikes momentarily upon our ears; we cannot analyse it for it is gone as soon as we become aware of it, but the next moment we see a slender grey figure speeding from our company and flitting wraithlike from mound to mound of reeds, further and further into the marsh. The wind veers again and the mist-creatures swing round, as if they and the wind that carries them were alike guided by some malicious external intelligence: they overtake and crowd upon the fugitive. Once again we hear that thin evanescent scream, ended before we can take in its entire meaning; then there is silence, the mist drifts on, and the grey figure has vanished.

Suddenly we realize that the mist-banks beside us are full of movement, turbulent with indistinct forms gathering within them. The silence is intolerable in suspense. A few more moments to wait, and we too shall be overrun, herded into the treacherous marsh-pools by our scarcely-discernable enemies. We think of that hideous fate, the slipping foot, the struggle with liquid mud which binds and finally engulfs, the vain seeking for foothold or handhold, the last useless fight for breath: we see how the fear-driven victim brings about his own agony. In this moment of horror, a strange new hope comes to us, for far off where the mists are less heavy we see a tiny flame of light coming towards us through the darkness. From side to side it moves, dancing as though carried by one unseen who treads cautiously over the marshy ways. Soon we perceive that this light is followed by another, which takes likewise a varied direction but slowly moves towards us.

Again from among us there is a movement as a dim grey figure goes forth, running this time to meet the approaching lights. Another and another springs forward, to be lost from sight among the mists. Shall we too run to meet our rescuers?

But no. We turn our eyes from the phantom shapes—for those who seemed to run from among us, whether to destruction or to safety, are as phantasmal as the mist-creatures—and we fix our attention upon our calm and venerable Guide. He looks at us with love and reassurance, and signs to us to look again upon the mist. We turn back our gaze to it, and lo!—it is now only mist in truth, and the shapes into which it drifts are abstract and meaningless, while the marsh-lights move away and flicker mockingly over the black water. Terrors flee when we learn to see only what is, whether materially or spiritually, without the additions and interpretations of an ungoverned imagination. We look up at the sky, and it has grown paler. We turn, and above the horizon the Sun is beginning to rise. We watch the sky filling with gold, red and purple; at this moment in time we see both the rising sun and the fading moon. All is beauty, peace and wonder. The mist is dispersing, and a myriad dewdrops upon the grass shimmer in brilliant prismatic colors. In joy and in awe we make our salutation to the Sun, then, after lingering for a few minutes more to drink in the loveliness of the scene, we turn to follow our blue-mantled Guide.

Our path now leads steeply uphill, and after some time we come again to the river, for its upper reaches have their course through the hills before descending in successive rapids and pools to the plain below. Where we rejoin the river, the rift in the hills through which it has issued is broad and shallow.

Here and there the slopes show uneven ridges and points of rock, and among these a host of many-colored blossoms have opened at the daybreak. We greet these fair children of earth and of water, called into beauty by the fire of the sun, for they make our path so much the more joyful! The music of running water adds to the gladness of our hearts. And now our guide bids us pause again.

The silver disc of the moon has vanished altogether from the sky. But see! Another token of her power comes towards us. A troop of horses, milk-white with large blue-black eyes, comes gently descending the further slope. We look to our Guide, asking whether we should accept the company of these exquisite creatures. He spreads his arms to express assent. By the ordeals we have already passed we have earned the right to ride the horses, but the adventures of this Path are not yet at an end.

We choose our horses, and mount them. The horses toss their heads impatiently, anxious to move on. Our Guide meanwhile raises his arms in benediction, and we understand that he is about to leave us. In that case, how are we to know our true direction? We look again to our Guide for counsel, but the genial and wise smile with which this dignified Spirit responds to us needs no words. We have found our authority over the natural forces, so we should learn to trust them to work for us in their own manner.

The light about our Guide becomes more luminous, even in this full daylight. It grows stronger and brighter until it is a blue effulgence in which his form can no longer be distinguished; then the blue light itself slowly fades away and he is gone from us.

Now we put into effect his latest counsel, and give our horses their heads to do as they will. At once they set off beside the river, carrying us joyfully on our way. After some time, on each side of the river valley through which we are travelling there rise steep and rugged banks, where grey rock gleams among small flowering plants and where an occasional tall cone-bearing tree looks into the hazy distance.

On and on we ride. The banks are steeper, they are more rocky and less covered with vegetation, and the distance between them and the river narrows. After a time we are moving along a stony strand at the water's edge, and the sound of hooves striking upon pebbles gives forth an insistent and hollowly-echoing staccato. We go forward into shadow, because high above us rise the rocky walls between which the river flows. Gradually the stony margin becomes narrower, until at last, ahead of us, we see a place where the strand ends and the rocky wall rises sheer from the river itself. But without hesitation our horses plunge into the water, and, with us still on their backs, they continue to make their way upstream, swimming strongly against the current.

The many voices of the river sing loudly around us, deep and bellowing, keen and melodious, high and chiming, so that we cannot communicate with one another, but collectively must be led by the natural powers as these can best fulfil our true wills. So we go forward upon the horses, rejoicing in their powers and in our own, rejoicing in the sense of liberation which comes with the success of our efforts and theirs, rejoicing also in our nudity and in the direct contact of our bodies with the horses and with the water. This passage through the deep and flowing river is indeed a test of endurance, but it is one in which we can be glad with the certainty of achievement and with the sense of participation in a strength greater than our own—both the strength of the river and that of the horses.

At last the water becomes shallower, and our horses are able to find foothold on the river-bed and to walk instead of swimming. In this manner we are carried onward to a place where the river has spread into a vast pool, which we enter, halting in the shallow water around its edge.

From the deep waters in the center of this pool, a pair of large and beautiful fishes come to meet us. They appear in the form of dolphins, for as spiritual beings they are able to travel where they please in the watery domain, in the river as well as in the salt ocean. As they come near we salute them as elder brother and elder sister. The horses know them too, and neigh in greeting.

The fishes swim back into the deep center of the pool, and there begin a slow and undulating dance, over and beneath, around and across; and now in the shallows our horses begin dancing too for pure joy of life itself. Faster now the fishes turn, leaping sometimes in glittering arcs from the waves; faster also our steeds, with us upon their backs, rear and plunge and whinny playfully, sending the water in a spray of shining drops up from their hooves.

O, bliss of life and of being! O, elemental ecstasy! O, precious kinship with every force of Nature!

The two great fishes circle about one another, then raise themselves up in the water as in salutation, and plunging into the deeps are gone. We and our horses alike have been refreshed by the caressing waters; now they and we together return to the land, to find our path again. The horses fling up their heads and neigh, and begin running, running like the wind. We make no attempt to check them, for surely these large-eyed and comely ones know their way; and we laugh and sing aloud in exultation. Distance rushes towards us, meets us and disappears. Our horses are running, running like the wind. How splendid is the impact of air upon face and breast! How joyful, when we pat the velvety neck or shoulder of our mount, to feel the warmth and movement of steely muscles beneath! Now the hoofbeats thud upon grass, now they ring out on rock, now it is grass once more and the smell of bruised herbs comes to our nostrils. One of the horses neighs again, loud and high, and another answers in the rapture of running, running like the wind.

At once the speed accelerates, we are one with the movement of the horses, and keenly we scan the ground in the distances ahead. What is that dark smoke which spreads across our path, rising unevenly from the ground? A fierce and fiery light illuminates it from beneath, grows in intensity, then dies slowly away to spring up again shortly afterwards. We are rushing towards a mighty volcanic fissure, and there is no other way to go. Beyond it the ground slopes gently upward, and the path looks easy and pleasant: but first we must attain to it by a supreme effort.

We know that in this journey we have the power to do what we will, if we will it in truth, and a feeling of great joy and power is with us.

Now the air that strikes upon us is hot and filled with the harsh smell of saltpeter, potash, and other mineral fumes. The moment of trial has arrived. Our horses leave the rocky ground, soaring high and higher, and as we are carried upward we too strive to soar, to fly, to be winged for our passage over the fiery chasm. We catch a swift glimpse beneath of a molten depth too bright to look upon, of flame which seems consciously to reach up towards us. ★

But we have passed over the place of peril. We take a deep breath of sweet cool air, and a great shout of "Triumph!" rises from all our throats as the horse-hooves thud and pick up their rhythm anew on the farther side. Soon we are traveling over grass again. Up a wide slope we gallop, in a high region where flowers grow in profusion.

Now in the distance we see a curiously-shaped building, looking something like a step pyramid. Our horses carry us swiftly towards this; as we approach it they slow down to a trot, then to a walk. We see that the building is, in fact, a massive ziggurat, shaped like those ancient structures in Mesopotamia. It is built on a square plan, and has seven terrances joined by flights of steps, each terrace being progressively smaller than the one beneath. This ziggurat, however, is built entirely of malachite, an opaque lustrous stone with bands of darker and lighter green. We ride slowly up to it, then we dismount from our horses, thanking them for their aid and letting them go free.

There is a portal at ground level leading into the temple: we go through this. After walking for a short distance along a low passageway, we arrive at the portal of an inner chamber. Reverently we enter. The walls of this chamber are of polished malachite, the floor is of translucent deep blue crystal. We pass between the two pillars, Machetes and Nomothetes. The sweet smell of incense hangs upon the air. In the centre of the chamber is the Bomos, draped in brilliant green: upon it is the Mystical Tessera. We stop before the Bomos and salute the East, which lies before us.

Above us shines the single Lamp of the Mysteries, symbol of the Eternal Flame. To the north-east is the Banner of the New Life. In the south-east, a copper bowl rests upon a tripod some forty inches high: from this bowl ascends the faint blue aromatic smoke of burning incense. In the center of the eastern wall is a square-cut recess, which serves the function of a shrine. Within this is something which stands in shadow, yet from which power rays out to us like beams of light. It is a holy power, a divine power, most august and elevated and yet penetrating every particle of body and soul. As our eyes become accustomed to the shadow, we see that in the recess is a mass of black stone, vitrified by more than earthly fires, not sculptured by human hand: this is one of those venerable rocks, meteoric in origin, which have always been held sacred to the power of the Mother. She who nourishes, She who sustains, manifests Her presence to us through this most primal of Her emblems, this wandering rock which told early man that he and his world were not lonely in the universe. Our whole attention is fixed upon it, our every emotion is laid bare to those delicate and penetrating rays. Our joy and our sorrow, our love and our fear, our hope and weariness, our pride and shame, are poured out as a cup of wine for libation, for they are sacred to Her. A mother knows every part of the body of the child she has borne: but She whom we revere has brought forth and cradled our souls also in the depths of Her being. Thus we give back to Her that which is Hers, and in the giving is a great and joyful peace.

We have come through flowing water and through fire, and both have been needful to bring us into the Sphere of Venus. We have contemplated the sacred Meteorite, one of the great emblems of the Mother-Deity of this Sphere. As Her power pervades us, we come to understand that that which represents Her, must in some wise represent us Her children also. For the Meteorite, which has traveled through space to be a visitant upon our planet, is yet a sister rock to the rocks of Earth. So we too are indeed one with all which we perceive, and all which we perceive is part of us. We need have no fear of failure, nor ever shall fail, while we know ourselves to be a part of the Kosmos which fails not; and in the strength of that certainty we go forward to Victory, which is of our Mother. For this Victory is not only the outcome of our endeavors, but is our birthright from the beginning. Ours is not to be the transitory triumph of the aggressor, but the true victory of that which is receptive to, and fructified by, the mighty creative powers of the Universe.

Battery 3-5-3

The Working of the 28th Path

(Correspondences)

SPHERE OF COMMENCEMENT: Yesod (Foundation)

Hebrew Divine Name: Shaddai El Chai

Planetary correspondence: The Moon

Element: Air

Symbols: Mirror, masks, perfumes, the owl, the arched doorways

Colors: White, silver, mingled harmonious tints

PATH OF THE TREE OF LIFE: 28

Intelligence: The 28th Path is the Perfecting Intelligence, so named because by means of it the nature of every entity below the Sun-sphere is brought to its own fullness and perfection.

Hebrew Divine Name: Yahu

Influence on Path: Aquarius (Water-bearer)

Planetary correspondence: Saturn, Uranus

Hebrew Letter: Tzaddi (Fish-hook)

Path Stanza: Tzaphqiel, Bright One beyond veils of the
night! Envoy and countenance
Thou of the Mother, all hail! Thine is that
far Fortress of radiance
Lighting the drouth of our way: fountain of
hope, water celestial
—Deathless our thirst for it!

Tarot arcanum: The Star (17)

Element of the Path: Air

Symbols: The man (Aquarius), the ship (vessel), the sistrum (for Air)

Colors: Electric blue, hues of air and water

Living beings: The spirits of the storm

Magical phenomena: Soaring flight and aspiration, the ambrosial rain

Philosophy of the Path: Enlightened Humanism

SPHERE OF DESTINATION: Netzach (Victory)

Hebrew Divine Name: Yahveh Tzabaoth

Planetary correspondence: Venus

Planetary number: 7

Element: Fire

Symbols: Beacon, garden, temple on circular mount

Plants: All fragrant blossoms, cypress

Minerals: Rose quartz, amber, copper, obsidian, emerald, pearl

Colors: Green, rose

Magical phenomenon: Manifestation of the power of Mother through
the inner aspiration of each individual

Comments

This Path begins in Yesod and takes us to Netzach, and the journey from
beginning to end is in the World of Yetzirah. Here we travel under the
zodiacal sign of Aquarius, whose element is Air albeit with watery con-
notations. The two ruling planets, Saturn and Uranus, each have their
influence; but each is further conditioned by the fact that Aquarius is
one of the zodiacal signs of the "quarters," which are traditionally symbolized by the "Four Living Beings" of Ezekiel's vision. In the case of
Aquarius, the symbolic figure is the Winged Man, or Angel.

An "angel" is, essentially, a messenger from a divine or supernal
source. That is why *The Song of Praises* invokes for this Path Tzaphqiel,
Archangel of the Sephirah Binah, whose high influence indeed brightens
this Path with a luster which is beyond the elevation of the Path itself.
The Hebrew letter Tzaddi, "the fish-hook," seems to relate to this high
influence: an idealism lifting us beyond our former level to the noblest
visions of what we as human beings should attain to.

On the 29th Path we had to find our reality at the astral level of
being. Now on this 28th Path, attuned to the World of Yetzirah from the
beginning, we can joyfully and courageously follow our dreams. There
are dangers, certainly. The greatest is the one indicated while we are
still in Yesod, although it could apply to the whole World of Yetzirah:
the danger of being shut in with our own partial echoes and reflections
when we seek to explore the astral environment. And, having escaped
from that self-enclosure, somewhere on the way between the Sphere of
Imagination and the Sphere of Nature we may encounter such entities
as the "energy vampire," which is not a real existence in its own right

but, with its stolen life forces, is not quite unreal either. Such phantasms, however, must yield before the resolution of the truly living.

The aspect of the Goddess of Love which crowns this journey is an inspiring manifestation of the Supernal Mother whose brightness has illumined our adventuring. If upon the Path of Pisces we found ourselves to be "children of one father," upon the Path of Aquarius we find ourselves to be "children of one mother." The experience is *humanizing* in the best sense of the word.

The Working of the 28th Path

As a person awakens from deep sleep, without sensation, without emotion, so our consciousness awakens in the Sphere of the Moon. Then, gradually, we become aware of the scene and the sounds in which we participate.

We are in a large hall, surrounded by the gleaming walls and high, arched doorways of a stately palace, all of highly polished white stone accented with borders and ornaments of silver. The tall windows are similarly decorated, but are filled with many-colored stained glass, in abstract designs which, as the eye dwells upon them, seem to form themselves into suggestions of primeval living shapes, through which shines brilliant moonlight.

Now the sweet sound of festive music strikes our ears. We hear the tones of violins and of flutes in a haunting, elusive melody with a romantic dance rhythm. A mingled warm breath of delightful perfumes meets us as, through the doors, hand in hand, streams a throng of happy dancers, men and women. All of them wear eye-masks; all wear beautiful and fantastic costumes in a medley of colors which, however, do not clash. The effect is like a chorus of voices together proclaiming Carnival; while, unconcealed by their masks, the light in their eyes, and their smiling lips, emphasize the carefree festivity of the occasion.

We mingle with this light-hearted company, we share in the dancing, the song and the greetings which are casually exchanged. We feel we are surrounded with friendliness, with happiness shared and with the beauty of the scene, and evidently our new companions have the same feeling. After a time, however, we begin to notice a peculiar cir-

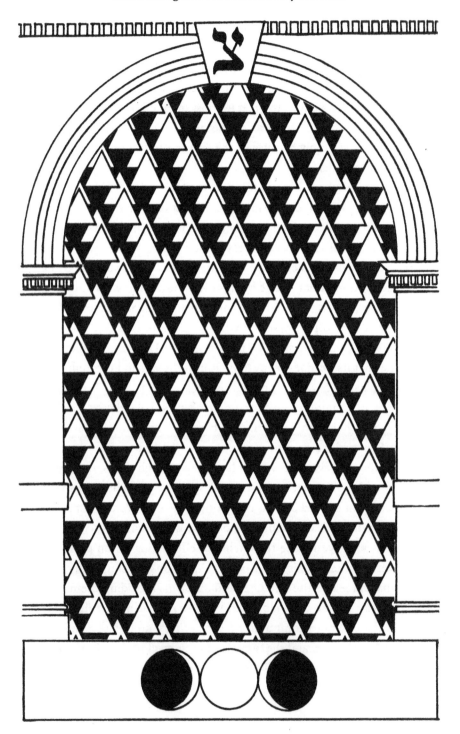

cumstance which makes communication far less easy than at first it appeared.

The highly polished walls of the palace have a singular power of reflecting shapes and echoing sounds. If we catch a glimpse of a smiling face beside us and we turn to greet it, most often it is only the reflection of our own features; if we speak to another person, we are not likely to hear that person's reply because of the echoing of our own words back to us from the walls.

Looking about, we can see that every person is affected by this confusion, the masked dancers as much as the rest of us. Every person, trying to communicate with another, seems as it were imprisoned with his or her own echoes and images; every person present, save one.

The exception is a slender young woman whose arrival nobody had observed, although her whole being is luminous. She wears no mask, and her eyes are bright and remarkably expressive. She is dressed-in-a diaphanous-robe ofpale blue, on which are scattered silver stars, and which is held at the waist by a girdle of silver. The tissue of her robe is so fine that its outlines seem to melt into the air, and through it she shines like pale ivory. Her long hair is deep golden and falls upon her shoulders; it is unbound save for a garland of small delicately colored flowers about her brow. Her arms are bare, and upon her feet are silver sandals. She carries a sistrum of shining pale yellow metal.

Watching her, we observe that luminous though she is, the shining walls afford her no reflection nor even a shadow; and when she speaks, her voice is not echoed back as every other voice is. Were it not for her personal radiance, we might consider these peculiarities to be sinister; but as it is, we realize the enchantment of this Moon palace has no power over her own greater power. After looking eloquently at us, she turns and leaves the building; and all of us, including the masked dancers, with one accord follow her. We all have one motive in this: for without the power to communicate with others, no one person's individuality is complete, and she over whom this spell of the Moon sphere has no power, must be our Guide to lead us to clearer levels of vision and knowledge.

As we pass through one of the arched, silver bordered doorways and walk out into the moonlight, a cool breeze is blowing. We go for some distance across a bare expanse of white rock which in some places rises up in wierd and picturesque formations, until we stand at the brink of a slightly sunken area in the rock, a natural amphitheater of roughly circular shape. Every detail of the landscape appears in clear definition in the brilliant moonlight; every detail stands out distinctly, too, of that which stands delicately balanced in the center of this circular depression.

It is a sailing ship, fully rigged and with white sails set ready for voyaging; a wonderful and beautiful sight, strange though it is to see such a ship poised upon bare, dry rock.

From where we stand overlooking the depression in which the ship rests, a narrow gangway leads across to the deck. With a sign to us our Guide crosses the gangway, and we follow her aboard. So far as we can see, there are no crew members nor anyone else in the ship but our Guide and ourselves; and there is no sound except for the slight movement of the canvas in the breeze. Only, as we watch, there settles silently upon the helm an owl with reddish brown plumage and black wingtips, to rest there with large eyes gazing forward into the moonlight.

When everyone is aboard, our Guide raises her sistrum and sounds it; it has a musical but commanding tone. The vigilant owl flaps its wings. Then, as the sound of the sistrum dies away, the ship rises almost vertically out of the rocky hollow into the night sky. Rising with the ship, we feel the breeze grow stronger and fresher; the owl looks keenly about to detect possible obstructions, but all is open and with a steady flying motion the ship goes forward through the clear air. We pass over white crystalline mountains and mysterious shadowed valleys, until at last, when again we look down, we see below us the luminous pale blue waves, lazily rising and falling, of an astral ocean.

Moving forward all the time, the ship descends, until a plume of diamond spray rises as her bows cut into the undulating surface. The owl mounts into the air and glides from the ship; but instead of soaring upwards as we should expect, it plunges down into the waters. No sooner do the waves receive it, however, than a transformation takes place: instead of the owl we see a tall man, naked—and with the beautiful musculature of a skilled swimmer, striking out strongly in the direction from which our ship has come. After swimming some distance he looks back, and raises an arm in a gesture of farewell; then goes on his way. The moon is rapidly setting, and sky and sea alike are illuminated by a myriad points of starlight in which the swimmer at once becomes invisible to us.

With a calm sea and a gentle wind, and no heed needed for guiding the ship, our dancers quickly decide to resume the festivities. Large, brightly colored lanterns soon adorn the masts, and delightful music sounds from several instruments and many voices. Part of the deck soon becomes a dancing area. The magnificent ship sailing onward under the stars, with the medley of gleaming colorful lights and sweet sounds, is a delightful spectacle. We are untouched by any breath of care. A wonderful sense of freedom possesses us. It goes to our heads; we laugh for happiness, without needing any more exact cause, while, each according to our own impulses, we dance, sing, converse or silently enjoy the total pleasure of the occasion. Only our Guide remains watchful, although she smiles at the festive scene, and the grace with which she glides among us has more beauty than the movement of the dancers.

Suddenly a startled cry halts the dancing, and we look to see the cause of the trouble. A number of long, gleaming tentacles, translucent and jelly-like, arise from the sea and attach themselves to the ship, so that the entity to which they belong is able to pull itself up by means of them. It has a multitude of limbs, whose length varies as they are required; its body, in the midst of them, is small and narrow, seeming to have no organs but a voracious and pulsating mouth. The ship is brought almost to a standstill by this clinging monster; some of its limbs reach out towards the lanterns and darken them instantly, seeming to drain the light itself from them at a short distance, while other of these limbs hover, quivering, over the heads of the assembled company. We begin to feel chilled and faint, and we seem unable to think clearly while we watch vibrant lines of light run up the tentacles of the entity, its body beginning meanwhile to expand and to grow luminous. Evidently we have to do with some kind of vampiric monster which is drawing our energy from us.

Our Guide acts quickly. A long peal of sound rings forth from her sistrum, and the ship rises rapidly, but this time with a backwards motion: no longer trying to press forwards despite the inertia caused by the monster, but unexpectedly snatching us away from it. Then instantaneously the ship darts forward and downward again, striking in the midst of the swelling light-filled body.

There is a crackling explosion, and a blaze of murky orange-yellow flame which seems to run from the disintegrated body back into the tentacles: we glimpse twisting threadlike fragments of that same dull flame reeling and spinning off in every direction before in an instant those too are gone. Indeed, only in a limited sense were they ever there, for this vampiric thing had no properly constituted existence. In the pure silence of the night, our ship continues upon her way across the gentle swell of that unfathomed sea.

All save one of the lanterns on our ship have been extinguished: a large one of electric blue still shines on one of the masts. The dancers have taken off their masks and we all sit quietly, regathering our energies and reflecting upon what has happened.

The Moon has set now, and without its light the stars dominate the whole sky. Overhead is the constellation Aquarius, which is often represented as a gigantic figure with a water jar, pouring down upon us some powerful influence: the influence of what lustration, we wonder, what initiation? Now that our friends from the Moon Sphere have put off their masks, we can more easily feel that they form one party with us on the ship, one band of explorers sharing the adventures of this voyage and the quests which possess our souls. A mighty magnetism has now entered into our questing, for, even more brightly than the stars of the constellation, and superposed upon the pattern of their twinkling lights, one resplendent planet shines with unfaltering luster: the planet Venus.

The sea has settled to a mirror-like calm, and upon its bosom the stars are imaged in perfect reflection. Our ship seems to be sailing over a sea of stars, under a sky of stars, through a universe of stars. The ship has become a small world traveling through space, and all of us aboard are the inhabitants of that world. The awesome wonder of this feeling touches all of us, uniting us in the telepathic bond of a shared emotion. The lovely planet which shines supreme in the sky above us is now duplicated in the waters, but this does not diminish for us her unique power and beauty. She is like a magnet drawing us, both forward and upward, but upward principally; even as a portrait of the beloved constantly impels a lover towards its original. The gaze of all of us turns more and more towards the skies, and we are not at once aware of what is occurring when the ship, in sensitive response to the concerted aspiration and desire of us all, gently leaves the surface of the ocean and inclines her course upward into the transparent currents of the air.

With a steady breeze filling her sails, the magick ship moves upward through the skies. Some of our friends again light the many-colored lanterns; again the sounds of festive music begin to be heard, and we sail like people returning from a carnival. Our new sense of unity gives our happiness a heightened, vibrant quality, while the joyful music lilts and dances as if entranced by its own fascination.

Upward and onward we fly, into the star-strewn night. Upward and onward. Faster now, and faster. O spiritual joy! Surely in the power of this flight we shall attain our heart's desire!

Suddenly our Guide moves to the bow of the ship and gazes attentively into the distance. At once the music ceases in response to her action. We join her, eager to know what she is seeking; and after a while we too perceive, afar off, an edge of thick storm cloud in which lightnings are playing. The storm seems very remote from us, but we are traveling at a more than earthly speed.

Our Guide sounds her sistrum, and the greater part of the sails furl themselves forthwith; but it is too late either to slacken speed or to change course. The mighty winds of the storm region catch and hold our ship, and we feel the pressure of the air as the ship, and we, are hurled forward into the tumult of the storm itself.

We are carried continually onward. The roaring of thunder is like the booming of a cataract, while lightning flashes and quivers all about us, crackling and hissing as it passes. Our ship is buffeted and tossed by the violence of the elements, but maintains her course. From time to time we catch blazing glimpses of the spirits of the storm: they are human in likeness, lean and strong, pale and almost transparent. Their features appear youthful but we cannot read their expression, and their timeless eyes flash forth a fire which is not human. Their hair is whiter than snow, and streams out from the head like a nimbus; gleams of lightning play in it unceasingly. So, hovering and soaring, they vanish and reappear with the surge of the storm.

Our desire is to rise above the chaos of the elements, to continue our upward flight to the serene and lovely star of our aspiration. Higher mounts our ship and higher yet, until the fury of wind and lightning forms a barrier of opposing force which brings us almost to a standstill. We look to our Guide, and before our eyes she is transformed. No longer is her robe diaphanous, for now it is one glory of blue light in which the scattered stars blaze with white fire. The flowers upon her brow are joyful sentient things, and her silver sandals outshine the lightning. She stands with her arms upraised in an attitude of dominance, the sistrum gleaming like a wand of power and sounding above the mighty wind that sings through it. Now the thunder crashes with a sudden rending reverberation, as if one mountain had been hurled to shatter upon another, and the lightning leaps across abysses of the heavens which open beneath our keel. The ship moves forward, and we ride unharmed through the raging tempest. On and on we travel across the tumult.

Suddenly, the elemental fury diminishes. Our ship has carried us through the main force of the storm but now continues upon a level course. She will carry us through the last throes of turbulence, and on into the night; but her magick will take us no higher.

Yet we, in the force of our aspiration, must still ascend; our very hearts leap upward to rise ever nearer to our Star. A single magnetic ray of the sovereign fascination of the Supernal Mother has touched us, and we must go whither it draws us. O wondrous exultation! O vision primordial! No other faculty nor power can match the soaring of such aspiration.

Our Guide turns her bright countenance towards us, and with a gesture she bids us to leave the ship, to go of our own volition. We know she will bring the ship, and our friends from the Moon Sphere, safely to their destination, but from this point our way is other than theirs. We respond to our Guide with a sign of acknowledgment and thanks; and now, with both arms upraised, we rise and soar forth from the ship into the currents of the air. The ship goes forward without us, our Guide standing like a brilliant blue luminary until all is rapidly lost to view.

The last drifting vapors of the storm depart beneath us at our ascent, like dark shadows whirling downwards. Exultantly we soar towards the stars, rejoicing in our powers, in the strength of our will and, no less, in the power of the divine attraction by which we are drawn: it seems that our gladness could be no greater.

Now another bank of clouds, purple against the night sky, appears over us. Here is no tempest, but as we rise towards these clouds a fine, cool mist falls upon us. Rapidly this downpour increases in volume; we are drenched in heavy rain. In our great joy of spirit, we welcome this gift of the heavens as we welcome all that befalls us in this adventure: we spread our arms to receive it, we raise our faces to it and open our mouths to drink of it.

But what do we taste? No earthly honey is so sweet, no fruit so refreshing, no wine so fragrant or so intoxicating. At once our senses reel. We have no awareness of whether we pass beyond the clouds or ascend through them, or when or in what manner the ambrosial rain ceases to fall on us. We do not know or care whether our garments continue drenched or if they are dry: the fragrance of that rain remains with us, and it lifts our hearts more than any tidings we could hear. Visions flash before us, visible and intelligible in an instant of consciousness: our perceptions seem expanded, so that we see beyond that which is for us Reality into other Realities different from ours, and these too we love. Our soaring flight becomes an ecstasy. We are raised out of ourselves by that wine of life; but better than the draft itself is our awareness of what it signifies, for we can only have received it as a token that we are approaching the last state of this journey: that the true thirst of our yearning will be assuaged, and we shall indeed be filled with the Brightness whose power has drawn us thus far.

With outstretched arms we continue rising swiftly towards the stars. Now as we mount the sky above us is filled with swirling flame, a glorious red-gold brilliance seething and flashing. Our ascent becomes less rapid, but still we approach closer to the coruscating vortex: more slowly yet but continually closer, although the flame above us is glaring, oppressive in its effulgence. Its intensity constricts us; inexorably, but with the slowness of a drifting feather on a windless day, we float upward and pass into the heart of that whirling fire.

Here we seem to be suspended motionless while the flames contine their vertical swirling around us; we feel their breath caressing us as they spin. They grow yet more luminous, their red-gold fire blanching to intense shimmering white light which still whirls and spins, flashing hypnotically around us. Time and space are remote and meaningless in the experience. ★

Gradually the light fades, the whirling recedes from us. Again the starry skies of night are above us. We are standing upon a hard rocky surface, near the top of a mountain. At the summit rises a stout, stone-built column, surmounted by a great hemispherical cup of burnished copper from which rise the flames of a beacon fire; the glowing luster of the copper bowl reflecting and augmenting the light of the flames.

Looking to the path before us, we behold a decorative gate of bronze, on which is wrought in gold the device of a rose.

The gate swings open and we enter. The upward path is continued by a flight of seven steps, leading to the summit of the mountain.

We reach the top of the steps and, passing by the beacon column, we go through an opening in a low parapet, into the circular area of the summit.

Here is a sanctuary, whose beauty and mystery is gently illuminated for us by the beacon fire. A band of garden, rising in a gentle slope towards the center of the area, is covered with rich green grass out of which spring all manner of beautiful flowering plants, each kind in a cluster not far from its neighbors: roses, daffodils, violets, lilies, in endless variety are growing here. At the center and apex of this circular area stands a building which glows like a gem. It too is circular in plan, with the roof sloping up from the eaves, and in the center of the roof is another elevation with its own pointed roof. The whole building seems to pulsate in the variable light of the flames, for the walls have the appearance of translucent rose quartz and its roofs are as if tiled with shining amber. An intense feeling of spiritual vitality reaches us in this place, a vibrant and deeply felt peace; we know that within these walls is to be revealed the objective of our journey.

A narrow paved path leads across the garden to this building, in which-a door of burnished copper, flanked by two cypresses, stands open. Adorning the lintel of the door is again the device of the rose. We take the path, and reverently enter the building.

The walls are rose-colored and translucent, within as without. The floor is like obsidian, bright as glass, dark green and mysterious as the deeps of the sea. Before us, to left and right, are the two pillars, Machetes and Nomothetes. We pass between them and pause, saluting the East, where stands the Bomos draped in brilliant green. Upon the Bomos rests the Mystical Tessera; and nearby, upon a plinth, stands an incense burner from which there rises slowly into the air the delicate smoke of a sweet, nostalgic incense. In the northeast of the temple hangs the Banner of the New Life, the high token of regeneration.

We have a deep yearning to understand the full meaning of the Path we have traveled, yet in this place we will not question; we will accept whatever we shall be shown. To the south-east is an arched opening as to a further shrine. Slowly we cross the temple and pass through this arch.

It does indeed lead into an inner shrine, and within this there stands before us a statue of extraordinary beauty.

Carved in warm-colored marble, of a tint between rose and honey, in the classical Greek style, is a superb female figure, robed and winged and at first sight to be identified with the winged Victory. This figure stands upon a globe: she represents victory over all. Her posture expresses sovereign authority, yet her countenance is full of compassion. But she is more than Victory: she has the intricate clinging robe of that flying figure, but around her waist is a real girdle of gold, studded with emeralds and pearls. This is a representation of Aphrodite, Goddess of Love, and her victory over the world is a victory of love. And, as a last difference from the classical Winged Victory, this Goddess carries a child in her arms: not a sleeping child, but one who leans upon her arm and looks about, wide-eyed and watchful. This child is represented as having a body and lower limbs draped in heavy wrappings, and the reason for this is twofold. In the first place, it makes the sex of the child indeterminate; for this child represents the whole human race, and at the same time it represents each one of us, each person, male or female. And, again, the heavy draperies represent the density of the material and astral wrappings from which we gaze out upon the universe. None the less, it is She, Celestial Love, who carries us, She who is also victory; and, if we will but let it be so, her victory shall be ours also.

To enter the sphere of Venus is always to know, and acknowledge, our unity with all that is. But to enter from the Path we have just traveled is to know by experience the impossibility of our separating ourselves, in our quest for perfection and for realization, from humankind, the race to which we belong. Yet herein is a seeming paradox. If each individual is to win to spiritual fulfillment through interaction with others, so, equally, humanity as a whole can only win to spiritual fulfillment through the striving of each individual.

These balancing truths are shown forth in the Star Path which we have traveled. Our relationship with our fellow beings is not a closed circuit of giving and receiving at the mutual level. Every normal being, human or other, has its right relationship with forces of a higher order, according to its own mode of being; without that contact it becomes merely vampiric, as was the energy-sucking entity which attacked our ship. We human beings can rejoice in the exchanges of love and friendship with our fellows, and can grow spiritually thereby: but when our aspirations summon us, we must follow, rather than choosing to remain among the number of our companions.

The very love which binds us together decrees this. While love is not altogether of the rational intelligence, neither is it altogether of the emotions. Reason and emotion alike are of the Lower Self, while love is of the Higher Self which governs and directs those other faculties. And from the level of the Higher Self, which is supernal, love needs to draw its sustenance. The qualities of vision, inspiration and faith are all needful for love: and all these gifts of the Supernal Mother are rayed down by her from the celestial heights of our inner being, from whence we must invoke them.

Battery 3-5-3

The Working of the 27th Path
(Correspondences)

SPHERE OF COMMENCEMENT: Hod (Splendor)

Hebrew Divine Name: Elohim Tzabaoth

Planetary correspondence: Mercury

Element: Water

Symbols: Books, scrolls, shrine, alchemical apparatus

Plants: Walnut trees

Minerals: Molten metal, white water

Colors: Checkered black and white, dappled light and shade

PATH OF THE TREE OF LIFE: 27

Intelligence: The 27th Path is the Awakening Intelligence, so named because by means of it the mental powers of all created entities of the lower created Worlds are brought into being with the awakening and activation of those powers.

Hebrew Divine Name: Elohim Gebor

Influence on the Path: Mars

Planetary number: 5

Hebrew Letter: Peh (Mouth)

Path Stanza: Play of the Breath and the Word, Life and
the Law, counterchange intricate
Weaving the ground of our days: this is our
strength, this is our jeopardy.
Spirit oracular, tell: knowledge and love,
will they keep unity
Or, opposed, shatter us?

Tarot arcanum: The Tower (16)

Element of Path: Fire

Symbols: The sword, lightning

Plants: Thorny trees

Minerals: Iron, lodestone, red sandstone, ruby, red jasper, corundum

Living beings: The horse of fire, the boar, salamanders, werewolves

Optical and other effects: Subordination of the powers of the five senses and the five elements to the influence of Mars

Magical Phenomena: Powers of the Sword and of the Horse, visions of destruction

Philosophy of the Path: Katharsis: purification through violent act or emotion, to attain the harmony of the Mother

SPHERE OF DESTINATION: Netzach (Victory)

Hebrew Divine Name: Yahveh Tzabaoth

Planetary correspondence: Venus

Planetary number: 7

Element: Fire

Symbols: Sea shells, pine cones, roses

Minerals: Amber, sandstone, blue-green marble, pink marble

Magical phenomenon: Manifestation of the power of the Mother through the spiritual disciplines of love

Comments

This Path is one of conflict, and of the resolution of conflict. It is the Path from knowledge—Hod—to love—Netzach—and the influence upon it is that of the planet Mars, whose element is Fire.

This progression can be interpreted in various ways, which do not exclude one another. *The Song of Praises* sees it as a trial of endurance, of courage or of faith, in face of a divergence of principles whether between individuals or within the one personality. *The 32 Paths of Wisdom* sees it as a traumatic awakening, which could be called a coming to birth from Thought into Life. Our Pathworking presents it as a convergence of emotional forces which, violently exploding, disperse their superficial excesses and leave the way open to true harmony and concord. As in the enigmatic legend of Eros and Psyche, the triumph of the lovers is in truth the victory also of the Queen of Love: and but for the influence of Mars upon the Path, the victory (which is Netzach) would not be realized.

The Working of the 27th Path

We have lifted our minds from considerations of the material order, not through disdain of all that is manifest in the material world but because

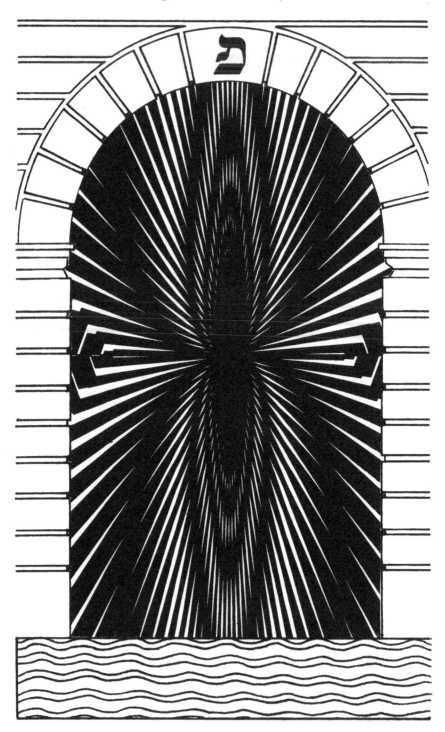

it is our will to look further, to pursue our quest into the deeper nature of that which is made manifest.

By degrees we become aware that we are standing in a spacious room. It is quiet and peaceful, yet it is the scene of much activity. It is a place recalling a long tradition of both operation and contemplation. The room is square in shape, and of considerable area; in each of the walls there are two lancet windows, filled with rounds of colored glass set in plaster in the Eastern manner. The colors of the glass are brilliant. There is no perceptible plan in the juxtaposition of each color with its neighbors, yet their brilliance and purity precludes any sense of wrongness or discord, just as in a garden scarlet blossoms may grow next to rose purple, sulphur yellow with deep blue. The walls of the room are white, the floor is checkered with black and white ceramic tiles.

Upon the window ledges and upon shelves in various places upon the walls there are books having a look of great age, with manuscripts and scrolls which seem quite timeless. In the wall facing us, between its two lancet windows, is a table altar upon which is a lighted lamp, a crown and an open book; before the altar is a kneeling bench. Across the middle of the room, directly before us, runs a bench of gleaming wood upon which is ranged, in actual use, some of the traditional apparatus of medieval alchemy. Here, from a vessel in a water bath over the glowing heat of a charcoal brazier, a liquid is being distilled; from the top of the otherwise sealed vessel containing the liquid, a tube carries the distillate over to a large glass urn filled with water, through which the tube is continued downward in a series of many horizotal coils. At the base of the urn, the tube again passes to the exterior, where the cooled and condensed distillate is gathered in a flask. The shape of the flask would not seem strange in a modern laboratory.

Further to the left along the bench, with less complex equipment, liquid metallic mercury is being heated and sublimated to produce the bright red crystals of mercuric oxide; while beyond the end of the bench, near the left hand wall, stands a small furnace. Amid the fiery coals rests a crucible, above which, in a kind of sieve, are some pieces of metallic rock. The veins of metal in the rock are becoming liquid with the heat and are flowing down into the crucible itself.

At the right hand side of the room opposite to the furnace, a wide doorway is open to the world outside. From a grove of walnut trees standing before the edifice in which we have found ourselves, a road winds into the distance, its tawny surface composed of gravel made smooth and sparkling by the action of the sea.

It is morning; the sky is clear and inviting, a slight breeze stirs in the branches, and mild sunshine dances upon the leaves.

The mist which hides the further course of the road is gleaming with sunshine.

Learning is good, but it is not the whole of life. Not all insight comes from study, nor does all power reside in knowledge alone. The painter, the musician, the architect, the technician need to understand the materials and the instruments with which they work; but that is not understanding merely in order to understand. They must understand so that in striving with those materials and instruments, all shall be brought into right order and just proportion, and the will of the artist shall prevail.

Let us go forth from this place and find what that shining mist conceals from us; let us discover how insight, allied with powerful action, can bring us to Victory.

We stand up and move towards the doorway. As we gaze at the scene before us—the clear sky, the walnut trees, the road—a bird flies up from the trees and speeds away with a shrill call, joyous and free. We step forth, aware of the kiss of the breeze, the beckoning smile of the sunshine. We are setting out upon a magical journey of discovery and experience.

Passing through the dappled light and shade beneath the walnut trees, we follow the bright and serpentine road. When we enter the region of the mist, we find a steep descent leading us into a chasm. Here the road changes its character, becoming a rocky track winding its way down among rushing streams and waterfalls, overflowing pools and slippery, precarious footholds. We need to be continually vigilant: now a promising path ends abruptly in a precipice, now we make our way round an angle to find our progress blocked by a spiring shaft of rock. The beauty of the scene is awesome and yet fascinating, each step successfully ventured leading us on to the next.

Now we reach the bottom of the chasm, and find our way barred by a torrent of white water, foaming swiftly and powerfully over a chaos of submerged rocks. On the side of the torrent where we are, we perceive there is no way to proceed along the edge of the rapids, either upstream or downstream; there is evidently a path on the far side, but seemingly we have no way to reach it. The sound and the flying foam of the torrent fills the chasm; even the air and the rocks themselves are part of this world of water.

At the brink of the torrent we turn and look back up the ladder of pinnacles and broken terraces by which we have descended. A broad buttress of rock which on one side had afforded us a welcome means of descent, now presents us with another face, the hollow of a forbidding overhang.

While we contemplate this shadowed hollow in the mighty rock, a strange shimmering of light agitates the mid-region of its surface. In a patch shaped like a long oval, the rock surface itself appears to be breaking down into seething and swirling particles of luminous energy, a curtain of shimmering light. Before we can make any account to ourselves of this marvel, forth from the center of the dancing disruption steps a tall and commanding figure, even more luminous in his own right than the shining energy particles which gave way to him. This Being advances at an even pace down the steep slope towards us, while the rock face has resumed its normal aspect behind him.

The newcomer ceases to advance, and stands a few paces distant from us and above us. We behold him as a warrior, and as more than a warrior: his presence radiates power. Upon his head is a dark but brightly polished iron helmet of antique design, surmounted by a flowing horsehair crest of scarlet. He wears a large cape of bright purple, extending to below his knees; this is fastened at the throat but is thrown back from his broad shoulders. Beneath the cape, down to his waist, he wears a kind of breastplate covered with lappets of heavy leather, overlying each other like tiles upon a roof and burnished like brown metal. A short kilt of similar material covers his hips. Beneath this armor can be seen the edges of a sleeveless red undertunic, leaving his muscular arms, his thighs and genitals bare. From a belt there hangs at his hip a heavy cross-hilted sword, of which the hilt and sheath are adorned with intricate design. His feet and calves are encased in boots of soft leather, bound from ankle to below the knee by crossing and recrossing thongs. All that is visible of his skin is tanned red-brown by sun and weather. Most conspicuously, however, all about him continually gleams and flashes an aura of blue-white radiance, so that despite his easy and relaxed demeanor as he regards us, the blaze and sparkle of light playing around him is a token of vigilance, of resolve, of action. Yet meanwhile the light of his eyes is calm and steady, with a strength which is inward and spiritual in its origin.

We have no need of words. This Being perceives that in order to follow our chosen Path we must gain the far side of the torrent, and that we lack any means to do so. He raises his right hand, and we see that upon it he wears what looks to be a shining black lodestone, graven with a mystic emblem and set in a ring of steel. Upon this stone he breathes, then whispers a Word of Power which we cannot distinguish; and now, raising his right hand towards the skies, he looks upwards. Our gaze follows his.

From the instant of our perceiving the shape approaching swiftly through the high heavens above us, we realize that it is larger than any bird and that there are no outspread wings. As it rapidly descends a sheen of red-gold gleams upon it. Now it is revealed as a magnificent chestnut horse with mane and tail streaming through the air, and with legs extended as to land from a flying leap.

The warrior slowly lowers his hand and points to the white torrent. The horse, completing its descent, gathers all its hoofs together and strikes them upon a large submerged boulder in midstream. Steam rises from the water. The horse dances and stamps again and again upon the rocks, then soars up into the air and disappears.

Tall plumes of white steam billow upward; the surface where the hoofs struck, and the surrounding boulders and fragments, glow red over a heart of incandescence, while the torrent, hissing and boiling, shrinks away from them. The warrior goes forward and, with a sign to us to follow, strides steadily across the glowing causeway from which the seething waters have retreated. But for his leading, the fiery rocks would have detained us even as the torrent did; with the luminous purple-cloaked figure going before us, we follow securely over them to the path beyond the rapids. Here the warrior goes along the same path, leading downstream. Confidently we take him as our Guide. Soon, as we follow that powerful and luminous figure, the chasm becomes a wide valley and the path turns away from the river. The sound of rushing water is lost in the distance.

Trees crowd upon us. The path has brought us into a forest, and the heavy damp smell of dead leaves and of mossy bark surrounds us. Above us rise the trunks and branches of mighty trees; some straight and vigorous, others gnarled and twisted, but all with the appearance of immense and silent strength. Among them has sprung up a thick growth of smaller trees. No obstacle hinders our luminous Guide, who moves easily some yards ahead of us; but here we have difficulty in following him. The leafy earth is full of hidden holes and little water-courses, and the thin branches of the smaller trees catch at us and hold us. They are like steel springs, with thorns which are like claws. As we try to move under them, a tangle of roots rises up from the ground, moving to snare our feet. We stand still and look about to see which is our best way of escape, and our Guide looks back at us, pausing also to see our decision.

A movement becomes visible in the shadows among the further trees, and the damp air of the forest fills with a new sense of danger. The energies of our earthly flesh and blood, energies which still accompany us at the level of the astral world where we now are, transmit their own invitation to such entities as are alert for them. The shadows move closer, and in the foremost of them we become aware of small eyes like embers glinting over a tusked and bristled snout, with the appearance of a wild boar; but the herd which follows this entity is a rapacious unindividuated medley of hunched shapes, red tongues between sharp gleaming teeth, pointed, dagger-like feet and savage eyes. Even as this becomes clear to our vision, the feeling of menace growing meanwhile as oppressive as the gathering of thunder clouds, behind its more individuated leader the whole shadowy mass begins to pour in a rapidly swirling circle of ferocity around us. At this our Guide unsheathes his heavy sword and, swinging it from high overhead, brings the edge of

175

the blade down as he strides towards us, cleaving through the eddying circle as through smoke.

The tension snaps; in a blaze of blue-white lightning the danger flashes away from us, and we from it. We are suddenly without weight, without dimension or direction, neither in light nor in darkness. Our sole awareness is of going outwards, far, far, far from our previous center, and then after a period of stillness there is an awareness of return; but not return to the same point. The difference may be the diameter of a world or the thickness of a leaf our consciousness tells us only that a difference exists.

We look about us. We are standing firmly and steadily upon a bare rocky plain, of red sandstone, with neither tree nor mountain in sight. Our Guide stands by a tall unhewn monolith near to us. We perceive, extending into the distance on every side, an ordered array of similar monoliths, great boulders set on end, each one about ten feet distant from its neighbors as if on a huge checkerboard. The sun is rising into a clear sky which already reflects a hot, brilliant light. The monoliths cast their long black shadows diagonally across their checkerboard arrangement, only the irregular shapes of the monoliths and the furrows and undulations in the sandstone terrain lending variation to the scene.

Our Guide leads us across the plain of monoliths at right angles to the sun's rays, so that at every few paces we move from dazzling light into deep shadow, then from deep shadow to dazzling light again. This rhythmic flashing of the sunlight is bewildering, hypnotic; but for our Guide we should be walking almost blindly. But we fix our gaze upon the shimmering, flashing radiance of his aura which is un-changed by sunlight or shadow; and thus gazing we move steadily forwards. Gradually as the sun mounts higher the shadows of the monoliths grow shorter and become less significant.

Now we are beyond the monoliths. The sun is high in a burning cloudless vault which is like a canopy of red hot iron over the naked red sandstone.

We keep our eyes fixed upon our Guide across the dancing and quivering heat. Suddenly he halts, and turns to face us; he draws his sword, raises it, and brings it down whistling through the air. From the cloudless sky crackles a mighty lightning flash in response: our Guide and we are caught as in a whiplash and lifted high above the plain. Without effort we rise through the hot dry air.

The sound of a huge rending and roaring crash comes from below. Looking down, we see that the landscape below us has changed. Under the intense heat the rocky plain has all at once shattered into a confusion of disarrayed blocks, riven by gaping crevasses. A thick cloud of dust, rising to a lesser height than we have attained, partly obscures the chaotic scene, until our ascent, the result of our Guide's timely action, carries us out of sight of it altogether.

Motion ceases. Again we seem to be without locality, without centrality. Fleeting images form and disperse around us: we recognize scenes in the life and action of some of the great armies of the past—of Alexander, of Caesar, of Napoleon and many another—and we perceive their magnetism, which is not unlike the magnetism of iron, the metal of Mars. For in the nature of Being itself, whether expressed in mind or in matter, there is the tendency to order, to relationship, to polarity. That which departs from one system, whether of atoms or of human beings, tends to inaugurate or to find a place in another system which in its turn develops its own gravitational force and its own magnetism. Every fragment of iron which is drawn to a magnet becomes itself magnetic, and even so does the fraternal magnetism of the great armies, fostered by the very austerity of order and discipline, reach out to us here as we glimpse it, and touch us with its power.

The images and impressions fade, the dazzling space encompassing us is resolved into other forms. We are surrounded with crystalline shafts of light, strong and flawless in their abstract beauty. Then these dissolve into pure elemental fire.

A landscape of fire takes shape around us. Our Guide takes the lead as we enter a cylindrical tunnel of fire, its walls ribbed intermittently with yellow flame. A continual low roaring rings in our ears. The fire moves and quivers, the roof of the tunnel opens above us into tall jagged pinnacles, golden tipped, which sometimes shrink downwards into fragile points of flame, sometimes tower to a height and then disappear upwards. Again the fire moves, and within it we find ourselves entering a forest of golden trees, where leaves of gold shine and flash upon the branches, or, carried by the wind, drift and fall in glittering sparklike showers. Strange Beings like tall and powerful bipedal lizards appear, and stand in the path before us, barring our way.

Our Guide addresses them, telling them that we are travelers upon our rightful way, not to be hindered, and that he is guiding us. These Beings are intelligent and not hostile, but since we have entered their territory they are reluctant to let us go. They are Salamanders, Spirits of the element of Fire. They have the strong and graceful beauty of skilled dancers, they have the candor and directness, and the tenacity, of their fiery nature, but their pride and anger are easily stirred.

With our Guide accompanying us, we are conducted by the Salamanders across a narrow fiery bridge beside which the flames now form a vibrating wall, now shift and part to reveal glowing caverns beneath us. Now we have been brought into an even more fantastic region of overpasses and caverns, high soaring bridges and branching, vein-like tunnels: a three-dimensional lacework of fire, red and golden with shimmering points of blue and green, and with everywhere the sound of a continuous roaring. Now and then this sound is punctuated by a subdued explosion or a transient hissing; and then some part of the landscape changes to a new pattern as in a kaleidoscope.

Suddenly before us there opens a huge circling vortex of flame, in the center of which at first we perceive nothing. We gaze into that wide gap of black space, from which we are separated only by the veering and changeful current of whirling flame; and now, immeasurably far away in the deeps of that space we behold another vortex, a vortex of stupendous cosmic fire, pale as pearl, seeming peaceful and cool in its awesome remoteness.

At this blazing portal our Guide turns about; that further adventure is no part of our present path. Courteously he thanks the Salamanders for their hospitality and for showing us some of the wonders of their secret abode; then once again he raises his mighty sword and sweeps it downwards with a power that cleaves the curtain of the world of flame wherein we stand.

It is night. Lightning fills the sky, for a moment illuminating a desolate slope where streams of lava have piled up and solidified in grotesque and unlikely shapes. From high over a cone-shaped peak which rises above us, a dull red light is reflected down by some transient clouds, telling of a volcano which is not in full activity. A cold wind sings around us and around the piles of lava: an insistent wind which stirs anger and hostility, whether there is cause or not.

A bright gleam shines from a narrow fissure a little distance from us. Within, we glimpse amid the quivering volcanic fires a group of Salamanders, gazing with rapt attention towards a narrow plinth of rock in whose concave top lies a cluster of rubies, more scarlet than the heart of the fire, more brilliant than the scintillating tips of flame. As moths give their whole consciousness to the light of a lamp, so the Salamanders are totally possessed by the glory of their treasure, the rubies of the fire-cave.

But other eyes besides ours have beheld them. Colder than the wind, greyer than the shadows, more insatiable than the empty abysses of Night, the Werewolves peer and whimper about the very entrance to the fissure. They can take at will the form of wolf or of man; they are savage as wolves, but theirs are not the simple needs of a wild beast. Nor do they adore the rubies for their beauty, as the Salamanders do through a natural affinity. The Werewolves desire the red stones only partly for their fierce effulgence; chiefly it is through the human lust to possess jewels of inestimable worth.

The Werewolves divide into two groups: the larger group in wolf form, the smaller group in the form of thin, wiry men, bold and cunning. Even as they do this, the Salamanders become aware of the approach of their enemies. Flames spring from the bare, gritty earth before the mouth of the fissure: flames in which the Salamanders can spring into manifestation, to defend their shrine. As the Salamanders appear in the open air, the Werewolves in wolf form attack them; they do not fear fire as natural wolves would, and the Beings of living flame grapple with these Beings of cold shadow which, as long as they retain their wolf shape, can equal the Salamanders in combat. Meanwhile, the Werewolves in human form, whose powers are human simply, have slipped behind the defensive fire, entered the cave, and snatched the rubies from the plinth.

Our Guide, who with us has watched the action, is of no mind to allow the Salamanders to be robbed so easily. He breathes upon the shining lodestone of his ring, then swiftly whispers the Word of Power to summon the Horse. Anxiously we watch as the marvelous steed descends from the night sky. The wolf Werewolves see him too, and gather to snap at his legs and prevent him from landing; but he gives them his hoofs, and while they run off howling with burning mouths he rises a little in the air, then descends to the ground at the cave entrance. Stamping and stamping again, he completes and widens the barrier of flame, then soars back into the heavens.

The human Werewolves, with the fabulous rubies in their hands, are trapped in the cave. In human form they cannot overleap the flames, which are steadily advancing upon them from the outside as well as from within the cave. In wolf form they can hope to do so, but then they must lose their grasp of the gems. The need to survive prevails, and they transform themselves to wolf. Even as they leap, however, the flames leap with them; more Salamanders spring into manifestation in the new fire, and here, too, Werewolf and Salamander are at once locked in combat.

Now those wolf Werewolves who for a moment can disengage themselves from the struggle raise their gaunt grey heads and send forth into the darkness their eerie, howling cry. Its echoes, or the replies to it, are borne back upon the chill of the swirling wind, which beats upon the flames as if to extinguish them and calls forth a swarm of sparks from the fire like angry wasps from their nest. And now in response to that shrill howling, into the combat rushes another pack of Werewolves, yelping and snarling in their eagerness to rout the Salamanders.

Still our Guide will not allow the Fire Spirits, whose guests we have been, to be outnumbered by their rapacious adversaries. Again he summons the Horse, who stamps upon the earth in a hundred places before soaring up again into the skies. Wherever the Horse has stamped, flames spring up; and wherever there are flames, a fresh contingent of Salamanders can come into manifestation. In the fierce struggle which follows, many Werewolves are reduced to ashes, and the survivors give up the contest. But they are wily and treacherous. As they depart, some take human form, and one of them cries out to another: "I rejoice for my brothers that they were slain by the true Salamanders, not by the spurious children of the Horse." The other Werewolf replies, "But I for my part shall boast for my kindred, that they were slain by the spirits of fire brought from Heaven, not by the spawn of the fires of Earth."

Hearing these words, the unsuspecting Salamanders begin to boast: the spirits of the volcanic fire calling themselves the True Salamanders, while the Salamanders who have sprung into manifestation from the fires struck by the hoofs of the Horse describe themselves as Children of the Fire of Heaven. And the cold relentless wind lashes them, so that from boasting they turn to quarreling, and from quarreling to strife. The Werewolves lurk on the outskirts of the new combat, urging both sides forward with taunting and jeering words; then, since neither party of Salamanders can defeat the other, the Werewolves urge the whole furious rout of the Fire Spirits against us as the cause of their dissensions. Before that elemental fury we can but flee, with the insensate Salamanders raging and hissing in pursuit.

Our Guide draws his Sword of Power. Again he cleaves the air with it to speed our departure; but this time he himself stays behind to cover our retreat, lest any of our elemental pursuers should speed between level and level of the Astral Light to follow us.

The lightning flashes and crackles. Above us extends a night sky of luminous blue-green in which the stars shine red. We know not in what region we may be, but an unutterable mournfulness seizes upon our hearts. We are standing upon the brink of a wide and slow-moving river. As its waves move and glitter in the starlight the waters shine bright crimson and their odor repels us. Nevertheless, we are thrust forward as by a force outside ourselves and we must go on. We step into the water. As we wade across a wind springs up, sighing and wailing; it keens and pipes in wierd lamentation, mourning the dead of every battle since the dawn of time. It voices, too, the implacable anger which lies beneath the lamentation: the anger which admits of no consolation because there can be no restitution.

Now we are across the loathsome river. We pause upon the bank, and the waters shrink and fall away from our limbs as if they had never touched us.

Before us upon a hill stands a tall fortress, stark black as we see it against the strange metallic sheen of the sky in which the stars burn red. The wailing of the wind is shriller now, with a voice not lamenting nor angry but lost and desolate. It sings of the waste places, of the loneliness of empty lands. The fortress looms above us; exerting all our powers we mount the hill towards it.

A massive turreted gateway, all of red jasper, receives us. Underfoot is a paved way of jasper blocks; the exterior of the fortress is all of that same material. No sooner have we passed into the deep shadowed archway leading into the fortress, than a portcullis descends with a thunderous crash into its place behind us, closing the entrance with an immovable grill of colossal iron bars. The echoes die away, and all is silent. We examine the huge portcullis, but no means are visible by which it can be raised again. We look attentively at the tall fortified gateway built of ponderous blocks, but no lesser door is to be seen in it. The fortress is a strong refuge but it is also a prison.

Now that we are becoming more accustomed to the darkness, the small spaces of light from the strangely colored sky and its luminaries seem bright behind the unrelenting bars. Even as we look, however, in one area of the portcullis, in a long oval shape, the contrast of light and dark becomes less clearly defined. The particles within the oval are dancing and becoming mingled together; then through that confusion steps our Guide, to stand before us while the bars of the portcullis are consolidated into dense blackness behind him, and the red stars gleam through the narrow spaces.

Our Guide, indicating that our way lies through the fortress, leads us to the interior. We find ourselves in a great hall, which has no windows; the only light comes from flaring pinewood torches set in sconces high upon the walls, so that many corners are thrown into a blacker obscurity. We perceive the foot of a grand staircase, but there is no other doorway. The air is dry and cold, giving a strange feeling as if we were underground. The walls are of unpolished granite, one area of which is devoted to a display of objects designed for punishment or penance: whips, scourges, hair-cloth cinctures, branding irons and the like, all intended to cause suffering through the sense of touch. We go to examine these articles, but an aura of pain and humiliation hangs heavy about them, a sense of the degradation which fastens upon the inflicter of such suffering much more than upon the victim.

A sudden dazzling flash stuns us, as if with the impact of a mighty blow. We struggle to regain our senses. The fortress is gone, and we are caught up in a strange scene, the legendary battle of the Centaurs and Lapiths. The Centaurs, half man and half horse, appear to have little advantage over their fully human but primitive antagonists. Both parties contend around us with straining muscles and huge blows; there are no weapons save here and there a rough wooden club, or a rock caught up at hazard. The muscle-tearing effort, the reiterated strain and shock of the conflict are with us; when swiftly the impression of the scene departs from us, and our awareness returns to the enclosing walls of the fortress.

With our Guide we move to the ornately carved grand stair of red jasper. On each side of the wide steps a broad balustrade sweeps upwards, each balustrade having at its lower end a human head of heroic size: that on the right sculptured with ferocious and violent aspect, that on the left stern, cold and forbidding. The shafts supporting the balustrades are sculptured, each into the grotesque semi-human form of a gargoyle, an imp or similar monster, so arranged that half their number look down with their distorted faces at a person ascending the stairs and the rest upwards to a person descending, with looks and gestures of rage or malice, vindictiveness, mockery or contempt, or the dangerous terror of a wild animal at bay.

We mount the stairway to the second floor. Here the walls are faced with polished bloodstone, dark green like marble but marked with irregular patches and sprinklings of bright red as if the stone had been stained indelibly with blood. This level of the fortress is lit by cressets, their flames springing from bowls of oil which are suspended by chains from the high ceiling; these flames give no perceptible warmth, and the air, although humid, remains chilly.

In the middle of the floor of red jasper blocks rises an ornamental fountain, its waters rising from a central piece of statuary and falling into a wide bowl of green serpentine whose base is in the shape of a scorpion, with claws and tail upraised, carved in the same green rock. The central sculpture represents Hercules struggling with the Hydra, the fountain issuing from the mouths of the great water serpent, whose several heads are lifted above the head of the hero. The dampness and chill of the place seem mysteriously to emanate from this fountain, and as we turn away from it a cold fog enfolds us. Swiftly the mistiness vanishes, but the chill of it remains with us like a foreboding although a scene of unexpected festivity meets our eyes.

We are in a banqueting hall of olden times. Nobles and knights, with stately and beautiful ladies, all clad in velvet and in silken gossamer, range themselves about a long table shining with plate and linen, with jeweled cups and dishes of unique artistry. The company in their joyfulness and splendor, and the attendants likewise in the pride of their office, seem a people set apart from the world's hardships. To a burst of merry music and of loud acclamation, a monarch, most richly clad and of truly royal bearing, takes his place at the head of the table, not far from where we are standing. Wine is poured into the richly ornamented goblets, the king's cupbearer presents the massive royal cup, and with the ceremonial of long-established custom the feast begins.

But no! The king takes one deep draught from that heavy cup, then lets it fall crashing to the floor. For a brief while he stands, his face contorted in agony; then he too falls and lies writhing. Screams and cries of horror arise from the company; some of the guests turn upon each other, drawing swords with mutual accusation and denial. Some stand too stunned in horror to accuse, but more, staring about as if they expected Death's hand upon their shoulder, swiftly gather out of the assembly their kindred and allies and make from the scene forthwith, even before the victim's frame has ceased to quiver. All is fury, fear and confusion.

Meanwhile, from the fallen cup the dregs of poisoned wine have flowed forth upon the floor. In imagination we taste it. We savor its fragrant sweetness at the first, expecting within it to find the genial fire of the grape; but instead there comes a cold and alien harshness, a bitterness that scarcely needs the consuming pain which follows, to declare itself a stark foe to the body's life. The whole visioned scene of the fatal banquet fades from our consciousness; but our last impression of it is of the taste of the poisoned wine.

We are back within the fortress. With one accord we return to the fountain, and dip our cupped hands in the basin. We long for the sweet coolness of fresh water to dispel the evil image from our imagination, and we drink eagerly. This water is not poisoned, but it is salt as the sea, choking as the tears of unassaugeable grief. As if we had drunk of those tears themselves, every spear-thrust of frustration, every sorrow we have known surges into memory, whether its cause be distinctly remembered or not. We hold fast to our self-possession. We know that these emotions must be accepted, however briefly; they have no power to harm us, but will sink again into their due place as strengthening fibers in our lives.

Again we face the scowling or mocking figures of the stairway, and with our Guide we mount to the third floor. Here the walls are overlaid with dark, shining plates of polished iron. One wall is adorned with a collection of old-time Japanese battle fans in all their exotic and intricate artistry; another with a number of daggers from many lands and different ages, many of which have beautiful damascene work of inlaid metals, and rich jewels on the hilts. On examining these things, we find that the iron plates of the walls are strongly magnetic and it is by the power of magnetism that all these objects are held in their place.

Now a hot, moist wind is blowing upon us. We turn away from the assembled weapons and look about us. The fortress and its contents have vanished from our view; the hot, moist wind is blowing across a tropical landscape. Tall trees stand amid rank grass or in marshy water. Large brightly colored birds dart before us with piercing cries, and from the swaying branches of a nearby tree a troop of monkeys descends, to disappear into the tall grass.

The pungent fragrance of an aromatic plant comes to our nostrils. A little way before us, a strange plant is growing from a decaying tree trunk; we approach it and look at it more closely. It is a plant of vigorous and prolific growth; its leaves are greyish in color and spined like those of a thistle, but its flowers have large petals of a clear light blue with a bright yellow center. The strong, hairy stems of the plant hang low, weighted down with their spiny leaves and numerous blossoms. We gather close to it and inhale the fragrance of the flowers.

It is a curiously exhilarating odor: something like vanilla or heliotrope, with a fire as of cinnamon in the first sensation but with a coolness as of menthol as we breathe it in more deeply. We feel as if awakened to a new awareness. The traditional Arab saying, that a man's destiny is written upon his forehead, comes to mind: if we had the full power of the Third Eye, which this fragrance stirs to increased activity, we should assuredly perceive all that concerns us.

As we continue to inhale the strange fragrance, the inner excitement produced by it increases, and with it the range of our perception. Then our elation changes to anger. We see the rigid limitations of the human condition, the cramping bounds of all earthly life; we see the blunders and wrong decisions which could have been avoided with foresight if we, or others, could but have known what now we comprehend. We would cry out in rage against it all, would shatter it all—

Our Guide draws his sword; it is necessary that we should continue upon our path. He raises the blade, and brings it down in a swift arc: lightning flashes across the sky in a blaze of dazzling brilliance. The strange plant, and the jungle, are gone from our consciousness. The anger leaves us. For a moment, outside time and space, the concept comes before us of an ancient and mighty tree, an oak or a cedar, growing upon a rocky mount and tossed, but not broken, by tempestuous winds. Not fury, but courage and endurance, is the answer to the cosmic mystery which has confronted us. The impression fades, and we are standing beside the grand staircase, on the fourth floor of the fortress.

The air is humid no longer, and its dry heat is harsh upon the skin. The walls here are covered with pumice, and this pale brown, porous volcanic rock adds to the cheerless and austere effect of the room. Life-size human masks of baked clay, each differing from the others and each more ferocious in aspect than any sculpture upon the grand staircase, are hung upon these walls at irregular intervals. This level of the fortress is illuminated by intensely bright but partly covered lamps, which revolve so as to cast their glaring light upon sections of the walls at random. From time to time, but always unexpectedly, they illuminate one or another of the masks; and the effect of these narrow, intense rays bringing suddenly into relief some hideous contenance is frightful. The mind knows that these masks are nothing but skilled works in baked clay; but the emotions do not easily grasp that cnowledge, and the instincts are even less able. Besides, the violent alternation between light and darkness confuses the eyes, so that after-images of the masks, spectral in their reversed illumination, snarl or glare inexorably from the empty shadows. We move forward, beyond them. For a moment we are lost in darkness; but now a great flash of surging flame heralds a scene of destruction. Now we witness the devastation by fire of a conquered and ruined city. We see the living captured alike with the bodies of the slain in an inescapable inferno, the despair of some victims and the madness of others. Glowing embers and spilt blood shine redly beneath the flames. Falling buildings engulf the mangled and charred remains of the dead and the frantic struggles of the living. The vision fades, releasing us. We are back in the fortress, but as we make our way towards the stair, the masks and their partial images cast by the flashing lamp light evoke and re-create the episode of horror. Now it is we who walk upon embers. We take care lest we stumble upon corpses, or lest the glowing walls should fall upon us. The ferocious masks in their unrelated malice are like demons of the night, drawn to the carnage without human comprehension of it. Other faces, too, look upon us and mock our revulsion, faces which we feel sure are not after-images from the masks.

The valiant and serene countenance of our Guide draws us to him upon the grand stairway; and, his purple cloak going before us like a banner, he leads us up to the fifth floor.

On this fifth and highest level of the fortress the illumination is faint, and we cannot determine its origin. There is no feeling of dryness nor of humidity, of cold nor of heat, nor is there any movement of the air. We cannot see the walls distinctly: only a subdued red sparkle, as of corundum, gleams here and there from their surface. The floor is thickly carpeted and gives forth no sound as we move.

The darkness and silence, and the stillness of the air, are oppressive. We await what is to happen.

A single hollow sound, not loud, but uneasy and jarring, strikes us. It seems to hang upon the air, coming from no particular direction. After it has died away, another similar sound is heard. Then, following more rapidly, another.

Our senses are alert, our attention fixed upon these sounds. When the next sound comes, it seems louder and even more jarring; and now they occur more regularly, so that we can distinguish a regular rhythm coming into being. Now the rhythm is steady and unvarying, and we can recognize the sound as the beating of a drum of unusual pitch and resonance.

This monotonous drumming in the still air and the darkness is oppressive. We speak, but the drum beats are just loud enough to drown our voices. We try to escape from the rhythm by moving about, but the sound comes from every direction equally and we are further troubled to find our movement synchronizing with the beat.

We cease to struggle against the sound, letting it pulse over us and through us. On and on it beats, on and on. Now another phenomenon occurs. As our consciousness rebels against the relentless monotony, the imagination weaves fragments of melody to chime with the rhythm The illusion increases. The single drum beat is multiplied to a hundred in unison. Shrill voices chant words which we cannot quite distinguish. Shrieking choirs, demonic orchestras hurl mean-ingless cascades of sound upon our ears, all reiterating the one relentless rhythm.

We know that the greater part of this frenzy of sound comes from within ourselves, but so long as the drum beat continues we cannot stop it. We try to distract ourselves from it by turning attention to our other senses, but no object presents itself: nothing but the faint red glitter of the walls, and from this we turn away and close our eyes as the flash of the particles seems to wax and wane with the rhythm of the drumming. We try to collect our thoughts, to summon our will, but every effort is absorbed and fragmented by the rhythm, and by the reverberating clamor of sound which it evokes. We feel as if our very spirit is being crushed by it.

Our Guide moves forward among us. The steadfast light of his aura holds our attention with its unvarying brightness. The sound of the drumming continues, but now it is again only a single jarring reverberation: its power is gone from us. With a sign that we should follow, our Guide leads us across the dark, carpeted floor to a narrow flight of steps which leads upwards, in one corner. We mount these steps to an open trap door, and stand with our Guide upon the roof of the fortress: a flat paved surface, surrounded by a crenelated parapet. The drumming has ceased. Above us the sky is black and starless, but we feel all about us the free air of night.

Raising the lodestone ring to his lips, our Guide breathes upon it and whispers the word which we do not hear. We look skyward, but in the darkness we do not see the approach of the Horse before, with the ringing thunder of his hoofs, he descends upon the roof a little distance from us.

Five times he smites with his hoofs upon the fortress, smites in the true power of Mars against that symbol of excessive force; and, at the last blow, our Guide draws his Sword of Power and raises it on high. For judgment and the redress of equillibrium are true works of Mars, and these qualities must be confirmed before we are free to complete this journey.

A deep thunderous roaring and rending sound comes to us from within the foundations of the building, which shakes beneath our feet as the sound grows louder and nearer. Suddenly the whole tower is rent asunder, and even as our Guide brings his sword down we are thrown high into the air.

We are surrounded by a bright scarlet light in which at first we see nothing else: but the magical power of the sword has supervened over the simple force of the explosion, and we are lifted to a great height and carried swiftly onward. And now before us we see our Guide, his purple cloak wrapped about him, as he rides the shining chestnut Horse. The Horse soars rapidly through the glowing light. Our Guide turns and lifts his sword to us in greeting and farewell. His aura blazes scarlet, brighter and brighter, encompassing his steed: then both blend into the surrounding scarlet brightness and are gone from us.

And now while still our flight proceeds a blaze of orange flame, brighter than the scarlet, springs into being before us. It encircles us and engulfs us. Its very brightness is bewildering, and yet it gives place to an even brighter radiance, an intense yellow light as of the sun itself. In this third zone of brilliance we feel as if suspended, almost losing our sense of motion: but suddenly, without warning, the color of the light is transformed into its complementary, a deep luminous violet. Still we move onwards, but slowly now. It is as though we had in an instant been plunged from the height of the skies into a violet ocean, and this sensation increases as the violet light gives place to blackness. Yet still. it is a luminous and transparent blackness, a blackness which is black light.

Now the blackness is tinged with blue, and quickly we are surrounded with blue light: not the color of sky or of sea, but a bright spectrum blue which shines all about us with a steady and perfect clarity. We are still moving slowly onward, however, and now in the midst of this world of blue light there grows a flame of vibrant and living green. It attracts us and draws us, growing larger and all-encompassing as we move into it.

The impulse of our flight leaves us, and we wait passively within a world of greenness which caresses and vitalizes. ★

Gradually the green light resolves itself into a bright landscape. We are standing within a scattered cluster of feathery trees, looking across a grassy space. Everything has the look and feeling of early summer: the freshness of dew and of rising sap pervades the life of this place, but the dew flashes with the fire of the sunlight, and the rising sap fills branch and twig with the flame of life.

Before us, under the clear blue sky, stands a building in the form of a classical temple. Upon a base of four steps which extend to the whole width of the building, seven smooth and unfluted columns support the architrave and, above this, the broad triangle of the pediment. The pediment is adorned with a sculptured group representing the Judgment of Paris. In this we see Hera, as Queen of the Heavens, standing majestically crowned and wielding the scepter of governance; and Athene as helper of mankind, offering symbols of the inspiration she gives in the arts which humanize our life; but the protagonist gives the apple of victory to Aphrodite, who appears as the undraped and inviting Queen of Love.

In the myth as it is traditionally given, Aphrodite is declared the most beautiful; but in this representation each of the three Goddesses, albeit carrying her own attributes, is shown with exactly the same exquisite form and face. Thus it is indicated that none is less than the loveliest. Ultimately, each in her own way manifests the same Divine Power. She who infuses life with love is also the giver of inspiration in every art; and she who governs the great forces of attraction and reciprocity, the polarities of the universe both physical and metaphysical, is Queen and ruler of all existences. But in our life on earth we see most clearly the Queen of Love, the gentle giver of desire and of fulfillment: she who brings man and woman together and who is likewise manifest in all fruitful concord.

The building itself suggests and echoes this interplay and unification of forces. From the four wide steps upon which it rests to its aspiring summit, its lines bespeak harmony, balance and peace. Yet at the same time the edifice is dynamic. Its exterior is entirely of marble in which varying shades of blue-green, light and dark, occur in undulating bands, across which fine veins of white form a network like foam upon the sea; and in this hard lustrous stone, inclusions of fossil sea shells display their delicate marine structures as if seen through the most limpid water.

Yet all this is but the exterior of the temple, the outer vehicle of that manifestation of Divine Power which we seek. Intent upon our purpose, but without haste, we cross the intervening space and mount the four steps. We pass through the portico and through the doorway within, and enter the temple itself.

Within the walls we expect to find darkness, or deep shadow. Instead, there is a soft golden radiance mingled with flashes of brightness. The flat roof appears to be fashioned of pieces of clear amber, varying in dimension from the size of a hand down to small gemlike drops, and in color from deep red gold to the palest yellow, all set in burnished copper. The interior of the walls and the floor are of sandstone, in color a soft and delicate rose red, and the walls are ornamented with large pine cones and roses in beaten and burnished copper. As the varied amber light dances upon these surfaces, the whole temple appears living and rejoicing.

We pass between the two pillars within the entrance, Machetes and Nomothetes, and stand in contemplation.

The Bomos, draped in brilliant green, stands in the center of the temple; upon it lies the Mystical Tessera, and above it shines the single Lamp of the Mysteries. Behind and to the left of the Bomos, in the north east, is the Banner of the New Life. Directly behind the Bomos, at the eastern end of the temple, is a raised dais before which upon a slender pedestal stands an incense burner, the smoke of sweet spices gently rising from it. Above the dais is a canopy of carved fruitwood, in which among intricate plant forms symbolic emblems are heightened with gold: heraldic trophies of the Triumph of Love.

Upon the dais itself is a sculpture, wrought in gleaming pink marble. Here, half reclining in their embrace of love, Eros and Psyche are represented in a total unity and harmony of reciprocal limbs and bodies. The delicately plumed wings which spring from the shoulders of Eros, spiring upwards, convey something not only of the ecstasy of the lovers but also of the sublime heights to which she who is clasped in the arms of Love himself will be carried.

This representation of Eros and Psyche, the inmost secret of this temple of the Queen of Love, is the revelation of a great mystery. We might be surprised to fmd it in this place, for in the legend Aphrodite shows herself so cruel a mother-in-law to the earth-born Psyche, chosen bride of the immortal son of the Goddess. Aphrodite sets the young woman one seemingly impossible task after another. Yet it is through, and by, her faithful perserverance in those trials that Psyche not only wins her acknowledged place as Eros' bride, but also gains her own immortality. The victory of Psyche is also the victory of Love, and of the Queen of Love.

As we contemplate the figures upon the dais, we become aware of a delineation upon the red sandstone wall behind the group, not intended to be evident at first. Painted in a deeper red monochrome, and standing tall above the sculptured lovers, Aphrodite, most voluptuous yet most regal, extends her hands over them in blessing and bestows upon them the supreme rapture of her smile.

In reverence we acknowledge this mystery, and salute the East.

It is by the Path of Mars, and by the trials of that path, that we have come to this place of joy and wonder. In this reflection, too, we can find a likeness to the story of Psyche. Even in an earthly setting it is ever seen that the victory of love in a human life does not come easily: much more is this true when the prize is recognized as Love Divine.

In the legend, the first trials of Psyche are caused by her own errors, in not knowing truly whom it is that she loves. For Psyche is the soul, and she has at first to abide only by faith in her lover and faith in herself, in the darkness of earthly night. Her sisters tell her she is giving herself to a hideous monster: the detractors of Love proclaim the same thing always. When Psyche catches her first glimpse of the beauty of Eros, he vanishes. Many great mystics, whatever name they give to the Beloved, have had a like experience.

But once Psyche knows the face of him she seeks, and sets out to find him, she comes within the hard testing and purification of the laws of the Mother. Yet thus it always is with the faithful ones of Love, who go with light in their hearts through the harsh places of earthly life. Thus it is with the soul which strives ever onward for union with the Winged and Luminous One who is her own fulfillment and perfection. So does love which is nurtured on earth come through striving and opposition to its realization in the heights.

This Path which we have just completed does not of itself bring us to that full realization. But the meaning of this Path is Deliverance: deliverance from the false security of lower existence, deliverance from the blindness in which we do not clearly perceive our true goal, deliverance from inordinate fears which would deform our vision of Love. The power of Mars, rightly interpreted, is the active champion of justice and truth, without which harmony and love remain unattained; Mars is the surgeon who frees us from all that prevents healing, the flash of lightning which shatters the tower in which we seek safety and fmd oppression. So have we trodden a vital portion of the road of Psyche, our soul; we have entered the temple beyond that path, and have seen imaged therein the high reward which awaits her faithful seeking.

So may we attain.

Battery 3-5-3

The Working of the 26th Path
(Correspondences)

SPHERE OF COMMENCEMENT: Hod (Splendor)

Hebrew Divine Name: Elohim Tzabaoth

Planetary correspondence: Mercury

Element: Water

Symbol: Caduceus

Colors: Orange, black, white

PATH OF THE TREE OF LIFE: 26

Intelligence: The 26th Path is the Renewing Intelligence, so named because by means of it everything which is capable of change is brought by the Holy One to a new creation.

Influence on Path: Capricorn (the Goat)

Planetary correspondence: Saturn

Hebrew Letter: Ayin (Eye)

Path Stanza: Out of the wellspring of forms filling the
wide spheres with its fashionings
Myriad images rise, wild or serene,
fleshly, ethereal:
Hail, O thou Eye that hast seen all things
that are, Knowledge to gaze on them
Blessing their goodliness!

Tarot arcanum: The Devil (15)

Element of Path: Earth

Symbols: Ancient kings, buried treasure, the sacrificial axe, the Well of the Eye, the lamp

Living beings: The human, animal and elemental participants in the "Sabbat"

Magical phenomena: The dance of the "Sabbat," the power of the Fountain of the Eye

---

The following material should only be included
in working this Path after the 25th Path has been worked.

CONCLUSION OF 26th PATH

> *Living beings:* (Additional to those above mentioned:) The Devourers, the Watchers upon the Heights
>
> *Magical Phenomena:* (Additional to those above mentioned:) The Lake of fire, the vision of the Philosophers' Stone, the vision of the Golden Age

SPHERE OF DESTINATION: Tiphareth (Beauty)

> *Hebrew Divine Name:* Yahveh Eloah V'Daath
>
> *Planetary correspondence:* The Sun
>
> *Planetary number:* 6
>
> *Element:* Air
>
> *Symbols:* the megalithic circle, the eight-pointed Star
>
> *Magical Phenomenon:* Vision of the world of the four elements in its essential goodness

Comments

In *The Song of Praises* the text for this Path seems to glance at the verse in Genesis (1:31) in which God beholds all of his new creation and sees it to be very good.

The goodness of all the Worlds, including the material universe, is an essential part of Qabalistic teaching. Yet at some points in the Pathworkings, as in the teachings of a number of exoteric religions, it appears that we human beings can endorse the Divine approval only "at our peril." This needs to be understood.

A foreshadowing of this warning occurred in the working of the 32nd Path, when we had to turn away from materiality to begin our upward progress. Our own body is a part of the material world, and linked closely to it is our emotional-instinctual nature, the Nephesh. Our rational consciousness, which is of a higher order, is committed in the unity of our personality to love and care for this subrational and childlike part of us. But to show true love for a child is not to submit oneself to its wayward impulses. One must govern the child one loves. One must also govern the lower nature that one loves, even though in both cases it is healthy and delightful to share sometimes in their play. The rational mind, as has been said, needs to develop into the full Ruach consciousness which is the vehicle of the supernal, Intuitive Mind: and as soon as it turns towards that illumination, the rational mind will begin to enter into the right ordering of its own relationship with the lower self.

If, instead of thus looking upwards, the consciousness were to habituate itself to being dominated by the Nephesh and by the physical body, then the Higher Self (the supernal level of the psyche) would be unable to direct the rational consciousness in the governance of the whole. Even rationality itself would fail. This possibility of disintegration within the psyche is, in general terms, the source of the grave warnings involved in the moral teachings of the various religions.

This Qabalistic doctrine indicates a uniquely human problem. Thus, in the present Pathworking, the elemental beings, the animals and the children below the age of reason who participate in the "Sabbat" are but enjoying the astral world in which they are fully at home. Our own Nephesh is at home in that World too, but as whole and adult persons we cannot find our guiding vision at that level. That is why the completion of this Path is denied to us until we have gained the Sun Sphere by the authentic portal of the 25th Path. Then, certainly, we can pass through the purifying Lake of Fire and, with our higher discernment, see the true mystical goodness and beauty of the material and astral worlds. The vision of the Golden Age, the transmuting power of the Philosophers' Stone, indicate the profound significance of the change of viewpoint. Thus *The 32 Paths of Wisdom* calls this Path the Renewing Intelligence, "because by means of it everything which is capable of change is brought by the Holy One to a new creation."

The Working of the 26th Path

We stand in a place which is dark and shadowy, although the light is sufficient for us to perceive our surroundings. This is a temple, octagonal in shape. Eight pillars, equally placed a few feet within the enclosing walls, are connected to each other by Gothic arches so as to form a colonnade surrounding the central space. High up in each of these eight arches hangs a small lamp which burns with an orange flame. In the center of the temple, directly before us, stands the Bomos draped with

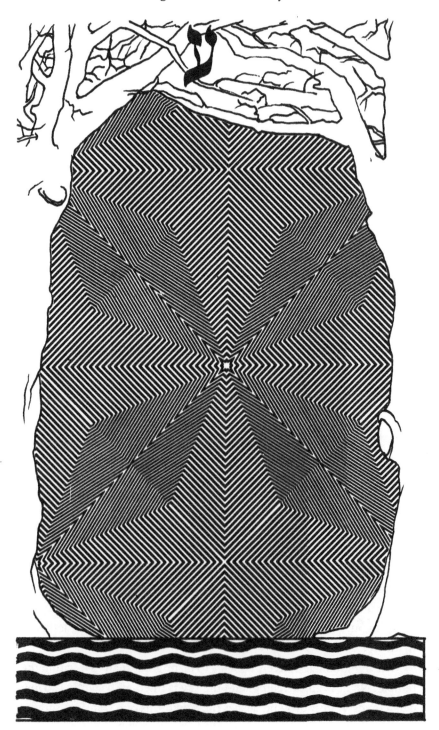

the same vivid color; upon it is the Mystical Tessera, and above it hangs the Lamp of the Mysteries, of greater magnitude than the other lamps and burning with a clear white flame.

Behind us, we know, is the doorway to the outer world, with the two columns, Machetes and Nomothetes. Before us, beyond the Bomos, in the arch directly opposite to the door, stands a tall Caduceus of marble, carved, and inlaid with stones of many colors. The two serpents, one dark and one light, are entwined about the central staff. Their scales gleam with lozenge shapes of iridescent luster: the dark one with black opal and hematite, the light one with aquamarine and mother of pearl. The staff is of brown marble, very plainly carved with the appearance of wood, but at its head are extended two delicately plumed wings, their glistening crystalline whiteness touched into splendor by the fiery radiance of the lamp in the arch above.

We approach the caduceus more closely, to consider it and to reflect upon something of its significance. The serpents cling tautly about the staff, their eyes of onyx shining lifelike. Their vitality gives force and meaning to the whole Caduceus: just as the person in whom the powers of sex are alive and equilibriated is an infinitely more dynamic individual than one in whom those powers are inert, even though both states could be described as conditions of balance and repose. But yet it is not from the serpents that the Caduceus gains its stability and unity, but from the central rod; and it is the rod, moreover, which is crowned with those white and shining wings of power. Even thus, in the diversity of magical knowledge and experience which we seek, we need also a central reality which shall give strength and unity to the whole, a reality which shall lift us on wings of inspiration.

Somewhat to the right of the Caduceus, in the wall of the temple, is a narrow door which stands slightly ajar, and which leads, as we perceive, to the outside. We gaze once more at the Caduceus to fix its image in our mind, then we move to this door and, opening it, look out to the open air.

The light outside scarcely appears to be brighter than that within the temple. Night is approaching, and the sky is filled with swiftly moving dark clouds. A gust of wind dashes the cold drops of a transient shower across our cheeks. The twisted boughs of a leafless tree nearby creak as they sway to and fro, and beyond the tree the road takes a slowly descending course through a bare landscape to disappear into thick forest below. Over this wild and gloomy scene, the sky between the flying clouds glows with the lurid fire of a diffused and fading sunset. Assuredly this is not a prospect to tempt the timid, but we recognize this Path as a needful part of our experience and we do not expect all our progress to be made beneath smiling skies. Resolutely we step forth from the doorway of the temple.

As soon as we are moving along the road, much of its threatened unpleasantness is gone. The brief shower is over, we become accustomed to the gloom, the air is invigorating and the slight downward slope gives impetus to our steps. It would not be difficult to travel a long distance in these conditions, and the austere countryside offers us no distractions. As our power of sight adapts itself to the shadowy road we fail to notice how fast the meager light is fading, until we enter the first fringe of the forest and find ourselves all at once in total blackness.

We stand still. The wind has ceased, and the darkness is silent, without stir. Wrapped in leaden night we remain thus motionless while long minutes pass. This deeper blackness does not become penetrable to us, nor do we have any idea what direction to take, if indeed we can take any. The forest is no longer present to us; in imagination we seem encompassed by a void which is empty and yet oppressive, a waste region of leaden air. A drowsiness as of sleep begins to settle upon our unoccupied senses. Our situation in space and time becomes less relevant, the mind begins to feel free to make its own excursions.

This sense of space and freedom is abruptly ended by a harsh animal sound which seems near at hand, yet without specific direction. A goose cackles, a goat begins to bleat, an ass brays; then all these sounds blend into what sounds like wild mocking laughter. Then abruptly again there is silence. Again we know we are in the forest, for now we are conscious of the odor of dead leaves which hangs in the heavy air.

All at once a gleam of radiance is reflected on the trees in front of us, and we turn to discover its source. We are not alone in traveling this desolate path. The grim nature of the place where we are, and the fact that the newcomer is indeed a Being of Light, make him very welcome to us; otherwise we might demur at the company of so strange a figure.

His features are thin and severe. He is clean shaven, dark of complexion, with narrow face, high forehead and bright, piercing eyes. His bearing is stately and commanding. His lean angular figure is wrapped in a heavy cloak of dark brown cloth, with inwoven geometric designs in red-brown, black and white, a wide border embroidered in rich, bright colors, and a tasseled fringe. Beneath the cloak he wears a robe of heavy unbleached linen, extending to mid calf. On his feet are sandals ornamented upon the instep with a mosaic of semiprecious stones. His hair is black, with a heavy forelock falling upon his brow; and at the sides of this there arise two tall spiral horns curving slightly backwards, each ending in a sharp point tipped with a sheath of obsidian. His whole figure is surrounded with a radiant nimbus of white light. He treads this wild path with easy grace, and soon comes up with us.

He passes us, then after a couple of paces he turns and looks at us inquiringly. His austere, resolute mouth remains closed, and plainly he intends no conversation with us. We ask him, however, if he will guide us upon this Path; and after regarding us a little longer he turns about and, with a gesture which bids us to follow, proceeds again upon his way.

Now, in the light shed by the nimbus of our Guide, we advance easily. We pass beneath the high vaulted branches of majestic trees, through thickets of lesser growth where our Guide unerringly finds the hidden trackways, through dim hollows in which we skirt the margin of black pools, and over ridges where mighty roots form the steps and terraces by which we mount.

At last we emerge from the forest, and, our luminous Guiide still going before us, we proceed steadily under the thick darkness of the night sky.

Our inner faculties overlay the darkness with forms and colors of pure light. We stop as we look at a high cone shaped mound, lonely and abandoned as it is to outward seeming. To it we behold advancing the rich pageantry of a great funeral procession, even though we know that what we are witnessing took place ages upon ages past, in most ancient time. It is the burial of a king or a mighty chieftain, and in the procession we see proud armored warriors, ascetic priests in fantastic and sumptuous regalia, barbaric banners glittering with gold and gems, totemic masks and effigies stained with bright pigments—each of which would have been prepared with its own mysterious rite. We see the corpse carried seated upright in a litter, crowned and robed magnificently, and accompanied by a host of incense-bearers, singers and flagellant dancers. With great solemnity the corpse is conducted into the prepared mound, then the entrance is sealed. The envisioned concourse of people fades slowly from our sight. Buts stationed even yet about the mound, we behold those elemental entities which in the funeral rites the priests invoked to guard the tomb: those beings which have long trumpet-shaped muzzles to proclaim the deeds of the departed, those others with diamond-shaped sea.green eyes to weep for his death, those again which have wings and talons of pure flame to menace mortals who would desecrate or plunder, and lastly those which have teeth of granite rock to crush such as will not take warning. These four cohorts of elementals remain, we perceive, couched even now at the four quarters of the forgotten mound; the place is most regal, most mournful and most desolate. Our Guide moves silently away, and we follow.

Now the path takes a slight upward inclination, leading through rough grassland where we might stumble but for the bright nimbus of him who goes ahead of us. As we move forward, once more phantasmal forms appear against the heavy darkness. Amid acclamations and feasting, a young ruler comes to power. He is dressed with showy richness which might seem simple-minded, but he is not that. His cool, sardonic expression masks a fixed resolve. The people extol him because the fountains daily flow with wine, and sweet oil burns night after night in festive lamps and beacons. But as he sits among the elders and sages, even in his silence his ironic smile and holiday attire mock their gravity; and when he is appealed to for judgment in matters of law, we see him with that same smile grant mercy to the merciless and bid the victims to learn wisdom. Everywhere he challenges institution and custom, so that at last even the assassin who slays him brings about no peace, but only precipitates civil war and ruin. These scenes fade from our vision in an instant of time, like a dream; but the conflict between law and lawlessness has sounded a timeless note of tragedy, for law and lawlessness both are in their nature Saturnian, primeval.

Now with the tall luminous figure of our Guide still going before us upon the path, we enter an avenue of venerable trees. Their lower branches spring from near the ground and their feathery leaves gleam with a luster as of dark bronze. Their bitter fragrance fills the air. We are in an avenue of ancient yew trees: trees associated by their very nature with the cult of the dead, yet, being evergreen and of vast longevity, emblems also of deathlessness and renewal.

We pass slowly between the two lines of these ancient trees. About their trunks a high ridge has been formed of their fallen leaves during the course of centuries, but beneath this ridge, and beneath the massive interlace of their roots, the earth has eroded away into hollows and cavities. One of these openings is larger than the rest, and we pause to peer into it. More than a man's height below us, and plainly revealed by the hazards of erosion, is a shrine of incalculable antiquity. We cannot guess how old it was when these yew trees were first planted in the earth which covered it. There, upon a rock-hewn altar, lie a massive cup and a sacrificial axe, both of them graven with mythic scenes and gleaming with gems.

A near movement catches our attention. Slowly traversing the surface of the altar is a large black serpent, which then coils itself in the shadows at one corner of the altar and rests motionless. Upon the floor of this shrine lie the white skull and some of the bones of a human skeleton: whether sacrificial victim or intending robber, whether laid low by the axe or by the venom of the serpent, we cannot know. Truly the burden of the past lies heavy in this place, and the breath of night is cold upon us. We turn away from that forgotten shrine, and our Guide who-has paused- to-await -us -moves ahead, leading us beyond the avenue of trees.

More steeply now the path mounts up and up. The night sky is covered with a haze which emits a faint and leaden light, and this is reflected upon the bare rocks of the region we have now entered. At last, keeping in the tracks of our silent but sure-footed Guide, we reach the level surface of a barren plateau.

We advance to the center of this space, where, in an elliptical depression, is the unguarded pit of what appears to be a large well. Near this our Guide halts, and as we follow his example we look down into the well. No water is visible, but the depths of the pit glimmer with what seems to be black, swirling light. Now we turn our attention again to the surrounding plateau, and become aware that this place is not empty. Presences which are not yet visible to us, both human and other than human, are gathering in this area. We sense their approach even as we might feel and hear the rushing of a great wind, but this is an inward feeling and hearing and no wind stirs. Over and above this movement, too, we have awareness of a force more subtle yet stronger, a watchful force which moves not but which is summoning and drawing those that approach. We feel the compelling desire with which this summoning force is pervaded, and as the atmosphere thickens and presses inward with the coming of the responding entities we strive to see them. We are eager to behold what manner of guests are awaited with such bodiless eagerness, such supra-sensual avidity. Striving to penetrate the darkness with our questing gaze, we discern only a transparent quivering of the air, only a brief and changeful movement of evanescent masses.

The mind's eye, however, clothes our inward impressions with vivid form and color that we may consciously know what is taking place. Some nude, some clad in fanciful garments, a number of youthful figures move gracefully across our vision. Their hair streams with leaves of vine and of ivy, and with huge blossoms crimson and gold; but they are not wearing garlands, it is their hair itself which has budded forth in this exuberance.

Now, with laughter and violent gesture, other beings less delicate crowd upon our consciousness: these appear as bearded men, powerfully muscled but of no great stature, who look at first to be clad in skins of animals. The rough fur, however, is their own, and their own are the short foxlike tails. These are Satyrs, male elemental beings who snatch every pretext for rough revelry and sexual enjoyment. Now, swiftly overtaking them and with shrill cries inviting their pursuit, are their female counterparts the amorous Nymphs of mountain, forest and river. Besides these, mingling with the increasing throng of humans and elementals, are a number of natural animals: horses, cattle, goats, pigs and dogs as well as some of the wilder sort. Now and then a cat rides the shoulders of man or woman, or a human rides a horse or a steer into the concourse, but far more numerous than these are the glimpses we catch of beings neither truly beast nor human: human countenance on bird or gliding serpent, velvety muzzles illumined with human eyes, human forms with clawed or hoof-like extremities. Yet no participant shows hostility to another.

Fleeting although our vision is of all these beings, we know they are all merging into a riotous dance which revolves, though at a distance, about the dark well by which we are standing. It is from the black swirling depths of the well, or rather from the quivering air above it, that the strange compulsion emanates which-governs this otherwise ungoverned assembly. At first the movement of the dance is confused, uncertain: some in the throng have arrived laden with provision for eating and drinking, some have musical instruments in which they delight. By degrees however there emerges a circling movement of complex and changeful involutions, in which the motley host of dancers proceed like the joyous procession of some great carnival.

The pace of the dance quickens as the confusion clears. Its rhythm, stressed by multitudinous footfall and by clapping hands, by drum, castanet and voice, becomes all-pervasive while the movements of the dancers become more extravagant and instinctual. Unreason holds sway.

Those beings who are not wholly caught into the dance itself, nonetheless show in their own manner their oneness with the joyous and heedless will of the gathering. Some participants leave its sweeping circle, to couple in obsessive embrace on its inner fringe, where also are gathered many less active sharers in the scene. There are children, too, in this astral festival, drawn simply as the animals are by its primal vitality, or by who knows what call of inherited race or of past incarnation? Here in this inner ring, among the drinkers and onlookers and lovers are young infants, contentedly drawing sweet milk from the breasts of young matrons or from the udders of she-goats, or sucking the juice of grapes or nectarines held to their mouths by playmates. The older children are for the most part indistinguishable among the adults, but here and there we see a small figure carried high among the dancers, bestriding the shaggy neck of a Satyr or seated upon the dimpled motherly shoulders of a Bacchanal. These children laugh and crow as they sway in the dance, looking with innocent acceptance upon scenes which many a hardened adult would repudiate. Every aspect of life that seeks fulfillment is here, the energies of all gathered up into the vortex of the rhythmic stampede which whirls, ever faster and more vertiginously, about the conscious, hungry and swirling Eye of the central pit. And we perceive by the pulsing of the air above the pit that all those beings who make glad sounds and dance, who eat, drink or dream, who lust and enjoy for themselves, as it seems, and for their fellows, are in truth yielding up the gathered honey and the smoking incense of their experience to nourish and to enkindle the questing and perfervid Well of the Eye.

In a sudden instant of silence the thread of frenzy snaps. Each entity remains as if frozen, all at once void of emotion and of impulse; then the still figures with one accord slowly turn their gaze to the center of the circle. We too, who are standing near the pit, look to it for a resolution of this juncture.

The silence is only of a moment's duration. The earth trembles underfoot as a mighty thunder sounds from the depth, then from the pit a vast fountain of blazing light mounts to the blackness of the heavens. At an incalculable height the light changes; it splinters and coruscates, spreading in all directions as if to create a new cosmos of fire, ablaze with every fragmented color of the spectrum. Then those whirling and scattered fires turn and rush downwards, descending upon every living entity upon the plateau. Beast and human, elemental being, astral traveler, dreamer—ourselves with all the rest—are overwhelmed and infused with this fiery rainbow of creative energy, the Fountain of the Eye. For a flashing moment of time we are aware only of the iridescent, dazzling light, engulfing us in its brightness.

The moment passes, but around us is changed. Now we are standing upon a small grassy hill in a deep valley. Our Guide stands nearby, holding a lamp which burns with a bright golden light. None of those other Beings whom we saw upon the plateau is here with us: all those lives are following their own proper Paths, we realize, as we are following ours.

The engulfing brightness has vanished, but we feel inspired, uplifted by it. Now to stand beneath the night sky is itself an intoxication, and the odor of wild herbs in the darkness is an exquisite and precious thing.

The Fountain of the Eye is not a phenomenon which we left when we departed from the plateau, if indeed we have departed from it. The Fountain of the Eye is deep within us: the fountain itself, and not only the inspiration which it bestows. Upon this Path, no matter what we behold, whether inwardly or outwardly, the Fountain of the Eye is the experiencer, and continually the fragmented spectrum of its experience is flung back into the soul to germinate and to flash forth in ever new developments from the original.

We recall the purpose with which we set out upon this Path, to find a central unity which would give purpose to all we might learn or discover. Does the Fountain of the Eye represent that central unity?—is the purpose of our life to be found in the continual flux and reflux of experience?—the giving of the will in all directions so as to make ourselves one with the universe around us, and in exchange to make the experience of the universe a part of oursleves? Whether or not this be our true objective on this Path, we each feel ourselves glowing inwardly with the glory of this concept, and mantled outwardly in the increasing resplendence of the rainbow light. We exult in its many-colored brilliance, and even more in the conscious creative vitality which expands within us with the light's increase. Each of us has a body, limbs, features, composed entirely of scintillating energic light, whose radiance spreads outwardly to form a splendor all about us. We stand proudly, as transfigured beings: transfigured, not by becoming other than we ever have been, but by coming to a conscious realization of the power of our selfhood.

Now our Guide raises aloft the lamp which he carries, and we understand that he is about to leave us. The golden light of the lamp becomes brighter and more luminous, increasing to an intense radiance in which his form fades from our sight, and we know he is gone from us. The effulgence of the lamp however remains. It encompasses us, shines into us, and for a while we behold nothing but its dazzling golden splendor. Illuminating us through and through, it strips away from us even the rainbow fire in which we have gloried, the astral light of the Fountain of the Eye which had seemed so powerful.

If this working is being conducted for the first time, that is,
in series and prior to the working of the 25th Path,
continue with the text below which concludes in the Earth Sphere.

If this working is being conducted subsequently to
working the 25th Path, continue with the normal text on
page 252 which concludes in the Sun Sphere.

The golden light changes gradually through red to an intense violet, then, its intensity fading, it becomes a deep but still luminous blue. At last even this fades, leaving us in blackness. Yet the blackness is not inert.

Emanating invisibly from us is a delicate whirling vibration which at first seems only to make more dense and obscure the night in which it spins. Then from that very density a glimmering aureole of light is emitted. Closely encircling us, it silently grows in brightness to a clear ring of white light whirling clockwise around us. Suddenly there is a momentary tumult of bell-like sounds, and in the same instant the shining aureole springs to an immeasurable circumference of which we remain the center. Now this immense, spinning circle of light pulses and quivers with inwoven rhythms of ever increasing complexity, and, swiftly though it moves, we catch in it glimpses and suggestions of colors, forms, of lesser orbits which are whirled about in that great circumference while they spin each on its own less constant axis. From its outer rim to its center, this great circumference becomes filled with more, and more intricate, manifestations of sound, movement, light, and evidently of life. A great breath of joy and triumph comes to us from it all, as from a universe newly brought into being. Even though we know that in all this vision we are experiencing nothing beyond the level of astral existence, the elation of it like a glorious wind takes possession of us and at a high point of ecstasy we shout aloud, acclaiming the beauty and wonder of our vision.

Again a change is taking place in that which surrounds us. Color is blending with color, form merging with form, so intricately that both color and form soon become indistinguishable. A uniform wall of greyish light surrounds us, and we lose all sense of its movement.

Our surroundings rapidly consolidate themselves. Beneath our feet is a smooth floor of large black and white checkers. Around us are walls of natural rock, with an open doorway through which the daylight shines brightly. The sounds we hear are coming in from the outer world: the sound of a flowing stream, and the call of birds. We have returned to the Sphere of Earth.

The adventure of the Path of Capricorn is a needful and valuable part of our inner life. The symbol of the Goat is essentially that which links the depths with the heights. To draw strength from the deeper levels of existence, and to aspire to the heights, is needful to the wholeness and balance of each individual as it is needful in every aspect of life. To draw upon the depths is always possible to us children of Earth, for the hidden channels necessary to our survival are kept open, often without our knowledge; but to aspire to the heights is not always immediately to attain.

None the less, aspiration is always an essential condition for attainment, and as each of the Four Worlds mirrors the others, so images and patterns of aspiration are always present to us. But the implications of this interchange between the Worlds are cosmic as well as individual. The non-material yearns to the material even as the material aspires to the non-material, the seed seeks fulfillment by falling to earth even as the tree seeks fulfillment by reaching towards the sun. The mystery of the Fountain of the Eye is one of the mysteries of the existence of the Universe.

Our experience upon this Path of the Goat, and above all our encounters at several levels with the Fountain of the Eye, have been most fruitful even though they reached no high culmination in the Sphere of the Sun. That they did not do so, was due to the containment of this Path as we have now traveled it, entirely within the Astral World. The Astral World has immense beauty, dignity, and power—it is essential to the operation of any magical power soever but it cannot confer the fulfillment of any high spiritual aspiration. Nor does the Path of Capricorn, of itself, afford us a gateway between World and World whereby we may rise above the Astral.

But this has been no failure: the Fountain of the Eye itself attests that every experience is precious. When in due time, and by another approach, the Sphere of the Sun shall have been opened to us, we shall tread this path again. The outcome, then, will be other than it has now been. But in order to find, we must seek; and we must travel in order to arrive.

Battery 3-5-3

The Working of the 24th Path

(Correspondences)

SPHERE OF COMMENCEMENT: Netzach (Victory)

Hebrew Divine Name: Yahveh Tzabaoth

Planetary correspondence: Venus

Planetary number: 7

Symbol: The planetary sign of Venus; the mirror

Mineral: Malachite

Color: Green

PATH OF THE TREE OF LIFE: 24

Intelligence: The 24th Path is the Image-making Intelligence, so named because it provides shapes for all created entities which are of a nature allied to its own complex beauty.

Influence on Path: Scorpio (the Scorpion). In Ezekiel's vision, the Eagle

Planetary correspondences: Mars, Pluto

Hebrew Letter: Nun (Fish)

Path Stanza: Nearest the heart of the seas watches the
Fish, shimmering, nacreous,
Moving with pulse of the tides, gliding far
down under their turbulence,
Crossing the fathomless caves, threading
the lost hulls of the argosies—
Shadow inscrutable!

Tarot arcanum: Death (13)

Element of Path: Water

Symbols: The torrent, the pit, treasures of the deeps

Plants: Deadly anemones

Colors: Mingled browns and greens, deep red, all lurid and warning colors

Living beings: The harpies (noxious bird forms), the sea monster

Magical phenomena: Vision of the Dark Mother, the death wish

The following material should only be included in working
this Path after the 25th Path has been worked

CONCLUSION OF 24th PATH

> *Magical phenomena:* (Additional to those abovementioned:) Visions of the Primeval Mother, and of the Mother as Isis, Cybele, the Mater Dolorosa, Kali; finally as the Ocean which is the source of life and of life renewed

SPHERE OF DESTINATION: Tiphareth (Beauty)

> *Hebrew Divine Name:* Yahveh Eloah V'Daath
>
> *Planetary correspondence:* The Sun
>
> *Element:* Air
>
> *Symbols:* The crystalline pyramid of spirit supported by the pillars of the four elements, the solar disc, the eight-rayed Star
>
> *Magical phenomenon:* Assimilation of, and transformation in, the solar light

Comments

On the Tree of Life this Path runs from Netzach to Tiphareth in symmetry to the course of the 26th Path from Hod to Tiphareth. This 24th Path is also in its significance a necessary balance and sequel to the other.

The Song of Praises celebrates for this Path the enigmatic Fish which symbolizes its strange and subtle nature. The Fish is the pictographic interpretation of the Hebrew letter Nun; it is also a variant of the zodiacal symbol of this Path, the Scorpion, brought into harmony with the watery nature of that sign which gives the Path its element.

The letter Mem, which signifies "the Waters" in the sense of the great Mother-Ocean, does not come into this series of Paths. We do indeed meet with an aspect of that great reality: but here the emphasis is not so much upon the source of Life as upon the shadow of Death which haunts it.

In the "comments" on the 26th Pathworking we have looked at the danger perceived by the Qabalistic philosophy, and by many religions, that the rational consciousness might make a wrong choice by clinging to the life of the emotions and instincts, instead of aspiring first to its own spiritual completion by the higher faculties. To make the latter choice will bring the whole pattern of life—including that of the lower self—into full and harmonious realization.

Because the rational consciousness (sometimes called the ego consciousness because it is what we most often designate as "I") has the possibility to bring the whole personality to ruin by making a wrong choice,[8] some thinkers in both East and West have come to the conclusion that not only the Nephesh is evil but the "ego consciousness" is also evil. They rightly perceive that we should choose to be governed by the Higher Self, that is by our supernal faculties: but they frequently fail to perceive that it is precisely the ego—rational consciousness—which has to make the vital choice. Neither the Nephesh nor the physical body can make it: it has to be the "I" which consciously wills and determines the matter, and which maintains that resolution.

However, this uneasy awareness of our personal autonomy is the youngest of our faculties, and there are circumstances in which its abdication can seem the simplest and best solution to the human problem. Confronted as we are upon this Path with the allure and the menace of the depths, and facing that confrontation entirely from the astral level—entirely from the level of the Nephesh, as we must do before the attainment of Tiphareth—a return to the womb, a cessation of personal volition, can seem a "consummation devoutly to be wished." Therefore, although we first take this Path "out of order" before the 25th so as to taste of its darker potential, its completion is necessarily deferred until after the 25th has been successfully achieved. We must have achieved our right of way through the Gate of the Sun before we can arise from the deeps of this night. It is in the Briatic vision of the "Four Living Beings" previously mentioned, that the quarter denoted by the sign Scorpio is denoted instead by the soaring Eagle. It is not by obliteration of selfhood but by illumination of vision that we find the Mother as bright sustainer of life rather than as dark destroyer.

The 32 Paths of Wisdom, while having allusions here which apply also to the Mother's essential nature in Binah, comprehends also her power of appearing according to the nature and capacity of those who seek her. She is the Image-maker, and her own forms are beyond our power to number.

---

8. Needless to say, the extent or permanence attributed to such ruin would also be governed by one's personal system of beliefs.

The Working of the 24th Path

We are standing in a temple in which our first impression is of light and vitality.

Seven hanging lamps, suspended at equal distances around the central area of the temple, burn with steady emerald-like points of green flame; while over the central Bomos, the Lamp of the Mysteries sheds its white radiance, illumining the brilliant green covering of the Bomos and the Mystical Tessera which rests upon it. And, pervading and finding expression through all these things is the feeling of serene and beneficent sunshine.

There is a clear sunlit sky outside, seen through the open doorway which, with the two pillars, Machetes and Nomothetes, is behind us. Yet now a glorious beam of golden light flashes towards us from the far side of the temple, across the Bomos. Passing around the Bomos,-we-go to seek the-source of this inspiring radiance.

Directly opposite the door of the temple is an alcove, which enshrines a large and beautiful symbol. A large equal-armed cross, standing upright, forms the lower part of this symbol. The four arms of the cross are of stone; that on the right colored olive green, that on the left russet, the lowest arm black and the highest citrine. Surmounting the cross, at a height slightly above our heads, stands a circular frame of malachite enclosing a shining mirror whose diameter is the same as the width of the cross. Placed in this way, the mirror reflects nothing but the brightness outside.

For some time we contemplate this symbol. It most plainly represents the powers and qualities of the Four Elements surmounted by the pure radiance of the Sun Sphere. But, since the Sun in its reality symbolizes for us the world of Spirit, a deeper mystery is hinted in the image we are contemplating. For the total image—the equal-armed cross supporting the circle—is the sign of Venus, the planetary power which not only represents the forces of Nature but also signifies Harmony; and here it can betoken especially the great harmony and equilibrium between our higher nature and our lower when they are brought into unity.

This suggests a further conclusion. Surely, by sincere aspiration, we can mount naturally and easily through the lower order of things into the higher, and find awaiting us in the spiritual world all the shining reality of which the beauty of the lower worlds is but the darker substructure? We are native to all the Worlds—the material world, the astral world, the worlds of mind and of spirit—and therefore, surely, we have but to take as our starting point the sphere of the forces of Nature, in order to go forth and to claim our inheritance?

Standing before the symbol, we look more attentively into the alcove which contains it. There is a space between the symbol and the wall of the temple. Stepping aside to look into that space, we discover therein a door; the door is slightly ajar, and it leads to the outer world.

We pass through the door, and find ourselves walking upon a path which leads beneath a heavy arch of leafy stems of climbing roses. These stems are laden with buds, but there are no blooms as yet; and as we pass beneath this arch, the sharp thorns catch at us.

We leave the shadow of the arch, but do not find ourselves in the expected sunshine. Here is a different region, a place of silver mist: an all-enveloping mist which hides even the ground beneath our feet.

We tread lightly, silently. Or do we float here, navigating unmeasured deeps of mist with neither bearing nor sounding to direct us? We would go more slowly if we could, halt if we could, yet still our ankles move and we glide onward.

Nothing here threatens us. We are not cold nor hot, not weary, not menaced by anything. Only, we are lost: lost to sight and hearing, bewildered, troubled. Nothing threatens us. We fear that Nothing. Nothing, Nothing.

We are oppressed by the silver mist, by the silence and the lack of form. If we could stand still awhile we might consider what course to take; but on what would we establish an opinion, by what reasoning would we decide? Still we move onward, our senses straining for any least impression to engage them. At last, searching through the bland barriers of the mist, they find contact: something which the sight sees not, but seems faintly to taste, something which the hearing hears not but seems delicately to brush upon. This presence is behind us, unseen, unheard as yet, but menacing, approaching stealthily. We would flee from it because of its mysterious approach. We are drawn to it, because it exists and moves.

We cannot halt our gliding progress forward, nor, we find, can we hasten it. As if we moved through some sluggish liquid denser than water, we advance only by conforming our pace to its slow yielding. During our first struggles against it, as if we were setting up an opposing vibration in the atmosphere, the mist surrounding us darkens from silver to a lurid deep greenish blue. We have thus made worse our condition for no gain. In the unbroken and seemingly unbreakable silence, it is as if our hearts cry aloud for aid. Even if we were to be answered by that which pursues us, even that would be welcome.

The stillness hangs heavy as if none had heard. But now, as slowly we continue to advance, a shaft of white light seems to dart down from the shadow above us to the shadow before us; it darts down, and there remains, gliding slowly onwards so as to maintain constantly the, same distance ahead. As we gaze at it, there is a movement within that light. Within the shaft, somewhat above the height of our own heads, a countenance turns to look upon us.

We see no form of a body, and the features are fashioned of the light itself. It is a commanding face, broad at the cheekbones, with aquiline features, eyes deep-set but penetrating, the mouth and chin austere and resolute. Then it turns away again while the shaft of light continues to move steadily before us; but we know, beyond any doubt, that those features of light have truly looked upon us, those deep-set eyes have seen even within our hearts. This luminous Being will be our Guide.

More confidently now we move upon our way. But the silence is no longer unbroken. Now a brief snatch of speaking, ended before we can begin to understand it, sounds suddenly in the air above us. Vainly we try to recall it, to hear it again in memory well enough to hazard at least a guess as to the words, but we cannot even remember the sound well enough to know if it was a man's voice or a woman's. We stumble, and lose time while we struggle in the heavy air. It seems to us that the shaft of white light has moved further away from us. We dismiss the disturbing voice from our consideration, and press steadily on towards the radiance of our Guide.

Now brighter than a star, yet lovely with all the gentle changeful hues of pearl, a burst of light shines forth above us a moment, and is gone. Our eyes seek after it, wonderingly, yet to no avail; and now, perforce, we turn again towards the austere shaft of light which guides us through this region of vapors.

Again a sound of voices: voices most musical now, uttering unknown words yet sweet to the ear as a soft sound of bells. At the same time a cluster of lights, high above, diffused by the mist, shines briefly upon us with a glow of rose-color and lilac. Now sound and light are gone, before we could fix attention upon either; but it seems to us as we remember that perhaps beyond the lovely gleam of light we saw for a moment reclining forms, faces that looked down to us. Perhaps they were only shapes of fantasy: we do not know, but we raise our arms to them as a sign in case they may have reality.

Again we stumble, and now we seem to be falling slowly forward. Soon, indeed, we cannot tell whether we are falling: we seem suspended, turning helplessly as we float in a void. Gradually the deep greenish blue shadow which has surrounded us begins to disperse. We are drifting in an atmosphere of milky light in which radiance moves and eddies, as if the mist were at each moment about to part.

Now all about us, sometimes coming close and sometimes fading, sound again sweet voices, with brief unrecognizable fragments of thrilling music. Away before us, moving steadily onward, we see the shaft of pure white light, the austere Presence which guided us through the murky shadows, but at this time we have little heed for it. A world of beauty and light is about to burst upon us, to overwhelm us with its wonder and bliss.

And now in visions through which we float, we are encompassed with delight. In slow succession we pass through landscapes of stupendous loveliness, palaces adorned with more than earthly slendor, swaying oceans, illimitable cosmic vistas. At one moment we look from sublime and awesome mountain summits, where the wind blows the white dust of eternal snow across the burning cheeks of skies filled with sunrise; at another moment we pass through green secret valleys where water murmurs all around under the heavy bowers and drifts of leafage, and the birds fly securely as in a primal paradise.

Now we gaze across a plain of gold, where black trees with a sheen of copper in their leaves stand like sentinels placed at random. Upon a hill beyond is a city, where the fortified walls are of white marble and the towers are roofed with blood-red tiles.

We glide to that city and enter into the topmost fortress. There within the spacious square of the enclosing wall is a garden open to the sky. There, too, is a shining pool whereon white swans float, and beside which peacocks walk and spread their plumes to catch the sparkling drops from the tall jet of a fountain. In this garden upon brightly colored cushions sit young men and maidens of noble form and feature, some playing musical instruments and some happily conversing. We hear snatches of their talk, and when it is not directly of love it is upon the great themes of beauty, truth and goodness; but always with delight. Then we are borne onwards from that place.

Everything we might conceive to exist of beauty, of whatever kind, is here disclosed to us, each marvel seeming real and tangible around us until it gives place to the next. There are no bounds, no measure in beauty: a galaxy whose birth we have witnessed in the splendors of space may seem intimate and precious like a cluster of gems to be held in the hand, or we may find ourselves walking softly through the wonderland of a single blossom, not to mar the dewy surface of the luminous living velvet beneath our feet.

Most lovely and most poignant among all these wonders, is the envisioned beauty of living beings human and non-human, earthly and unearthly. Forms known to us, loved by us, appear among the rest, even as they are known to us and yet transfigured: princely, heroic, angelic in their appeal. And continually the delicious haunting music besets us, breaking and changing when we would listen to it, elusive, fitful, incomplete.

Time after time it seems to us that we are about to make that transition which seemed so possible and so easy: to pass from the world of beauty which can be aprrehended by the senses, naturally and without effort to the world of spiritual beauty which is of beauty's essence. Yet the transition does not come. That which we perceive, see, hear, become aware of no matter how intimately, still remains external to us. We do not, cannot, touch it soul to soul, essence to essence. Yet that is what we desire, which truly beongs to our highest and most inward nature could we but achieve it. Without that, all the vision of beauty or loveliness of body, soul or mind which surrounds us is frustratingly, heartbreakingly unattainable. Our contact with it, which should be immortalized, is but transitory. We feel saddened, wearied, cloyed but yet infinitely dissatisfied. We try to turn away, but the thrilling sounds are still about us as we go, although the soft radiance fades swiftly to the darkness of night in which we see only the light of the guiding presence still going before us.

Now we have become aware of another presence accompanying us: other than the visible light of our Guide, other than the vanished beings of beauty. Like a slow beginning of warm rain, like the first deepening of shadows towards evening, this presence has impinged scarcely at all upon our consciousness until we give attention to it. We feel certain it is the same which was pursuing us previously, only at this time it is less strange to us and we feel less threatened by it. It is like something familiar from long ago even though forgotten now, something that attracted us perhaps in childhood: the whispering voice of a forbidden playmate, the bitter fragrance and the imagined flavor of bright red berries or of pallid mushrooms. We cannot name this presence, but it is with us almost palpably.

Our Guide pauses and turns to look at us, then goes forward again. As we follow, we find that at the place where that luminous Being paused, the level surface underfoot abruptly ends. Now we must make our way upon a bridge: a narrow bridge which trembles and sways beneath our steps. In the darkness we can see neither the depths of the chasm we are crossing nor its further side, but from far below we hear the roaring voice of a torrent. As we advance, we become accustomed to the movement of the bridge, and more boldly but at an unhurried pace we move forward at some distance behind our Guide's bright shaft of light.

Suddenly, out of the dark sky, a flock of birds assails us: strange fiery birds with glowing blood-red plumage and fetid breath. Raising our arms, we ward off the attacks of beak and claw, but the birds, alternately darting in and retreating, shed from their flapping wings red hot feathers which sear our skin as they drift against us. These birds, while they attack, continually reiterate a shrill, harsh cry which pierces our ears and pours forth upon us a stench of carrion.

While we are defending ourselves from these horrible entities it is impossible for us to move forward upon the narrow, swaying bridge. As we struggle to defend ourselves against our assailants, the movement of the bridge becomes a dangerously increasing rhythmic swing. We look to our Guide for aid in this desperate situation, and as we fix our gaze on the bright shaft of light it swiftly moves out a little way to the side of the bridge, it hovers for a moment above the chasm, then, becoming elongated downwards, it descends, flashing, until the foot of the column seems to rest upon the surface of the dark waters rushing far beneath us.

The message is unmistakeable, and we perceive that longer reflection will add nothing to our resolution. Facing the side of the bridge where the darkness of the chasm is illuminated by our Guide's shaft of white radiance, we choose a moment when the swaying of the bridge impels us forward and then, adding our own impetus to the movement, we plunge headlong down into the dark water. The fiery birds follow us, giving forth more violently than ever their repulsive shrieking and fluttering their wings so that the burning feathers shower upon us; then, as we sink below the surface of the torrent, they dart away and are gone.

We are not in darkness as we move submerged, for the light of our Guide goes above us upon the water, and the whole body of shimmering fluid around us is transfused with that radiance. Even though the light becomes less distinct as the powerful current carries us onward to greater and greater depths, its source remains always above us as our Guide constantly watches over our course.

Soon it appears that however wide may have been the torrent into which we plunged, now we have been swept into a far greater expanse of rushing water. Huge boulders are piled beneath us, their surfaces polished so smooth by the immemorial current that their dark colors seem almost translucent as the light strikes upon them: the obscure brownish grey of flint, the angry red-brown of jasper, marble of mottled green and brown and black, the inscrutable green of obsidian, slatey blues of other rocks. Among this chaos of boulders there appear as we move above them impenetrable caves and crevices, at the entrance of which strange life-forms await us with menace or with cautious hunger.

Here, clustered upon the rocks overhanging a deep cavity, are a number of seeming flowers, each with a disk of petal-shaped rays some seven feet across or more and brilliant with concentric bands of vivid color: bright greenish blue with violet, or rose pink with deep orange, or sulphur yellow with magenta. At the center of each flaunting disk is a steep funnel whose mouth, about a yard across, is guarded by a dense ring of vertical spines, greyish in color with green tips needle sharp; among the spines arise five pale filaments, spaced evenly around the flower, each filament having at its tip a small darkly gleaming sphere. At first we take these filaments to be the stamens of the flower, but as we approach the dark globules turn in our direction and follow our movement, and we realize they are the eyes of an almost animal organism. Evidently in response to what the eyes have seen, the sharp spines turn outward to form a horizontal ring, and we become aware of a strong suction pulling us towards the central funnel of each of the giant blossoms. These gaudy predators, of whom the sea anemones of Earth are but a tiny shadow, would evidently devour us. Once we were drawn into the funnel, the spines with their poisonous-looking green barbs would turn inwards to prevent any possible escape, and we should feel our energies, consciousness and life itself being slowly drained from us by the enveloping organism. As we gaze in fascinated horror at the concentric bands of lurid color, we allow ourselves to be drawn almost inperceptibly nearer until the increased pull of the funnels warns us of our danger. Then, struggling with all our strength, however, we regain enough distance from them so that the current sweeping us onward outmatches the strength of those living vortices. Without thought and without hesitation we entrust ourselves once more to the embrace of the onrushing current, as to a deliverer.

But now a predator of a different kind appears stealthily out of the further shadows. It moves serpentlike, curving from side to side, then pauses to watch from the outer edge of the faint circle of light which contains us. This entity has its own greenish glow of luminescence, in which we see it clearly: with its body colored a mottled dark red above and pale nacreous blue below, it has its head shaped into a narrow snout in which, at each side of the ferocious armory of teeth, a long, incurved ivory fang projects downwards from the upper jaw. A spiny scarlet fin, like a crest, extends through the midline of the skull down the back-bone. Despite its generally serpentine form this entity has several fish-like fins, but its tail lashing from side to side as it swims is not fishlike: it ends in a tapering point from which now and again the tip of a quiver-ing steel-blue barb appears. The unchanging yellow eyes which watch us from the sides of the head are bright with a cold intelligence greater and quicker than that of either fish or serpent.

As this monster looks at us, its green luminescence becomes brighter and stronger, and the spines of the scarlet crest rise more erect. We want to escape at once from its threatening presence, but at first we are at a loss how to do so. When we maintain our position or simply drift with the current, it does the same. When we actively move away from it, it begins to close in on us. To move faster is to speed its pursuit. We have to beware not only of the powerful fanged jaws, but also of the whiplike tail which from time to time lashes suddenly sideways and forward, pro-truding its vicious and certainly poison-dealing stiletto. We move this way and that, frantically conscious that our movements are too slow to outdistance such an opponent, but hoping at least to evade it. A deep gully, which runs away to our left among the boulders below, catches our attention: we impel ourselves downwards as we strive to reach this gully. But our pursuer divines our intention, and, throwing off ripples of green phosphorescence which shimmer away like flakes of pale emer-ald, it moves swiftly in a graceful zig-zag to intercept us before we reach the desired gully. We abandon that hope of escape, and turn again to the course of the current.

As we are carried onward we see, to our right, arising from the depths, a group of great rocks set almost vertically, as if tilted up by some subsid-ence in the underlying bed. This formation appears to offer us a refuge, and quickly as we are able, we turn our course towards it. Again, how-ever, our pursuer moves more swiftly; and a streak of green light flashing through the water gives us warning that we cannot reach that stronghold. Once more we allow the course of the current to guide us.

We resolve to move downwards through the water, so that the wilderness of boulders may afford us some protection. The boulders will impede our progress and we know not what other foes may lurk among them, but at least that voracious fanged snout cannot dart forward upon us here, nor can the lethal dart of the tail make its lashing sidelong swing to strike at us. The monster follows us at a distance, and we strive desperately with all our faculties to hasten our descent.

At the depth we have reached, the white radiance sent forth by our Guide is hardly visible to us; but suddenly among the boulders there appears a bright gleam as of sunshine. It is made up of every faint ray transmitted from above, every straying glimmer of light and phosphorescence in the waters, garnered, reflected and magnified among wonderful objects of gold and gems which lie scattered here. As we make our way among the boulders, in one deep crevice and another we behold more of these gleaming splendors, revealed at the very limits of our power to discern them. It seems to us that the monster has impelled us to discover these things and to look upon them. Sometimes, too, a slight variation in the strong current will cause some of these hidden treasures to stir and shift, and momentarily a jeweled cup, a ring or some other object will be mysteriously lifted and turned about as if for our particular notice, and will then sink again into obscurity. In spite of the fascination of these marvelous things, however, we do not linger, for whenever we glance back we see our pursuer still inexorably following, behind and above us.

Now as we move deeper we find ourselves in the irresistible grip of a flow more powerful than that which carried us along at a higher level Almost in darkness we are swept onwards, battered by rocks as we are borne from one narrow channel to another, our limbs tossed violently this way and that. We have no knowledge of where we may be in this world of waters, nor whither we are bound; until, unexpectedly, our movement changes to a swift, smooth course which seems to cradle us in a haven of peace.

It comes to us that we are very weary of the violence and harshness of this journey. As if in a dream, we recall vividly the fair forms and colors, the sweet and thrilling sounds of the earlier part of this Path, when we were almost, but not quite, able to transfer ourselves into the blissful world of spiritual loveliness. From that point, through no choice save the necessity of each moment, we have descended further and further from those shining heights.

Now in the dim light we perceive that we are being carried helplessly forward and down towards the brink of a gaping pit. The monster has followed us thus far, but now with a final glint from its cold eyes it turns away and leaves us. We, held fast in the current, are powerless even to struggle. As we reach the brink, the pit below us appears to be the crater of an extinct and long submerged volcano, a portal to unimaginable depths. Again, however, even here, there comes to us the certainty that we are not alone. Again we are aware of that unnameable presence, known from aforetime: a presence comforting and yet alluring, filling us with that sweet desire of what appears inevitable, which is so often called a sense of destiny. How it sings to us, calls to us!

In fascination we look down into the rushing depths of the pit. Their further distance is filled with a dark, intense green-blue, mysteriously reflected within itself to an infinite degree. In the heart of that most profound color is a remote circular space of ultimate blackness. We are falling towards it with what feels like a lethargic slowness, and with exactly the same slowness the blackness sinks to yet further depths.

Gradually as we gaze into that blackness the contours of a face appear to us, even as they might appear when a dark surface is used for scrying. It is the face of a woman: a face neither young nor old, but immovably calm and strong. The darkness against which we see that face appears suited to its natural complexion. The sorrow and wisdom of all the ages, as well as their voluptuous joy, are in those deep eyes set wide apart beneath their heavy brows; the high cheekbones, aquiline features and firm chin are those of a woman accustomed to rule, a matriarch whether noblewoman, peasant or prophetess. And even though we have not seen this face before, we recognize her. This is she whose unseen presence has haunted us for so long on this Path. We cannot turn away. The intense magnetism of those eyes draws us, calls to us irresistibly, so that we reach out our arms to her as to a mother. All our yearning is towards that face, forgetting totally in what fatal ambience we behold it.

O the bliss of encounter with this mystery, of mingling our being with it! Would not oblivion therein be the ultimate ecstasy?

If this working is being conducted for the first time, that is, in series and prior to the working of the 25th Path, continue with the text below which concludes in the Moon Sphere.

If this working is being conducted subsequent to working the 25th Path, continue with the normal text on page 260 which concludes in the Sun Sphere.

We welcome the profound sweetness of this surrender. Receive us, O Mother!

But no! In an instant the pit is transpierced by a shaft of dazzling silver radiance. We are caught into that beam of light: we know not whether we are lifted up or whether all the vision of darkness is stripped away from us, but at once we stand face to face with our Guide upon the swaying bridge. Yet the darkness, the wrenching and battering of the current among the boulders, the measureless depth of the crater, the allure of the Dark Mother, are still fresh in our memory; in our hearts we ask, *Why had we to endure these things?*

It appeaars to us that our Guide replies, *Only by enduring them could you know their power.* But, the next moment, we cannot recall the tones of that voice. We look again upon our Guide, and it appears to us that that countenance of light, and the remembered countenance of the Dark Mother, are the same. But we dare not to ask, *Who are you?*

And now we are not gazing upon any face, but upon a whirling spiral of silver light, rippling and flashing. We are drawn swiftly into this spiral, surrounded by its bright convolutions, until suddenly it expands and becomes all-encompassing.

The whirling motion ceases, and we see only the gentle undulations of silver light extending in every direction. We stand motionless, reverent and wondering, while gradually the ripples of silver light become edged and tipped with delicate traces of violet.

All at once we feel smooth rock beneath our feet. We look down and see beneath us a translucent lustrous surface which gathers the light into itself like a moonstone. We look about us again: the silver ripples have formed themselves into a distinct image. Around us as we stand upon the moonstone floor is a wide circle of nine tall crystal columns, equally spaced; their transparent shafts gleam in the soft light, and from within them sparkles the random brilliance of scattered flecks of gold. Before us, in the center of this circle, is a round pool in which the water is still, black and fathomless.

We look to the space outside the ring of crystal columns. Except in one direction, all is obscured in a soft blue luminous haze; but directly before us, some distance beyond the columns, is the foot of a mighty stairway which ascends until it too is lost to our sight in the blue haze. At each side of the foot of this stairway stands the colossal rock-carved form of a Kerub represented as a man-headed, winged bull, indomitable in strength and serene of countenance like those of Assyria. These figures have eyes of crystal which flash piercingly through the misty atmosphere; and they stand each with the wing further from the stair upraised, but the wing nearer the stair extended across it. Thus the two sculptured Kerubim stand with wing-tips touching to guard the stair from access.

Thus have we returned from our journeying, and now we rest in the Sphere of the Moon.

We have traveled the Path of the Scorpion towards the Sphere of the Sun. We have not on this occasion entered that Sphere, for this Path which proceeds from the Sphere of Venus—the Sphere which governs the forces of Nature—does not of itself give access to more than the mysteries of the Astral World. Therein lies the great enigma, and the glory, of human life: that in order to realize our nature in its fullness, we must transcend our natural powers.

None the less, this dark and perilous Path has revealed wondrous things. We have truly looked upon the treasures of the Deep, the gold of the Unconscious which never sees the light of day. Our Guide upon this Path has not sought to spare us its experience, and in this we can discern at least one sign of the kinship, or identity, of that mysterious luminous Being with the Dark Mother, upon one of whose countenances we have also looked.

For She who is here the Dark Mother (but who can also appear as the Snow Queen, or as that "nightmare Life-in-Death" whose "skin is white as leprosie"[9]) is indeed a mother to us, since it is She who lures us into incarnation to taste again the fruits thereof: who tempts us into the way of Life which brings us also under the yoke of Death. In ancient Qabalistic lore she is also Lilith the Serpent Woman, holding out to us the fruit of the Tree of Knowledge whose taste precipitates us into the bondage of the material world, even as in Greek lore Persephone is lured by Hades or Pluto, her male tempter, to eat of the pomegranate which makes her half-subject to the Kingdom of Death. Always the whisper is "Taste and try!"—but if we were to refuse the experience and the penalty, we should also miss the glory to come. Only after passing through the lesser Mysteries of Yetzirah can we come to the Greater Mysteries of Briah.

Not foolishly, therefore, did we entrust ourselves to our luminous Guide, whom we may perceive as either the son or the other self of the great Ocean Mother. Nor are we mistaken to desire union with her; but a return to the instinctual life of the natural world, or of the womb, is not the way. Not through disillusionment, nor through weariness, nor through the fascination of self-immolation can we prevail.

However, the treading of this Path, even as it has been, marks a progress. Returning from the Path of the Goat, we arrive in the Earth Sphere. Returning from the Path of the Scorpion we arrive in the Sphere of the Moon. And directly above the Sphere of the Moon on the Central Column of the Tree of Life shines forth the Sphere of the Sun, the glorious objective of this present series of pathworkings. When once we have attained thereto, when we travel again this Path of the Scorpion we shall find—as with the Path of the Goat—the conclusion of the

---

9. *The Rime of the Ancient Mariner*, by Samuel Taylor Coleridge.

adventure to be other than it has been. By these Paths also, when that happy time comes, we shall pass as victors and the gate of the Sphere of the Sun shall stand open for us.

To gain this consummation, may we mount securely upon the Stair, and may we speed swiftly and freely as the Arrow!

Battery 3-5-3

The Working of the 25th Path

(Correspondences)

SPHERE OF COMMENCEMENT: Yesod (Foundation)

Hebrew Divine Name: Shaddai El Chai

Planetary correspondence: The Moon

Element: Air

Symbol: The crystal cube

Magical phenomena: Astral visions of the four elements

PATH OF THE TREE OF LIFE: 25

Intelligence: The 25th Path is the Path of Trial, the Critical Intelligence: so named because it constitutes the principal trial set by the Creator for all those who aspire to perfection.

Hebrew Divine Name: El

Influence on Path: Sagittarius (the Archer)

Planetary correspondence: Jupiter

Hebrew Letter: Samekh (Prop)

Path Stanza: Stone of the Patriarch's dream, pillow
       austere couching the wanderer
    While between heaven and earth glorious
       Shapes came and went ceaselessly:
  Hail to thee, Gate of the Worlds, column
       unhewn set for memorial
       Pointing the Arrow-road!

Tarot arcanum: Temperance (14)

Element of Path: Fire

Symbols: The thyrsus, the straight path, the arrow

Living beings: The Lovers, the Angels of ascent and descent, the Centaurs and other bi-formed ones

Magical phenomena: Divine intoxication; visions of the Androgyne, the Eternal Child and the Lion

SPHERE OF DESTINATION: Tiphareth (Beauty)

Hebrew Divine Name: Yahveh Eloah V'Daath

Planetary correspondence: The Sun

Elements: Air; Spirit (the fifth element)

Symbols: The solar mirror, the truncated pyramid Mineral: Topaz

Magical Phenomena: Vision of the Self-made-perfect, manifestation of the Day-Star, apotheosis of the four elements in the unity of spirit

Comments

This is the crowning Path of the present series: the Path by which Tiphareth is to be attained, and, with that Sephirah, entrance to the World of Briah. Small wonder that *The 32 Paths of Wisdom* calls it "the Path of Trial, the Critical Intelligence." *The Song of Praises* makes reference to the traditional identification of the letter Samekh, "the prop," with the "stone of the patriarch's dream" (Genesis 28:10-22), and also to the straight flight of the arrow to the mark which is suggested by the zodiacal sign for the Path, Sagittarius.

In fact the name "the Path of the Arrow" refers not only, of right, to this Path itself, but to the Paths 32, 25, and 13 taken as a single straight course. In the latter sense, "the Path of the Arrow" is traditionally understood to be the route of the dedicated mystic, passing without digression through the Gates of the Worlds to the divine consummation of the mystic's existence in the white brilliance of Kether. Here upon the 25th Path itself we are treading only a part of that way, but reflection upon the mystic's singleness of purpose may help us understand the nature of the "trial" of this Path.

What has to be attained here is a major change—the major change—not only in the *mode* of consciousness but at the same time in the *level* of consciousness. A new way of looking at things has to be effected, a new and spiritually-based self-responsibility has to be won: and this by a specialized use of the normal means of alterations of consciousness, that is, total absorption in an activity. The nature and direction of the Path, with its symbols, are to do the rest: to produce the "upwards fall" which is to take the aspirant through the Gate.

Upon this 25th Path, as upon the 26th, there is a pageant of revelry: but this is Dionysian and fiery while the other was Bacchanalian and earthy. These attributions are deeply relevant. Fire, not Earth, is the element of severe testing. Bacchus is a rustic divinity, whereas Dionysus means "The Lame God," and Jacob—he of the dream—is, by reason of his wrestling with the angel, the lame patriarch. Both these heroic figures are thus types of the Sacred King, one of the great embodiments of dedication in the Western Mystery Tradition. Here the beings whose procession joins with our progress are, like ourselves, hastening directly forward on the uphill Path.

Many of the entities whom we encounter, or see in vision, upon this Path are of dual form: the centaurs, the androgyne and others. These foreshadow for us one of the characteristics of the World of Briah, that in it the divine and the human modes of creative thought meet and mingle. Other entities, of single form—as the Lion—are symbols of solar and Tipharic power.

In the episode of the truncated pyramid in the latter part of this Pathworking, it is made very plain that our whole progress towards the Sphere of the Sun, towards Briah, and towards adepthood, is by an ascent through the levels of our own being. Like the spider (a living eight-pointed star) we have spun from our own substance, in our involutionary descent into matter, the very thread which is now our stairway of return. We set out upon this path, in Yesod, with astral visions of the four elements, the components of the world in which we live and of which our lower nature is a part. We close it in Tiphareth, with a vision of the spiritual realities underlying the four elements. That which we have left has become ours more truly: and in our continued journeys upon the Paths, with our gaze drawn ever to a newer wonder, we shall find ourselves more truly yet.

The Working of the 25th Path

We stand in impenetrable darkness, enwrapped in a total silence. We try to see around us and above us, but there is nothing visible. We look down, and find we are standing upon a large cube of crystal, colorless and almost perfectly transparent; it would be invisible in the blackness but for a faint glimmer of light which emanates from the rock itself. This crystal cube rests upon nothing, seeming to be suspended motionless in the void of space. We raise our heads and stand passively. The heavy darkness around us is still totally and completely silent.

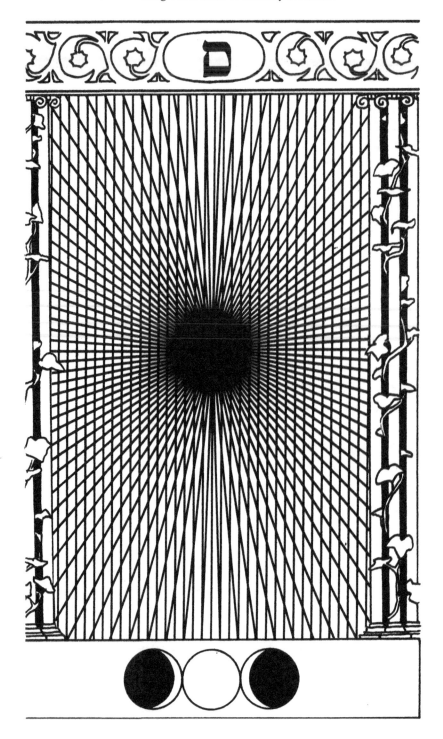

Gradually, from the darkness before us, comes the delicate breath of a gentle breeze. At first we scarcely feel it; quickly it grows stronger, caressing our cheeks and carrying the sweet refreshing fragrance of innumerable flowers. From behind us comes a sound of water cascading from a height. We turn to look, and there meets our sight a sheer fall of translucent water, descending as if over a towering precipice; a cataract which shows itself pale blue and gem-like against the darkness. Ever and anon a flashing trail of droplets, sparkling like a necklace of sapphires, is thrown off into space, or a sudden mist of smaller drops hangs for an instant like a veil, filled with bands of intense violet and scarlet and bright yellow light of incredible loveliness, until at once the colors shimmer and are gone. As we watch the waterfall, we see its changeful beauty reflecting a stronger and more lasting red-gold brightness than any prismatic splendor. We turn back to our original position and find, on our right, the manifestation of a great fire whose hot and glowing heart is open to us, surrounded on three sides by tongues of yellow flame rushing madly upwards. The roaring and crackling of the fire dispels from us the murmur of the breeze and the voice of the waterfall alike.

Expectantly we look to our left, confident that in that direction some other manifestation must meet our gaze. Nor are we disappointed. On that side there lies open a wide, smiling valley. Beyond an orchard of small trees laden with ripening fruit, we see low slopes of rich pasture land, through which runs a line of darker and denser vegetation evidently marking the course of a river. Above this peaceful scene stands a ridge of steep hills covered with forest trees; and above the hills again, edged with lines and scrolls of light like a silver filigree, rises a wall of snowy mountain peaks. Above the summit of a cone-shaped peak which overtops the rest, directly above the beautiful valley, a dense black cloud holds a glare of reflected fire; but here the reflection does not come from the leaping flames which are at our right side. This illumination is the hectic warning hue cast upwards from a raging volcanic furnace which seethes deep within the mountain.

We remain for a moment surrounded by the sweet gentle wind, the waterfall, the roaring fire and the vision of Earth in which all the elements are combined; then all these manifest-ations together begin to fade from our consciousness, returning slowly to the silent darkness from which they came forth, as we perceive directly overhead a faint speck of light, far distant. We fix our attention on this new phenomenon. At a great speed it approaches, and at last it seems to increase a little in size and distinctness. Still it is directly above us, but now it loses velocity and looks as if hovering there, growing slowly larger and brighter, until we perceive it as a central white light, pulsating and brilliant, surrounded by an aura of gold. Suddenly it leaps downwards and stands before us, not resting upon the crystal: a tall flame of living white light, radiating the glorious golden aura which now appears as a long ovoid surrounding it.

As we gaze upon this wonderful Being, the golden aura begins to emit a secondary region of brightness, also golden and shining although less intensely brilliant than itself. This outer aura rapidly spreads outwards until it reaches us and encompasses us. We are surrounded with its living warmth; it pervads us, we breathe it in and feel a radiant wave of vital strength, wellbeing and happiness surging through us with the golden light. We feel drawn by the magnetism of joy and love to the central Being of white flame, but we are not overwhelmed: the boundary of the inner ovoid of golden brilliance, within which we cannot pass, keeps us in the outer region of power. Nevertheless, the light holds us in a mighty attraction. As suddenly as it descended, the Being of white flame leaps and soars upwards again; and all of us, held securely in its outer aura, feel ourselves drawn upwards from the crystal rock, soaring through space as if in the train of a living comet.

We know nothing of the course of our journey, but the mere motion is bliss. To try to reckon time would be meaningless. A sound like rushing wind sings around us, and we are moving onwards; that is all we can tell.

As we continue our journey, the encompassing light of our Guide's outer aura fades gradually from our sight. We are moving now by our own inner impulse, and by our volition to follow the bright Being which goes in advance of us in the form of a shining white flame enveloped in its own golden aura. But, since the veil of radiance which previously closed us away from the space around us has disappeared, we are also able to look above us, beneath, and to each side as we proceed; and gradually we are able to discern numbers of wondrous Beings moving diagonally in front of us and all around us, some ascending towards the left, some to the right and others descending in the contrary directions. These beings appear as having tall slender human shapes of great beauty, garmented in pale luminous tints: their swift continuous motion seems to form a network of nacreous light all about us, rose and blue and saffron. Yet never do we directly encounter these shining travelers, although sometimes a fragment of music or of chanted song reaches us from them as they appear to come level with us. It is as if we had impinged upon another dimension of existence. So joyful and inviting is the sight and sound that we pause in our flight, uncertain, almost tempted to leave our course and to follow after such enchanting company. Our Guide, too, pauses in this moment of our decision. But no: we have chosen our Guide and our way, and we realize that in changing either we could win no true benefit upon this Path.

During our brief hesitation, however, the scene around us has begun to change. On all sides a mighty forest is spreading. Shafts of sunlight descend through heavy green foliage, to paint patterns of dappled gold upon the rich brown underfoot. Beneath the trees are dense thickets of fern and young saplings, climbing plants and bushes; we should hardly know there was a path through this wilderness, but for our Guide going forward luminously above it. With our feet going quietly over the soft mold, we follow. The voices of birds, the hum of bees, the sound of rustling leaves, together with the warm fragrance of moss and fern and of a myriad tiny blossoms, give life to the summer beauty of this magical forest scene.

Other sounds too drift to our ears as we move slowly along the faint winding track which leads us gradually uphill among the trees. From the green bowers on every hand come sudden stirrings of the leaves; and the soft and fragrant breeze carries broken snatches of speech, with the sounds of secret laughter and of candid kisses. Surely the forest is full of lovers, and of the sweet and sacred rites of love!

Eyes that we do not see, eyes intoxicated with love watch as we pass; lips afire with kissing whisper that strangers are nearby. But when we hear the whisper we ask ourselves, How are we strangers, when this enchanted forest and all it contains are a vital part of our own nature?

All at once we halt as an outburst of voices arises, voices male and female, joyfully calling one to another. Then, from a point close at hand but hidden from us by greenery, we hear the sounds of a happy throng breaking from the undergrowth and speeding, with swiftly thudding footfalls, through the forest in a direction away from us until the clamor is lost in distance. The magnetic pull of their running is almost physically palpable: it wellnigh carries us from our path as our imagination rushes forth, following those happy lovers, hand reaching for hand as they race through shadowed glade and across sunlit clearing, turning from obstacles, leaping over small streams, perhaps to plunge at last into some sweet lake or river, to bathe and swim together in the collective embrace of its waters.

But that is not upon our present path. The brilliant white flame which is our Guide, aureoled in golden light, hovers some distance ahead, silently awaiting us. We resume our progress through the forest. The birds still sing and the blossoms give forth their fragrance, but we no longer feel ourselves to be at one with the scene as we did before. Our goal is further on.

In a short time we find ourselves climbing a grassy slope beyond the wood, under an overcast sky. The leading flame goes before us as we mount steadily; we are facing into a cool wind which does not impede our progress, but which, rushing past our ears and catching at our garments, gives us the feeling that we are advancing at great speed. In fact there are no landmarks by which to measure the rate of our progress, and each one of us seems rapt into his or her inner consciousness as we mount onwards, onwards, aware only of our Guide going before us and the song of the wind flying past.

From behind us comes a crying and a wild chanting, with a thunder of hoofs. We are overtaken by a host of strong and gladsome beings: not as with the lovers in the forest each seeking beyond all else one other of their company, but each linked with the rest in equal love and fellowship. Here are graceful and stately nymphs, each one the Lady of a healing spring, a sacred grove or prophetic cavern. Here are Fauns—beings of the nature of the rustic Pan—some who teach, at need, the arts of survival in the wilds, some who are skilled in music and in the language of all the voices of Nature. Here are Centaurs, in form part horse and part human, mighty in strength but skilled in the arts of peace and wisdom: healers by knowledge of herbs, musicians, watchers of the skies. With these come

Sphynxes and Hippogriffs—entities with eagle-like head and wings upon the body of a horse—and eagle-headed Genies with human body; and many more besides in which the powers of humankind are supplemented by others typified under the form of lion and eagle, horse, ox, goat and reptile. All these entities, no matter how diverse in nature, have one characteristic in common: they all represent powers of inspiration, whether these are expressed in prophecy or through the other arts of life: directing and supporting our upward strivings, helping our lower nature to form and attune itself as a true receptacle for the Light from above. All these come garlanded with flowers, and some adorned too with the luster of massive ancient gems; and with them come human attendants, some of whom bear sistrums and rattles of every description, and singing in time with their sound. Others of the company bear each one a thyrsus, a tall festal wand made from a slender reed topped with a pine cone. With the revelers come likewise, running, prancing or flying, the beasts with which these entities have a partial affinity, drawn, with the whole procession, as if by the spirit of some great festival.

The mighty beings who have overtaken us pause and greet us, since we are traveling the same Path. Quickly we find garlands placed upon us: we have become part of this great progress, part of its joy and part too of its growing spirit of inspiration. The white flame which is our Guide goes ahead of us, and has now become the leader of the entire cavalcade. As we follow among our strange and marvelous companions, we begin to realize that they overtook us for this very purpose: to follow the wondrous Being of Light who is leading us.

Above us the sky is clearing again, and long shafts of bright sunshine strike downwards. To the right of our path rise gentle tree-covered slopes; to the left, low ridges of sandstone appear among the grass. The sky continues to clear and brighten, and the scene takes on a primeval and magical aspect.

Among the joyful company in which we move, excite-ment mounts higher as the chanting and the rhythm of the sistrums becomes more insistent. We find ourselves joining in the song, uttering melodious and resonant words whose meaning is unknown to us. The sound blends with the chanting of our companions, and in raising our voices we feel exhilarated, lifted above ourselves and made truly one with the mysterious festival in which we participate.

The procession becomes ecstatic. Sometimes a great winged being which has followed its course from on high will swoop down, and with loud ringing cries and beating pinions will encircle the concourse before mounting swiftly to the skies again. Sometimes a group of Fauns or Centaurs, or other entities, will break from the advancing throng, leaping and gyrating in a frenzied dance of delight before returning to their companions. Sometimes a voice, deep or shrill, will overtop the rest in powerful ringing utterance of phrases which fix themselves in the memory even though their meaning is unknown.

Now the space between the tree-grown slopes and the path widens into a circular clearing, a natural amphitheater. Towards its far end, the Being of Light who has led us here rises higher into the air and hovers there, a steady column of white flame enclosed in an aura of gold.

The onward journey ceases. Some members of the great processional gathering still chant rapturously, while those of the revelers who bear the thyrsus lead the assembly into a joyful dance. With one accord these emblems of the festival are raised and flourished with cries of exultation, while overhead the winged beings who are part of the company reiterate these cries as they hover and soar.

Spontaneously we are all caught up into a whirling celebration of pure cosmic gladness. Suddenly a renewed cry of delight from the thyrus bearers causes all eyes to turn towards them; and we see O wonder of wonders! Each slender reed, topped with its swaying pine cone, has burst into leaves which are neither of reed nor of pine. Thick clusters of vine leaves, with their sinuous stems and spiraling tendrils, gird them around; and, even as we watch, those leaves turn from green to gold and to scarlet, and among them sway heavy bunches of purple grapes.

This marvel lifts the spirits of the dancers to a frenzy. Faster and faster the throng moves, and we with it, until the surrounding scene spins and flashes, and the images and sounds of the festival, with even the presence of our Guide, fade from our consciousness. We who in the beginning of this adventure stood upon the crystal cube now find ourselves in a silent and all-encompassing ambience of intense luminous blueness; and here we remain motionless, passive and watchful.

Now a shimmering pulsation, seeming to come from afar off, sounds upon the air. Swiftly it grows louder and closer, until it is like a rapid clashing and ringing of cymbals all about us; and with it there sweeps across us a mighty wind, rushing and crying. Scattered flames of fire are carried in the course of this intense wind, streaming, flaring, scorching, as if they were nourished upon the air itself.

In the midst of this tempest of wind and flame there grows before our eyes a sphere of light, pulsating powerfully within itself with no reference to the surrounding tumult. This sphere of white light hangs before us, becoming stable as a large brilliant globe within which we can perceive another form coming into manifestation.

This form is a nude and vigorous human figure, androgynous in character. The strongly muscled legs are set astride, displaying male genitals, the penis erect. Up each leg is twined a serpent, with head turned outwards at the level of the hips. The necks of the serpents are grasped by the smooth hands of the upper torso, of which the arms, shoulders, upper abdomen and breasts are distinctively female. The whole of this androgynous figure radiates its own brightness, and the head is so luminous as to be indistinguishable to us.

Amid the clashings of cymbals, the rushing and crying of the wind, and the transient roaring of the flying flames as they pass by, this figure in its globe of light shines serenely. But now a voice is heard: a voice which may be carried to us upon the wind, or which may emanate from the visionary figure before us, or which may come from the unknown depths of our own being. In resonant and measured tones it chants strange, potent words which have the quality of a Gnostic invocation:

ZA-GOU-REH. ECh-AB-NETh-PhROM.

BI-ATh-I-A. BI-ATh-I-A-ChA. LA-I-LAM.

BAL-BA-OTh. ShA-BA-O. MEN-HOTh-PhRA.

ZA-GOU-REH. ZA-GOU-RI-EH.

I-APh-ChA-U. ATh-UM-I-OPh. SA-BA-ZA-I.

As the chant ends, a sudden loud clap of thunder shakes the atmosphere and at the same time there flashes a momentary burst of intolerably bright light. The thunder is gone as swiftly as it came, and instantaneously we are enwrapped in silence and in the blackness of a night without moon or stars. But in that same moment we have a sure sense of rising, rising, rising swiftly upwards, as if the void had drawn us up into itself. We come to rest, waiting, passively and without question.

High up in the blackness a shining white speck shows like a star. Rapidly it descends toward us, glorious in its living light and pulsating power. The origin of this light and the source of this power, is disclosed as a young child, crowned, but naked and luminous in beauty, standing upon a superb and equally luminous white stallion. The child carries a golden bow and a single shining arrow.

Smiling, the child turns his mighty mount at some distance before us, to look up into the same unbroken black expanse at which we gaze. Deliberately he fits the arrow to his bow, takes aim and releases it upwards into the viewless night.

The arrow leaps forth at an immeasurable speed. We can trace its course, for as it flashes to the heights it leaves behind it a searing line of light: a light which cleaves asunder the universe of darkness which it traverses. For a long moment this edge of burning brilliance hangs unchanged. Then an explosive electric crackling echoes across the sky, and along that line the blackness is riven asunder, to be swept away by the prismatic effulgence which bursts through and floods the dark void with its light.

With the explosion, horse and rider are gone from our perception. In a world overbrimming suddenly with radiance we are borne aloft to a new height, while as we ascend we hear again the chant which is like a Gnostic invocation:

ZA-GOU-REH. ECh-AB-NETh-PhROM.

BI-ATh-I-A. BI-ATh-I-A-ChA. LA-I-LAM.

BAL-BA-OTh. ShA-BA-O. MEN-HOTh-PhRA.

ZA-GOU-REH. ZA-GOU-RI-EH.

I-APh-ChA-U. ATh-UM-I-OPh. SA-BA-ZA-I.

We come to rest amid the splendors of this world of light. With no determinate shapes to meet the eye, and no distinctions of earth or heaven, this region is yet filled with movement: the movement of continually changeful masses of prismatic color, undefined as to shape and contour. Each of these masses flashes with a distinctive range of colors, which however changes with every movement. We watch one such mass of color change from predominating hues of deep gold and brilliant rose, to predominating hues of vivid sapphire and fiery orange, while flashes of emerald green, clear yellow and scarlet pass fleetingly across its surface. Then from no visible cause, a section of orange light detaches itself from this mass and moves away, changing meanwhile to blue-violet flashing with rays of golden green, and unites itself with another mass of light which until that moment was predominantly crimson. Next, across the whole visible scene broad bands of varying shades of blue spread and mingle vibrantly with the other colors.

Suddenly these random movements of abstract color cease to hold our attention as a living, recognizable form appears in their midst. Even more luminous than the prismatic radiance, a majestic and magnificent lion stands before us: a being formed of pure golden light. Flakes of pale golden light shimmer from his heavy mane and from his slowly swaying tail. With eyes of red-gold fire he looks about him, then he opens his golden jaws and emits a vibrant and tremendous roaring. We feel rather than hear the first thunderous reverberations of that sound.

The lion roars a second time. And now we can see his utterance in the form of golden flame issuing from his vermilion mouth in swirling gusts, and as golden flame echoed back from every quarter of this world of light.

A third time the golden lion roars, and this time so mightily that his whole form quivers, loses definition, and vanishes in the vibration. From the center where the lion had been, great waves of golden radiance reverberate outwards. The masses of prismatic color receive it, and all in turn are changed to flashing and vibrating golden light. The expanding waves strike us also: we feel their vibration as we felt that of the lion's first roaring, but far more violently. The vital golden light, the power and majesty of the lion, sweep through us and flood our whole being while once again the chanted invocation sounds in our ears:

ZA-GOU-REH. ECh-AB-NETh-PhROM.
BI-ATh-I-A. BI-ATh-I-A-ChA. LA-I-LAM.

BAL-BA-OTh. ShA-BA-O. MEN-HOTh-PhRA.

ZA-GOU-REH. ZA-GOU-RI-EH.

I-APh-ChA-U. ATh-UM-I-OPh. SA-BA-ZA-I.

We float in the all-pervading glowing light, which slowly changes around us to the hot whiteness of a noonday in high summer. The sun, masked in a blaze of incandescence, looks down from its zenith.

Now at this height we look again for our Guide. There before and above us the white column of flame, surrounded by its golden aura, hovers poised in the shimmering air. We await the direction of this luminous form; but a greater wonder comes to pass.

Before our eyes, our Guide changes in aspect. We behold the white flame transformed into a glorious personage of angelic beauty and power. We see a tall figure which gives an impression of great strength and of youth, clad in a robe of brilliant blue belted with gold. On the breast of this glorious Being is a huge gem, like an amethyst, deep violet in color, which continually gives forth flashing beams of intense blue and scarlet light. The feet are bare, but the hands are adorned with jewels which flash and sparkle with every hue. The head is most radiant, shining with golden hair and crowned with a garland of deep red roses. The aura of golden light still encompasses this Being, but it shines even more brightly than before.

Scarcely have we perceived this sublime transformation when our Guide ascends, higher and ever higher, and we find ourselves likewise lifted up and up towards the Sun, into the dazzling heavens. Nothing has reality for us at this time save the presence of our Guide, and the sense of rising towards the Sun; we have been transported beyond every care.

The light and heat of the Sun become intense, and our skin tingles and burns, but in the bliss of our ascent we pay no heed to this. We feel our garments being stripped away as if they were shriveled to nothing by the ardent rays, into whose power we are rising more and more swiftly. Those rays do not only burn, they seem to penetrate our flesh, slowly but steadily devouring all that gives us weight and density. We are being refined and transmuted in a crucible of air. We feel more than naked: we feel transparent and then invisible, consumed, without substance. We are aware at last of no feeling save for a great sense of freedom, and a joy which seems to be centered outside of ourselves: a joy which becomes forgetful of self as we keep our gaze upon the ever mounting, ever brightening form of our Guide.

Surely the Sun is drawing us upwards to itself! Our consciousness almost merged into the clear air which surrounds us, we ascend swiftly and more swiftly yet.

Suddenly, while still we rise upwards, the shining figure of our Guide flashes to a dazzling, incandescent brilliance and, together with its golden aura, is gone from our sight. Our ascent continues without pause, directly upwards towards the Sun. To that we aspire, to that we will mount up!

Upwards and upwards we proceed, perceiving no obstacle between us and our goal, until all at once our flight is halted. We are free no longer. It is as if the force of light and heat had been condensed into a massive crushing weight, pressing upon us from all directions. Held up as we are at this height, we are helpless in its grip: we have no power of resistance, no way of escape. The pressure increases beyond endurance, while at the same time a screaming and jangling tumult tortures our ears. We feel as if we shall be annihilated. Then, just as suddenly, with a blinding flash, the pressure and the tumult are gone, and we are caught up into a supreme and imageless brilliance. ★

In this brilliance there is a feeling of untroubled and peaceful suspension, a quiescence which seems like a complete absence of movement but for a sense of slowly turning upon a vertical axis. Now, even more gradually, an awareness of surroundings begins to return. The sense of turning ceases. Out of the brilliance is formulated, little by little, the interior of a temple which seems at first to be constructed of shafts of sunlight. In this temple YOU are standing entirely ALONE.

As your perception becomes more distinct, you see that except for the eastern wall, which is facing you, the entire temple—roof, walls and floor—appears to be composed of crystalline golden topaz which sparkles with inclusions of metallic silver. The eastern wall has a quality which is not easy to determine: it shimmers like a slivery mist, at some moments seeming thin and vaporous, at other moments opaque and palpable, but changing continually as if it were barely existing in the same dimension of being as the rest.

The temple is cubic in form, with its roof rising overhead in the shape of a pyramid. You are standing between the two pillars, Machetes and Nomothetes, which are situated to the west of center. From the apex of the roof is suspended the Lamp of the Mysteries, hanging above and just before you. In the center of the floor and exactly below the lamp, inlaid in the sparkling topaz surface is a small equal armed cross of red, enclosed in an octagon of yellow. This in turn is surrounded by the white eight-pointed star of the Ogdoadic Mysteries, whose nearest points extend to within a pace of your feet. The temple is filled with a sweet aromatic odor, a fragrance of roses and of frankincense.

Having contemplated this scene, you move forward into the very center of the temple. Now the Lamp of the Mysteries hangs directly above your head, and beneath your feet is the red equal-armed cross at the center of the Star. The light of the lamp surrounds you, bathes you, permeates you. It grows continually brighter, filling your consciousness although you do not gaze directly up at it.

You turn your attention to the mysterious eastern wall of this temple. As the light from the lamp grows progressively brighter, so your perception of that wall becomes more distinct: slowly the misty, changeful surface settles and resolves itself into a clear, silvery mirror.

You see your own reflection in this mirror: standing in the midst of the Glorious Star of Regeneration, with the Lamp of the Mysteries above your head and the radiance of the lamp illumining you, transforming you. You recognize your own features and form, but the light of the Lamp of the Mysteries sheds not only an outward brightness upon you. Its brilliance seems to irradiate you from within, giving your whole appearance a gentle incandescence which is expressive of spiritual beauty and strength. You see yourself, not as you are now, but yet as most truly yourself: yourself made perfect, timeless and serene in the power and the unity of your Higher Self. This transformed reflection is clothed in garments of splendor which give further expression to your inmost being, enhancing in grace and grandeur the luminous manifestation of your perfected reality.

Still the lamp above your head increases in brilliancy. You perceive its growing light reflected in the mirror, for a time showing the ideal image of yourself in more and ever more marvelous clarity and excellence. Then the glorious reflection gradually becomes merged in the dazzling silvery whiteness which engulfs it; and as the intensity of the light still increases, the details of the mirror and of the temple itself cease to be distinguishable. At last, just when the unmitigated dazzling brilliance is becoming intolerable, this too begins gradually to diminish, and a further formulation presents itself to you.

You are no longer within the temple of topaz. You are standing alone at the center of a square, facing the midpoint of one of the sides. Your bare feet are resting upon the surface, which is of smooth—rock, warmed by the heat of the sun, translucent and deep red in color. Without leaving the center you turn about, coming back to your original position. Beyond the edges of the square, in whichever direction you look, you see only the sky: a sky covered with a thin veil of mist which is filled with sunlight, so that the effect is like mother of pearl, luminous, flooded with delicate changeful tints which slowly, endlessly gleam and swirl. No sound is heard: the platform of rock upon which you stand might be floating, suspended in space.

You are conscious of great peace, and of great power. You stand at a center of equilibrium, but it is a dynamic equilibrium of magical action, not a static harmony. You look upwards. Directly over your head, a small circular area of light is more brilliant and more constant than any in the rest of the sky. Conscious of its presence, you again. Align yourself to gaze across the midpoint of the side of the square, and, standing thus, you steadily raise your arms at your sides until they form a straight line level with your shoulders. You stretch out your hands, feeling the balance of forces at whose center you are.

Instantly, from the luminous point above you, a shaft of white brilliance darts down, through the crown of your head, filling your Brow Center with light, and your Throat Center with a great impulse of understanding, and descending in that same flash to your Heart Center. A great radiance illuminates your Heart Center, so that a beam of light darts forth along each of your arms, and also from the center of breast and of back at the level of your heart. Thus you remain, with the vertical shaft of light from the zenith above your head to the Heart Center, and with the equal-armed cross of light, at whose center you are, reaching out to the horizon across the four sides of the square. A wonderful feeling of inspiration, comprehension and cosmic love fills your heart, pulses through you and radiates from you through those horizontal beams of light.

As you stand thus, your consciousness is expanded. Your feet remain firmly grounded at the center of the square, but your perception extends further and further in every direction, your inner faculties awakened, vibrant and active in the light which streams through you and goes forth from your Heart Center.

With your heightened perception, you realize that the square platform upon which you stand is the summit of a truncated pyramid. From the base of this pyramid, far below you, at each of the four corners a river of light pours forth, clearly visible from its brightness although the details of the ground are lost in mist.

Seen from above, these four rivers form part of an eight-rayed solar star, a living model of the Glorious Star of Regeneration: since you yourself, with the four beams of light which go out from you supply the rays of the quarters, and the four rivers carry powers of life, understanding, inspiration and aspiration to the four half-quarters of the universe.

However, the vertical shaft of light from the zenith no longer halts its course at your Heart Center. You now become aware of it descending completely through you. Your two arms, your breast and back, still give forth their vital rays which have their sources with this shaft of light, but now your Sex Center and the Center at your feet are irradiated as the mighty shaft of light descends through them into the pyramid itself. Your Sex Center awakens to awareness and vitality in the presence of this shaft of light, your feet renew and intensify their sensitivity to the surface beneath them. The translucent red rock glows more warmly, and you sense a pulsating force ascending from within it, whose rhythm answers to the beating of your heart.

Your Sex Center is immersed in this rising power, and glows and pulsates in response to it. From that Center, a rhythmic tension swiftly spreads through your consciousness.

Suddenly from the Sex Center a current of immense power darts upwards into your Heart Center, so that the Heart Center is instantly suffused with molten golden fire. The descending shaft and the four beams of light now fade from your consciousness as this glowing radiance expands outwards from the Heart Center, becoming an aura of intense golden light completely encompassing you. You stand with your feet firmly upon the pyramid; you are strongly aware of your radiant golden aura, now vastly expanded, and of yourself within it as a Being of life, of joy and of ecstasy. In this rapture you love, but you do not define any object of your love for there is no existence you would exclude from it.

Blissfully you raise your arms above your head, your hands separated by rather more than the width of your shoulders, the palms open and facing forwards. You feel yourself to be transfigured in the radiance, effulgent, and realizing the perfection of your human nature. In the void above and around you, beyond your powers of sight and hearing, you are yet conscious of mighty spiritual presences which hover there: Watchers and Holy Ones and Elder Brothers and Sisters in the Great Work.

Of your own free will and choice, in the abundance of that love which goes forth from you with the golden light of your aura, you purpose to give form to your universe.

To the East before you, by an act of will you invoke into being in that quarter the pure nature of elemental Fire. This is the most magical of the Elements, for its very nature is to set apart and to transmute. You call it forth to burst into being from an infinitesimal grain of intense heat. Like a germinating seed, from the first instant of its intelligible identity it draws upon the unconditioned ethers around it, transforming them into that resplendent yet austere beauty which is itself. You bid it to dance in its naked magnificence, so that proud and invincible Presences find their fulfilment therein; iridescent metallic wings and armored limbs flash forth reflections of the burning light, scarlet, gold or blue, and exultant voices ring out in clamourous chorus to the void. You contemplate the triumphant glory of elemental Fire, and within yourself you find responsive powers of enthusiasm, of assimilation and transmutation, and of ecstasy.

With hands still upraised you turn to the South, and by an act of will you invoke into being in that quarter the pure nature of elemental Earth.

This is the most peaceful of all the Elements, for in tranquility and silence the great works of Earth are performed. Far in the depths of Earth, you formulate dark and hidden caverns. Mighty and indomitable Presences, ponderous but shadowy of form, move therein; with slow finger they trace out the unmoving streams of metallic rock, and with patient eyes they watch for centuries the delicate growth of stalactite and stalagmite in inaccessible chambers and galleries. Above ground you formulate fertile plains and valleys, with their teeming richness of plant and animal life. Here other Beings of elemental Earth touch your consciousness, with an impression of swift-moving, slender limbs and delicate mouths: with a caress or a breath enhancing the scattered harvests of the wilderness, with evanescent silver laughter rejoicing in the keenest moments of life's multiform gladness. Now you call forth visually the high mountain peaks, which seem themselves to rest in perpetual meditation; and here sublime Beings of elemental Earth gather in silent and viewless session. Yet still they make their presence known alike to those who mount the steeps, and to those who meditate their awesome beauty from afar. You contemplate the strength and stability of the great forces of cavern, plain and mountain, united in the character of Earth; and you find within yourself like powers of constancy and of unconquerable resolve, and of that generosity which is born of the sure knowledge of your own inner abundance.

With hands still upraised you turn towards the West. By an act of will you invoke into being in that quarter the pure nature of elemental Air. This is the most mystical of all the Elements, for it is the breath which sustains life, and the means of all utterance. Its blue mantle of protection is ever about us, and to it belongs every soaring flight, every aspiration. You summon the marvel of its immeasurable distances; and in them move glorious Beings. These you discern riding the winds or floating in stillness, with plumed wings and vaporous garments of radiant whiteness, of saffron and of purple. Yet you see them without dimension, in a prespective which fluctuates: now small as flying figures graven upon a cameo, now vast of countenance as the spread of dawn or sunset. As you contemplate them, a soft wind breathes upon you carrying a sweet, ethereal but invigorating fragrance. With a new intensity of awareness, you find within yourself the freedom which belongs inseparably to the realms of spirit, the sense of eternity and infinity which transcends all limitations.

With hands still upraised you turn to the North, and in that quarter by an act of will you invoke into being the pure nature of elemental Water. This is the most powerfully transmissive of all the Elements, for it carries all influences and nurtures them to fruition. You summon before you the fluid curtain of the waterfall, and the fragile rainbow which quivers in its rising spray. You call forth the shining expanses of lakes and rivers, and, beyond all these, the illimitable vistas of the ocean. You call into reality those powerful and tremendous waters, with billows rising to tips of diamond, foaming and sinking to deeps of emerald and violet translucency. And in all these worlds of waters—in lake and river, in waterfall and mighty ocean—there gleam into manifestation ever and anon a host of graceful and ethereal forms, fluid as their native element, here rushing together in a rapture of seemingly everlasting union, there individuating, separating, realizing new inner vortices of identity, exulting in the bliss of selfhood until a new current carries them into even more joyful reunion. As you contemplate these beauteous beings of elemental Water, you can recognize within your own nature these two equally vital tides: the impulse towards union with other beings, which produces a higher level of individuation, and the impulse towards individuation which produces a more spiritually fruitful power of union.

With hands still upraised you turn again to face the East, completing the circle of this creative act of will. You lower your hands and cross them upon your breast, right over left. The harmony of rejoicing throughout all the Worlds of your universe, of which you yourself are the directing power and the focal center, sounds triumphantly about you and within you.

Gradually the sounds blend into a single chord, sonorous and thrilling, while the forms and colors of your vision are mingled into an abstract swirling of prismatic light. Gently the sound fades to quietness and ceases, while the swirling of prismatic light changes to a dazzling whiteness. Now the brightness fades, and the light formulates itself again into the temple of golden topaz, sparkling with points of bright silver. You become aware once more of the blended odor of roses and frankincense.

Above you hangs the Lamp of the Mysteries, beneath your feet is the red equal-armed cross at the center of the eight-pointed star. You look before you, to the eastern wall of the temple: it has become once more as you first saw it, a shimmering luminous veil of silver mist. The whole temple is suffused with radiant brightness. You salute the East!

Most happily you stand in this place of Light, to which you have traveled by the Path of the Arrow.

In this adventure you have tasted that high and joyous ecstasy of abandon to the Powers of Light, which transcends rationality but in no way sets aside reason; even as you have seen the vine, emblem of mystical rapture, burst forth from and entwine the thyrsus of Nature's jubilation, to support and be supported by it.

You have seen the indomitable force of this ecstatic transcendence shown forth in vision: first, as a glorious and triumphant androgynous figure grasping and controlling the Twin Serpents which represent the two sides of the Holy Tree of Life. This figure is seen as androgynous because dominion over the forces of Nature must imply an inner equilibrium, a potent acceptance of both polarities and thus the ability to work with them.

In vision you have seen darkness rent asunder by the power of the Eternal Child, that you might be lifted upward in the ensuing deluge of Light; since not by its own power is the adult intellect carried into the realm of the Good, the Beautiful and the True. And, once again, you have seen in vision the golden Lion, symbol of the Sun—and of your Higher Self, of which the Sun likewise is a symbol—and you have experienced the tremendous radiating vibration of that manifestation, flooding through you and awakening its counterpart in the depths of your psyche.

You have entered the shining temple of the Sphere of the Sun. You have stood upon the equal-armed cross, where, in a certain sense, you were, as you are ever to be, the Bomos: the dedicated focal point where the things of the lower worlds are employed to create a means of encounter with the forces of the higher worlds. You have looked into the mystical Mirror, and have beheld yourself supremely transfigured by becoming a channel and an instrument for the glorious power and action of your Higher Self.

You have stood upon the square top of the truncated Pyramid: the completion of Nature, or of your lower self, by the dominion of Spirit.

Visualize the truncated Pyramid as seen from above. If opened from the base upwards, along the juncture of its four oblique faces, and laid flat, it would form a Cross Pattee with a central square covering the union of its arms. See this central square as occupied by a large, brilliant yellow topaz which reflects and radiates the light of the Sun in every direction. Here, therefore, you have an image of the Cross of the Four Elements governed by the Fifth Element, Light, or Spirit of which Light is the symbol. As you envision this jewel, the cross with the central topaz, recognize it as a showing of the destiny of your entire being.

For what is betokened here is not an emancipation of the higher nature, so that it might cast off the lower nature and return alone to its native heights of divinity; nor is it a glorification of the lower nature alone and in its own right. What is in question is the fulfilment of the total unity of your being, a unity to be infused and governed by the glorious presence of indwelling divinity which is at once the inmost flame and the apex of your total individuality. No less than this is the objective towards which you have followed the Path of the Arrow into this temple of the Sun-sphere: the spiritual realization of your whole person, abundantly at every level.

See yourself therefore as a person capable of the highest ecstasies of divine perception. See yourself likewise as one capable of the boundless joy of knowledge and understanding fortified by true intuition. See yourself as capable no less of the raptures of emotional happiness, love, wonder and the sense of adventure. See also, added to these qualities, those heightened and exquisite sense perceptions whose pure pleasure the mystics often describe.

Rest not, therefore, upon the achievement of this journeying, but aspire! Aspire, and with all your will aspire to the realities which this adventure foreshadows.

Battery 3-5-3

Conclusion of the 26th Path

(For use subsequent to working the 25th Path)

Gradually, however, the light partially gathers density and materiality. All at once it darkens, and we find ourselves in a visible locality. Around us rise the irregular sides of a crater-like rocky hollow, near the center of which we stand. The floor of the crater beneath our feet is dark and lustrous, like a smooth surface of obsidian: the crags and boulders forming the walls of the cup are of rough greyish rock, with no distinctive feature save at the four quarters. At each of those points, carved in high relief as if looking at us out of the living rock, is a fearsome and repellent head. These heads, although each differs from the rest in individual detail and character, yet are all of one general type: a crested saurian, beyond any natural crocodile or other reptile in ferocity, bestial comprehension and intensity of vigilance. So vigorously are these characteristics indicated that the images seem almost to be more than lifeless sculpture. They represent the Devourers, nightmare beings of the Capricornian road to the Sun-sphere, watching for the unpurified.

The heavens above us are no longer radiant: instead, a lurid sky is filled with dense turbulent vapors, dark and menacing.

A movement in the center of the floor of the crater in which we stand attracts our attention, a stirring beneath its lustrous surface. There is an appearance as of a small spring gushing at that spot, sending forth not water but flame which spreads outwards in a circle: yet all is beneath the surface, a process apparently within the substance of the glassy rock. The smooth floor beneath our feet remains unimpaired and cool. We watch the fiery circle expanding outwards, the dark obsidian green changing within its widening circumference to a deep glowing red through which run sparkles and flashings of bright flame yellow. The circumference of the fire passes beneath our feet without causing us any sensation, and we continue watching as it proceeds outwards to the very edge of the floor of the crater. It reaches the rocky walls: the whole gleaming floor is of a vivid glowing red, like a window into the heart of a furnace, and we perceive that the vertical boundary of grey rock will halt its outward progress.

For a moment it seems as if no further development is taking place. Then at some points round the circumference a thin film of smoke arises, followed by transient sparks and delicate tongues of flame. Soon the entire circumference surrounding us is covered with upsurging molten fire, which begins to flow back upon the surface towards the center. We are caught within a converging circle of liquid fire.

Even at a distance we feel its scorching breath upon us. We see the random wisps of transparent flame going up from it into the quivering air. An incessant sighing and crackling goes up from it, and the heat as it draws nearer becomes intolerable. So as to delay the contact as long as possible we move to the very center of the lake of fire, for such it has become; thus, when it reaches us, it strikes from all sides at once.

The liquid flame laps about our feet and we are powerless in its grip. The very air burns around us, with a fire which consumes us, not outwardly but inwardly. Our mouths are parched, our lungs scorched, our strength is drained from us. We feel ourselves to be burned, charred: yet our garments are not even singed.

Flame dances before our eyes so that we do not see, but images of horror present themselves to our mind as if visibly. With a dizzy sensation of falling, we seem to be slipping down limitless burning precipices into illimitable seething gulfs of flame. The heads of the Devourers, animated now with a mocking semblance of life, leer at us with cunning eyes which seem to read within us every imaginable evil, or lurch towards us champing ravenous jaws, which would seize on any prey within reach, guilty or innocent. And in the flickering shadows beyond, innumerable other heads lift themselves, hyena-like, to see what feasting the Devourers may leave for them.

Yet all these shapes of horror are within ourselves, and the fire consumes them. The fathomless gulfs of fear are gone, and we stand in the midst of the lake of fire. In place of the hideous Devourers, four noble gazelles now gaze upon us: beautiful deer-like creatures of the goat kind with long backward-pointing horns, and eyes of topaz. But these are not simply natural gazelles, for each has a third topaz eye which looks serenely forth from the middle of the forehead. These four images, like those of the Devourers, seem to have some qualities of life: but with these we are glad, for they represent the Watchers upon the Heights, sentinel beings who make known the approach of newcomers upon their way.

Now the burning flood gathers itself into a swift eddy, swirling around our feet at first, then rising up about us with a roaring and crackling like incessant thunder. Soon we are totally encased in this column of liquid flame: we breath it, we radiate its heat as if we were one with it. We feel that we are utterly consumed, reduced to nothingness. A great sense of tragedy and loss overwhelms us but the fire whirls away the cries we would utter, and scorches the tears we would shed. Then it burns away the grief itself and the cause of the grief, so that we know these things too were but nightmares within ourselves. We feel that a great weight has been burned away from us, yet we are by no means destroyed. We are joyful, and truly ourselves.

Suddenly the whole whirling column of fire in which we are contained lifts into the air and, light as we are and burned free of the dross which would have weighed us down, we rise within the flame. Rejoicing in our ascent, we are carried higher and higher: then, all at once, the column of fire disperses and is gone, leaving us free and poised in equilibrium, but also in darkness. The dazzling after-images of the flame vanish in their turn, and no doubt is possible: we are as if sealed in a silent and velvety blackness, in which no trace of stimulation from without reaches any of our senses. There is not even the slightest breath of sound, although we strain our ears for it, which might let us know whether we are still floating at the same spot, or rising up, or perhaps are drifing onwards or settling slowly down. As far as we can tell, our position remains unchanged.

We remain passive, since we have no alternative but to await the course of events. At last, still without any sound reaching us, we become aware of a light shining upon us from above. We look upwards to see its source.

In the darkness there shows forth over our heads a glittering arc of light, like a crown, shining with every rainbow color in far greater brightness than we saw those colors previously in the aura of each of us. As this glorious light ripples and flashes, we catch now and then a momentary glimpse of a beautiful and joyful face appearing out of the darkness, and illuminated by the brilliance: the face of some delicate spirit being, which has drawn near only to rejoice briefly in the splendor.

Now there appears more distinctly and constantly a winged and noble being, seemingly composed altogether of translucent crimson light, and bearing a torch whose flame is of the same color. This being touches with the flame the many-colored light of the crown, and each prismatic ray and spark in turn begins to change to that intense crimson. The winged shape vanishes, but the process of transformation continues: the arc of light, now completely crimson, begins to flash inwards, converging to a center, gradually forming there into a sphere which is at first misty in outline but which is entirely of the same wondrous color.

The color itself has an emotional quality of fascination which holds our attention. It is poignant as the heart's desire, yet sweet as desire fulfilled. We would wish to grasp and hold it, to inhale it like the fragrance of red roses, to drink it like wine: yet we know it is ours already, near and dear as the blood in our veins.

While we reflect upon this paradox, the diffuse sphere into which the crimson light has been gathered becomes suddenly condensed, clear in outline and in character. All at once it is a perfectly spherical stone, translucent and lustrous, and of the same pure crimson color.

Now another winged being appears, flying powerfully as if from a great distance. This being seems as if composed entirely of clear transparent crystal, and carries a wand of pure whiteness. With this wand, the winged being, hovering, touches the crimson stone and then departs. The stone seems to tremble through its entire substance and turns slowly opalescent, then white as milk: but as we watch, the transformation continues yet further.

The white sphere becomes more and more intensely luminous, and gives forth heat as well as light. The heat and light increase until the stone becomes a globe of white-hot incandescence, overwhelming in its intensity. That which had previously, as the red stone, seemed to be a part of our own nature now appears as quite other, alien and even menacing.

Yet we cannot turn away from it, and each person's heart begins to glow with white heat and light in response to the burning white stone. We look for some further visitant to come to our aid, but there is none. Only the searing white light itself is present to us. ★

Suddenly with a deafening crash as of thunder, the white stone and its incandescence are gone. Bewildered and dazzled, we remain without moving until we can look about us. We are no longer in darkness: a new landscape surrounds us, and our feet rest upon a solid surface, although the sound of thunder is still heard until it dies away in the distance, and each of us still keeps at heart a spark, no longer menacing or alien, of the strong radiance of the white stone.

We are looking upon a pleasant country scene, the strange quality of which does not at once impress us. The sun shines brightly from a blue sky. Before us lies a bountiful field of ripe grain, ready for harvesting: but as we consider it we wonder how it was sown, for it is not growing in the straight lines which, from time immemorial, mankind has made by one means or another for sowing grain. This field has grown of itself, and needs but the gathering. Near by stands a clump of unpruned trees in all their natural glory, laden with rich fruits, while birds of bright plumage sing delightfully in the branches. A group of humans walk in a leisurely way across our line of vision, accompanied by playful animals which appear to be, neither domesticated nor savage: the garments of the people are extremely simple without any suggestion of poverty, while men, women and children are all radiant with good health and outdoor living in a genial climate. Soon the music of strings and pipes is heard, and we realize that some rustic festivity is beginning.

Of all the ages of human story, whether real or fabled, which have ever been described, the idyllic enchantment of this scene can belong only to one, and that is the true Golden Age itself!

Mingled with the sounds of music of human making, a sweeter, shriller sound impinges on our ears. It holds the essence of sadness and of laughter, it is most delicate and subtle yet its piping is most masterful: it both suggests and inspires the human music which entwines with it. For a moment we feel impelled to go and seek the unseen musician, yet we do not move. We know we would go uphill through the trees, through a region of dappled sunlight where we should be astonished at the myriad forms of life thronging around us. Then we should come to the limit of the woods, and no bird nor beast, no basilisk nor chimaera would venture further. But if we ourselves went on, there where the bare rocks lie under the sun we should find the Player, the Rustic Pan: we should look upon the terrible innocence which remains at the heart of the world. But to look into that infinite gulf of stark simplicity and unqualified truth is not part of our quest.

We turn towards a stretch of level grassland, and take a faintly marked path which leads across it. We are approaching what at first we take to be a low-roofed but extensive building: but as we draw nearer, it proves to be a large circle of roughly squared megaliths, each upright being linked to each by an equally massive lintel. This is a temple of the Sun, as of ancient times, in all its primal simplicity and beauty.

The rocks here are of a pale yellow opaque stone laced with veins of metallic gold, glinting and sparkling in the light of the sun which shines from high in the sky. One group of megaliths however is more finely finished than the rest, and is evidently intended to form a ceremonial entrance to the circle. Of these, the right hand upright shines with the blaze of burnished gold, while the left hand upright is entirely of bright translucent green: while the lintel uniting them is of deep scarlet rock.

We pass in through this ceremonial circle, and marvel at the noon-day stillness which at once takes possession of the peaceful scene. The air moves only slightly, so that the grasses stir and nod occasionally without noticeable sound: both we and the rocks are almost without shadow, for the sun is virtually at the zenith.

Concentric with the large outer circle of rocks there is a. small inner ring consisting of only eight megaliths with no lintels: four tall white rocks alternated with four red ones. We advance and reverently enter this central circle, which is the inner sanctuary of this solar temple. Within it the palpable energy of the enmeshed lines of force is intense, as if we stood in the midst of the Mystical Tessera: from each red megalith to the others of the same color in this circle, and from each white megalith to the other white ones, the lines of force flash so as to form an eight-pointed star. At the same time we feel another current which surrounds us, circulating from each rock to the next around this inner ring.

Yet the power does not shut us away from the world of life outside, but on the contrary it unites us with that world more closely. The sun now stands at its exact noonday height above our heads, the sweet breath of summer blossoms fitfully reaches us, and now and then the stillness is accentuated by the musical call of birds. In the distance, between the misty slopes of wooded hills, the brightness of blue sky and clear sunshine flashes in reflection from the surface of tranquil water. Over the grassy plain nearer at hand the hot air dances, filled with a myriad tiny sparkles of prismatic light. From this double ring of megaliths—another emblem, if we will have it so, of the Eye whose Path we have now completed—it is easy to look forth in peace, seeing with the vision of the spirit all that exists, and blessing it because of its essential goodness.

Now, having followed the Path of the Goat to its happy conclusion, we can look back upon some part of what we have attained with eyes which have already, upon the Path of the Arrow, come to see from the viewpoint of the Sphere of the Sun.

We have passed through the purifying lake of solar flame. The burning away of dross in that lake of fire brings about a renewal, not a deprivation, of all the treasury of the lower nature. The rainbow light which is distilled from our life experience has become the basis of the very transmutation which has brought us to this temple of the Sun sphere.

The rainbow light is essentially the same as the colors of the Peacock's Tail marking the first stage of success in preparing the Philosophers' Stone. We have gazed in inward vision upon that wondrous Stone, in its ensuing stages of the Red and the White: and when the White Stone has passed from our sight, something of its effulgence and ferment has found place in our hearts. There it is to increase, glowing with its own spiritual incandescence, to set up its own traditional ferment so that it will ultimately transmute not only ourselves, but every person and thing which comes in contact with us, all according to their own nature. For the Philosophers' Stone is itself a symbol, a presentment of the *Summum Bonum*, that Highest Good which is the supreme goal of every destiny.

From the viewpoint of this temple of the Sun sphere, we contemplate all things in the glorious truth and beauty of their inner reality. The Golden Age is neither lost to us in a remote antiquity nor tantalizingly lodged in a equally remote and unattainable future time: it is a spiritual reality which rests now and continually at the heart of all phenomena. Its light irradiates all that we love, for the vision of love does not stop at externals: it irradiates all that we see with the vision of the Sun sphere, for in that vision too the essential is seen within the play of circumstance, the external within the grace and beauty of change.

Battery 3-5-3

Conclusion of the 24th Path

(For use subsequent to working the 25th Path)

We welcome the profound sweetness of this surrender. Receive us, O Mother!

With arms outstretched we plunge headlong, helplessly, into the unfathomable pit. The torrent engulfs us: the alluring contenance vanishes, and in its stead our field of vision is filled with an infinity of streaming particles of every color, which appear to spring from the central depths, lengthening into twisted ribbon shapes as they rush towards and past us. They grow stronger and more violent: mighty streams of blue, green and scarlet light which thunder and shriek as they pass, as if menacing us with buffets of physical impact. Through this tempestuous chaos we feel ourselves falling, falling, falling for a time which seems interminable. Then gradually the tumult and the rising streams of many-colored brightness diminish, until we are left in utter darkness and silence.

We seem to be falling no more: but in all this, where is she whom we seek, and why do we seek her face no longer?

After another interval a small, steady glow of light, warm in hue but too faint at first to have any recognizable character, appears before us. We have no means to judge in what direction we are looking: but our attention remains fixed upon this luminescence which swiftly grows in size and brightness to become a long oval of delicate bronze-colored light with a more intense inner region of ivory whiteness.

Subtle, isolated snatches come to our ears, of a music which is not in itself incoherent but of which only scattered notes and phrases reach us. At the same time a warm breeze stirs fitfully in our direction, bearing a fragrance which as it comes and goes reminds us now of citrus, now of roses, now of pine woods beneath the sun and, occasionally, even of the 'resh bitter tang of the ocean. These sounds and odors strike von our stunned senses, awakening them to a new intensity awareness. We seek to press forward upon our quest, but we are unable to move.

A rhythmic piping, consisting only of three notes continuously interwoven, sounds as if from a great distance. At first it seems childish: but then its very simplicity, together with the sense of vast remoteness which it conveys, produces a strange fascination. As this sound holds our imagination, the soft light before us partly resolves itself into a misty shape, human, female, nude, but still phantasmal. This figure faces us, but the head is bowed and the thick hair falls forward, hiding the features. The arms are unseen as if the hands were clasped behind the back, and the whole body is curved forwards so that the full breasts and wide hips entirely lominate our view of it. We try to see more clearly, we wonder whether the figure will move: but instead it dissolves again into the oval area of light, and at the same time the strange piping changes back to the fitful many-toned phrases of music which we previously heard. The awesome and almost daunting vision has vanished as if we had never ieheld it, even while we are still seeking its place in the context of our conscious mind.

For that which we have glimpsed is an image whose spiritual meaning is scarcely accessible to us at this distance pf time: it is that image of the Mother which human hands in neolithic times fashioned in fragments of stone or bone, or represented in even more stylized form in sacred and secret shrines. We can venerate the archetypal simplicity of the concept, but yet the psychic language of the culture in which it developed is strange to us: we cannot enter into the full emotional significance of such an image. We would desire to open our hearts to that which we have beheld, because assuredly it relates to her whom we seek: but, O Mother! extend your arms to us in love and guidance! O Mother, show us your face!

The warm breeze stirs around us again, vibrant as a wind of early spring. The changeful music is like the song of birds mingled with the shimmering sound of gongs: the oval of bronze-colored light expands and contracts, now seeming to come close as if to overwhelm us, now receding so as to seem an incalculable distance away. Now it expands to a vast extent.

Once again we see a figure within the light, but now the vision is immense, and awe inspiring in its dimensions. This time there stands before us the figure of a woman completely draped in richly embroidered robes; a veil upon her dark hair: but her eyes are hidden in the shadow of the veil, and she does not look upon us. Now the vision shifts and is changed, and her robe is of the finely pleated linen of Egypt. Her gaze is upon a young child clasped in her arms, and still she does not look upon us.

She sets the child down beside her, and suddenly he is a youth grown almost to manhood. She wears a golden crown and he a shepherd's cap, but as each regards the other her features and his are identical, are one. Then he sinks down as in death, and she takes the crown from her head and laments as a woman distraught. The birds are mute: the strident insistent danger of the gongs is deafening. She bends over his body. Swiftly now it is the corpse of a grown man, now it is a skeleton, now it is gone. The gongs cease: we hear only the gentle rhythm of a single drum, like a heart beat. The Mother rises up, swaying in a slow dance of change and renewal. She lifts her graceful arms, and at once they are innumberable. Her infinity of fluttering hands cover the skies, then become remote and shining like stars. Momentarily they shed a pearly light upon us, then they vanish away. We are left in empty darkness: but the sound of the drum continues.

O Mother, wise in the intricate ways of joy and of sorrow, where shall we find you?

The soft bronze light is all about us now, although for some time we see nothing clearly in it: we drift without volition through tendrils of faint mist. Fleeting images of her whom we seek, in many forms, appear insubstantially before us and vanish away: now we glimpse her in a chariot drawn by cats or by lions, now she herself appears in feline form, now she is a she-bear protecting her cub, or a wild mare speeding afar over misty plains. These shapes are but as garments worn by her at one time and another as she may choose to figure forth something of her purposes, and each vanishes in its turn.

The tones of a stringed instrument, varying between entreaty and determination, are added to the gentle insistence of the drum, and a rich oriental sweetness fills the air. Now the mist dissolves as a scene becomes clear before us. We find ourselves before a huge temple, built of massive blocks, whose entire surface, from the foundation to the pin-nacled heights, is carved over with figures, emblems and leafy scroll-work in intricate profusion. A wide doorway into this temple stands open, and we atempt, in the drifting and dreamlike manner in which we are progressing, to enter the building.

Some unseen influence, however, prevents us from doing so, and the elaborate sculpture of the wall catches our attention as in a maze. We follow with our power of vision the convolutions of one branch of the leafy scrollwork, and find that the onward movement of our glance is checked as we examine stem growing out of stem, detail out of detail of ornament. At last we are contemplating a cluster of tiny but exquisitely carved flowers, whose petals are perfect in every vein and contour.

All at once, in one of these minute blossoms we behold a figure enthroned. Indeed, by what standard can we say these flowers are small, or large, or of any size? Here we behold her whom we seek, majestic and powerful as if we saw her seated above the rainbow and sending a manifestation of herself through the Worlds in each of its seven rays. We would do reverence to our Mother as she sits enthroned within the sculptured flower, but as we gaze the light quivers, and ten thousand such blossoms meet our eyes. Nor, now, are they sculptured. The temple has disappeared, and the blossoms are true blossoms, living and growing—red, yellow, white, purple—while the song of the birds rises triumphantly to silence every other music. Then that sound too fades away.

O, Mother of us all!—are we to seek you through all that lives? And if in this way we find you, how can your regard be upon us, how can you hold out to us your strong and gracious arms?

While we stand bewildered, a tinge of blue appears in all that we see. Rapidly the color spreads, until the flowers and foliage shine with every hue from pale sky blue to deep sapphire, and even the light which surrounds us becomes blue. The intensity of its color increases until the leaves and flowers disappear in it, seeming to melt away as ice melts in water. A total silence enfolds us, and the deeper blue shadows of the distance grow more mysterious.

This intensely blue ambience is both peaceful and stimulating. We fmd in it a quality of her whom we seek, and without resistance we await what is to follow.

A gentle and caressing pressure holds us on every side, and, as we entrust ourselves to it, slowly and steadily we are lifted upwards in its embrace.

Higher and higher we rise through the marvelous blueness. Now it becomes filled with ripples and sparkles of, brighter luminosity which are charged with an energy and vitality of their own. We catch fleeting glimpses, scattered among the sparkles, of shapes in vivid changeful colors: delicate shapes which might equally be living things or abstractions, long spirals, plant-like forms, radial patterns, cell-like mosaics and innumerable variations on these types. All flash forth in beauty and are gone before we can consider them. At the same time, however, there is infused into us a great and potent joy: it is not death, but life, which holds and constrains us! Still we rise, and our joy becomes ecstasy: until with a sudden swirl we are thrust upwards to break the surface of the blueness. ★

For a moment the impact of the transition bewilders us, but swiftly we begin to contemplate the new environment in which we fmd ourselves. We are standing upon the surface of a wide expanse of intensely blue water. Above us, a jet black sky is so thickly gemmed with stars as to give a light almost as bright as day. The gentle, almost imperceptible rise and fall of the blue water, in which this diamantine starlight is reflected, stretches as far into the distance as we can see: only in one direction is another object visible. At a distance from us a massive and glittering structure, which itself flashes blue in the starlight, rises sharply from the waters.

Gliding easily over the luminous blue surface, we move towards the edifice. As we draw nearer, we see that it rests upon five square tiers of black onyx which rise in steps from the surface of the water. Four massive columns of translucent crystal stand at the corners of the uppermost platform: the height of each column is the same as the distance which separates it from its neighbors, so that the four frame an open-sided cube. Upon these columns, and fashioned of the same translucent crystal, all gleaming pale blue in the reflected watery light, there rests a pyramidal roof.

We mount the five onyx steps to the level floor of the edifice, and pause there. So lustrous is this floor that the light of the stars is palely reflected there: but in its center, an elaborately wrought symbol claims our attention.

This is an extensive inlaid star of gold, at the center of which is a large burnished disc. From this disc there extend eight equal rays, long and tapering, but each strongly curved in the form of abroad reversed S shape, so that the star has the appearance of revolving in a sunwise direction: each of these long rays has its surface adorned with an intricate raised pattern of circles and ellipses, as if the burnished central disc in whirling on its axis were shaping the course of a host of lesser luminaries to its motion.

We approach this golden symbol and stand at the center of its burnished disc. At the corners of the spacious area surrounding the star, the huge crystalline columns rise high above us. We are at the point of balance of mighty forces. We begin to feel a powerful sense of centering within ourselves, a settling and ordering of our faculties in orientation to an inner point. We look before us over the luminous blue waters, while the starlight turns to yellow fire in the golden symbol at our feet.

Suddenly the star in whose center we stand begins shining with a brighter golden light. No longer is its luster a reflection from without: now the star has become luminous, emitting brightness of itself. As its radiance continues to increase it seems to stand forth from the onyx floor as if from a midnight heaven of its own. Soon we gaze down at it with wonder that our feet can rest upon it, it is so truly transformed to pure light. Even more luminous it becomes, brilliant as the noonday sun. Its effulgence blazes forth on all sides, turning the translucent columns and roof to shimmering luminescence, and passing through them as easily as through the open spaces.

In the increasing radiance of this mystical light, the gently swelling surface of the water turns from blue to a bright sheet of molten gold. The light grows even more intense, spreads further yet: it paints the sky with bright hues of sunrise, with rose purple, gold, green and cerulean blue. The stars fade from sight, all save one: the beautiful Morning Star hangs like a silver lamp in the glowing heavens, even though the only visible dawning is that of the brilliant star in which we stand. We gaze down into the incandescent fire about our feet, and marvel that our eyes are not dazzled: we can gaze into that blazing whiteness as the eagle gazes into the sun.

All at once we realize how it is that we can do so: both inwardly and outwardly we ourselves have become as luminous as the effulgent light whereon we gaze. Without our observing the wondrous change, the whole of our being has taken illumination from that golden fire. Now, too, we realize that the spiritual equilibrium in which we are poised is no longer a balance of tensions: it is an entire unity. We are radiant, vibrant wih power, blissful in this extended dimension of being. Each of us is the reality of that Star upon whose representation we stand. All our faculties are gathered to move in harmonious response to the central splendor, even as the design of the symbol prefigured: and in that harmony is both power and peace.

We have come through the darkness of the deeps and the shadow of Death, into the radiance of day and of a light which is other than the light of the external sun.

This golden star in whose central disc we stand is eight-rayed. It is both eight-rayed and indicative of motion, of action. In its balance of forces, in its solar splendor and power of interior regeneration, we find a symbol of the reality of life.

For no life, of whatever degree, is static. It is through that very faculty of change which is represented to the eye of understanding, even by the path of Death itself, that the life of the lower self comes nearest to the life of the spirit. The life of pure spirit is pure dynamism. Flame, starlight, the pearl, the diamond, all the symbols for spiritual life show this essential quality of inner movement, of vibrant luster: the quality of perpetually *becoming*, perpetual newness, rebirth. And all birth is of the Mother.

Thus the power of the Mother is ever with us, whether it is seen as menacing, seductive, or saving: not only to bring us through the births of our lower evolution, when the limitations of the material world can seem as fetters, but also in those higher births in which pure spiritual force is molded to lofty forms and purposes. In the pattern of our own being, and in the pattern of the cosmos, the power of the Mother carries us onward through birth and rebirth: and that power will ever more fully be with us in the bliss of that limitless Becoming to which all existences ultimately aspire.

Battery 3-5-3

chapter 8

Pathworking
and Practical Magick

I. Practical Purposes

Pathworking in Series

Pathworking is primarily, as we have seen it to be in the preceding chapters, a powerful mode of awakening and directing the inner faculties of the psyche for the purpose of spiritual progress and initiation. For this primary purpose, Pathworkings are most effective when performed in series, as given in Chapter 7: experience shows the ideal rate for the series to be one Pathworking per week. (If the series is being worked for the first time, both forms of Paths 26 and 24 will necessarily be included in their due sequence.)

A series of Pathworkings of this kind is self-balancing within the pattern of the Tree of Life, and no concern need be felt with regard to the effects of any energies which may have been released by the workings and which may have remained unassimilated. Sometimes, however, it is desired to perform a particular Pathworking out of series.

Selective Pathworking

CATEGORY 1. A group may decide to perform a Pathworking on the occasion of a reunion or similar gathering. Or an individual may feel a need to perform some particular Pathworking on account of an instinctive or intuitive impulse, with no desired result of the working either specified or even clearly known. One may feel for instance a sudden "nostalgia" for a particular Path.

CATEGORY 2. Having experience of the kind of "soul sculpture" which takes place through the deep level action of Pathworkings, an individual may decide to make use of a suitable Pathworking for the purpose of enhancing or developing his or her inner potential on some specific line, or in order to combat some inner weakness or defect. This is a special development of the normal use of Pathworkings, and only requires, to implement it, a steady resolve to go along loyally with the desired outcome of the working: the working itself can be repeated for the same purpose after a week, or, if desired, a longer interval.

CATEGORY 3. An individual or group-may decide to use—a Pathworking to help gain a purpose which is definably *magical*: that is, it is intended to produce change in the outer as well as in the inner Worlds. In that case the use of a Pathworking will be supplemental to another operation which is of an actively magical nature and is directed to the same purpose. This use of Pathworking is appropriate only to individuals or groups proficient to carry out the related magical operation.

In categories 2 and 3 above, and in 3 most distinctly, a specialized and practical use is made of Pathworking which is not envisaged in the procedures for Pathworking for general spiritual progress simply. Certainly these categories represent a natural and reasonable progression from the concept of pathworkings in series, but none the less they carry special requirements.

In order to determine which Path should be worked to further a given purpose, in either category 2 or 3, consideration should be made not only of the influences upon the Paths but also, with due regard, of the Spheres of commencement and destination. As a general guide, we list here some of the objectives for which the aid of Pathworking is most suitably sought in the two categories under consideration, with the recommended Paths for these purposes:

Category 2—For the individual operator, to gain access to particular sources of inner power.

(Purpose)	(Path)
Constructive attitude in human affairs (for)	28
Depression, despondency (to overcome)	32
Diligence in acquiring a skill (for)	30
Domineering, to overcome tendency to	26
Family disputes, to have healing influence in	29
Fear, to face one's greatest	27
Fortitude generally (for)	31
Grief, to assimilate	24
Harmonious influence, to spread	29
Healing, power in (to gain)	30
Higher Self, to strengthen bond with	25
Inner conflicts: for insight to resolve one's own; for understanding of other people's	24
Intuition, general (to develop)	32
Quarrels generally, for skill to avert	27
Selfishness, self-conceit, to overcome	26
Self confidence, to develop	25
Spiritual progress, to promote	25
Studies, for application in	28

The objectives mentioned in the list just given have been placed there because they are altogether "inner" matters which your deep mind, when once it has been "put on the right Path," is plainly competent to deal with. There are many other objectives which your deep mind is, at least potentially, equally able to deal with: but since, for most people, special training and/or special practices are needed to bring into action the deep mind's natural potential, these matters are placed with the "magical" objectives in the *next* list. Such are, for instance, astral projection and prophetic insight. Apart from this type of exercise of psychic faculties, this next list is focused strongly upon objectives which depend upon action outside the range of one's own personality, and which thus generally necessitate means which can validly be called "magical."

At the same time, be it remembered that you are quite entitled, should you wish, to take an objective from category 2 and to perform the appropriate Pathworking as a supplement to a magical rite for that purpose, exactly as for category 3, either alone or with your group: a Pathworking and magical operation to gain power in healing, a Pathworking and magical operation to strengthen the bond with your Higher Self, or another to promote harmony within the family. To put it succinctly: the list for category 3 could include all of the contents of the list for category 2; but the list for category 2 could not so effectively include the contents of the list for 3. Here, then, is the list for category 3:

Category 3—For the individual or the group, when Pathworking is to be used in conjunction with other working:

A—For specifically magical or spiritual objectives

(Purpose)	(Path)
Alchemy, for all works of	30
Assumption of God-forms *(Or, if practicable, choose the most suitable Path to the Sphere of the deity concerned.)*	25
Astral Projection, for general practice of	25
Astrological work, to acquire intuition for	28
Banishing, major rites of, for psycho-spiritual equilibrium	27
Body of Light, to strengthen (for such practices as astral Projection or the Watcher)	32
Bondage rites, for enhancement of spiritual consciousness	27
Exorcism/Sublimation	26
Holy Guardian Angel, for invocation of	25
Invisibility, rites of	32
Kundalini, arousal of	31
Mirror magick	29
Past Life Recall, works concerning	31
Prophetic insight, to gain or increase	30
Protection of the Home (rites for)	26
Protection while traveling (rites for)	25

Psychism, to gain or increase higher forms of	25
Scrying	29
Sex Magick	24
Visualization, to develop power of	32
Visualization, to make fruitful the creative power of	30

B—*For magical work related to life situations*

(Purpose)	(Path)
Adolescents, for understanding towards	24
Animals, for work on behalf of	29
Artistic inspiration, to gain	30
Career, for insight in planning	28
Debate, for effective skill in	27
Education, to promote any form of	28
Emotional fetters, for freedom from	31
Emotional problems, to help sufferers from	24
Generosity, to promote a spirit of	26
Healing, for a specific	25
Justice, for success in regard to	27
Love, for its triumph over obstacles	27
Partner in life, to find a suitable	27
Patterns-of-destiny, analysis of	32
Peace, to promote (at any level)	28
Prosperity, for increase of	29
Tolerance between partners (marital or other) to promote	26
Work, to find suitable	28

II. Resolving or Balancing the Forces

In Chapter 9 of this book will be found a series of Magical Images representing certain aspects of the archetypal powers of the Spheres, together with a series of simple Sephirothic workings. These images and workings are not required for use with Pathworkings which are performed in their ascending sequence: as has been explained, this mode of Pathworking is self balancing within the pattern of the Tree of Life. The material in Chapter 9 is required, however, for use in various ways with the three categories of selective Pathworkings previously given. The principles of usage are as follows:

For Category 1

In this category, the Pathworking is performed without the operator or group having conscious knowledge of any precise magical need which requires fulfillment, or any imbalance in cosmos or microcosmos which requires correction. There may indeed be such need or imbalance, or there may not: or, again, the energies evoked by the Pathworking may even overcompensate some slight lack.

Therefore, following upon any Pathworking in this category, there is performed a simple *balancing working* of that Sphere which, of its nature, balances the Sphere of Destination of the Path that has been worked.[10]

This simple working will not in any event cancel or negate the effects of the Pathworking. For one thing, Sphereworking and Pathworking are not of the same order. Moreover, spiritual or psychic influences do not in any context cancel or negate one another: just as an artist cannot cancel or negate the red paint upon his palette by adding blue or yellow in whatever quantity. So in spiritual matters, "The Gods themselves cannot recall their gifts," nor (as we find alike in Homer's epics and in the story of the Sleeping Beauty) can one Power simply wipe out the edict of another.

By no means, then, will the balancing Sphereworking annul the effects of the Pathworking. This balancing Sephirothic working is, however, desirable for the purpose of neutralizing any overplus of energies of the Sphere of Destination which may have remained unabsorbed by the need which motivated the working.

---

10. One series of simple Sphereworkings is given in Chapter 9. These same Sphereworkings are equally referred to as "balancing" or "resolution" workings entirely according to the context in which they are to be employed, since it is this context which determines the effect they will produce.

The Balancing Workings and Images for use in connection with category 1 are as follows:[11]

Path worked	Balancing working	Sephirothic Image No.
32	Binah	8
31	Netzach	4
30	Netzach	5
29	Hod	2
28	Hod	3
27	Hod	3
26	Malkuth	9
25	Malkuth	9
24	Malkuth	9

For Category 2

Here we have Pathworkings performed by an individual for the purpose of bringing about change within the compass of that person's own psyche.

This use of Pathworking differs from category 1 in two very important respects. There is a known and definite need to be met, whether this be a positive quality to be developed or a defect to be remedied. Additionally to this, before performing the Pathworking, the operator should

---

11. In the specific context of "balancing" the forces of the seven planetary Sephiroth, the authentic and traditional Qabalistic pattern is as follows:

Binah-Yesod. Chesed-Geburah. Geburah-Chesed. Tiphareth-Malkuth. Netzach-Hod. Yesdd-Binah.

Here it will be observed that Binah is balanced by Yesod, Tiphareth by Malkuth: the balance is not Binah-Malkuth, Tiphareth-Yesod, as some contemporary writers on Qabalah advocate.

The soaring spirituality of Tiphareth needs to be "earthed" in Malkuth, even as he who attains to adepthood in the Solar Sphere is bound to impose his will upon the world of the four elements.

The formative and restrictive influence of Binah should be counterbalanced by the astral vibrancy of Yesod (this is reflected in the reciprocity existing between the brow and genital chakras of the astral body). Inexpertly handled, the current Binah-Malkuth could result in complete magical inertia.

make, aloud, a specific and carefully planned *Declaration of Intent:* stating in unequivocal terms the resolve which the Pathworking is intended to implement The conscious personality of the operator is here calling his or her Higher Self to witness, and the emotional/instinctual nature to give heedful attention, that such-and-such an inner development has been resolved upon, and that, to aid the inner harmony needful to this development, a working of the (*whichever*) Path will now be performed.[12] The Declaration of Intent should be incorporated into the *Formula for Opening a Pathworking* which is given in Chapter 5, to replace the simple proclamation indicated in Section 2 thereof.

The energies evoked by the Pathworking will thus be utilized and absorbed within the psyche of the operator, and there is here no question of an "unused surplus" of Sephirothic influence. After a Pathworking in this category, however, a confirmatory *resolution working* should be done: this relates to the Sphere of Destination itself, to add force and resolve to the Pathworking in a manner which will impress itself upon the Deep Mind of the operator.

The Resolution Workings and Images for use in connection with category 2 are as follows:

Path worked	Resolution working	Sephirothic Image No.
32	Yesod	1
31	Hod	2
30	Hod	3
29	Netzach	4
28	Netzach	5
27	Netzach	6

---

12. It is NOT desirable to change the text of a Pathworking so as to introduce a reference to a special intent of this kind. In accordance with a sound magical principle, which applies here although this is not strictly a ritual working, the intent once declared should not be adverted to again. While the work is in progress, don't reopen the camera!

Path worked	Resolution working	Sephirothic Image No.
26	Tiphareth	7
25	Tiphareth	7
24	Tiphareth	7

For Category 3

In this third category a more complex situation is encountered. In practice, the salient factor is not the type of purpose for which the Pathworking is performed, but the fact that to attain this purpose a practical magical operation is also employed. In such a case, the Pathworking inevitably becomes ancillary to the practical magical operation.

Here, therefore, no Declaration of Intent should be introduced in the *Formula for Opening a Pathworking* nor, equally, should the Pathworking text be in any way altered to accomodate the purpose of the magical operation. That operation alone must carry, within its own structure, all that is needed for the direction of energies to the desired objective.

The relationship, as regards the order of events, between the Pathworking and the associated practical magical operation will be determined not only by the nature of the objective but also by the methods and expertise of the director of the operation. No matter what position is allocated to the Pathworking, however, when it is given it should be concluded with a resolution working: this to be chosen in accordance with the list given above for category 2.

The *balancing workings* and *resolution workings* for categories 1, 2, and 3 should be performed immediately on the completion of the Pathworking to which they relate, so that they may be contained within the evoked ambience. To this end, everything necessary (as detailed in Chapter 9) should be previously placed near at hand, so that the place of working can be quickly set in order for the balancing or resolution working, as the case may be.

Magical Images
and Sephirothic Rites

The material in this chapter is for use in balancing or resolution workings according to the principles set forth in Chapter 8. This material comprises:

(1) descriptions of nine sephirothic magical images which are to be visualized in those workings, and

(2) simple rites of Yesod, Hod, Netzach, Tiphareth, Binah, and Malkuth, designed to follow Selective Pathworkings, for the balancing or resolution of forces.

Magical Image 1
(Yesod, approached by the 32nd Path)

Visualize before you a clean shaven young man, with longish dark hair. A crescent moon, quite slender, is in his hair: the crescent is open towards the left, slightly tilted, and much light radiates from it. About his neck as a living necklace is a light-colored serpent, tail in mouth. Otherwise the figure is nude, with erect penis. You perceive in this figure great comeliness, but also powerful strength and stability. The bare feet of the eidolon stand upon a cube of translucent quartz, within which, at its center, is seen a dark serpent, coiled but beginning to rise up. The left hand of the image is placed as if to support the head, the right hand as if to encircle the waist, of the onlooker in a welcoming embrace.

Magical Image 2
(Hod, approached by the 31st Path)

Visualize before you a delicate male figure, graceful with a suggestion of effeminacy. The hair is short and dark, bound with a fillet. Great sweeping wings, each with countercharged black and white plumage, spring from the shoulders. The image has both hands upraised, the left hand higher than the right: water is flowing down from the palm of the left hand, flame is rising up from the, palm of the right. The figure wears a breechclout, half black and half white divided vertically, supported by a belt of alternated octagons and eight-petaled flowers. The winged sandals of Hermes are on his feet.

Magical Image 3
(Hod, approached by the 30th Path)

Visualize before you a delicate male figure, graceful with a suggestion of effeminacy. The hair is short and dark, and, springing from the temples, there are small wings with black and white plumage. The eidolon wears a long robe, girt at the waist by a belt of alternating octagons and eight-petaled flowers. The robe is black on the figure's right side, white on its left side, the line of division of the colors being straight down the mid-line. Upon the breast is a starlike jewel of eight rays. The arms of the image are raised with the upper arms horizontal, the elbows out from the shoulders but slightly forward. The forearms are raised at about 45°, the palms facing forward and vertical but not rigidly so. The fingers are slightly spread. The bare feet of the eidolon rest upon a sphere, from which two great wings with black and white countercharged plumage rise to frame the figure. You should feel that you are seeing this figure as it flies forward in space.

Magical Image 4
(Netzach, approached by the 29th Path)

Visualize before you a female form with long, dark hair flowing loose over her shoulders. The image wears a richly jeweled girdle of emeralds, pearls and six-petaled flowers: otherwise, her voluptuous figure is nude. Her feet are bare, and she stands with her left foot on the back of a lion, her right foot on the back of a lioness. With her two hands the eidolon supports her full breasts, as offering them to nourish and sustain all beings.

Magical Image 5
(Netzach, approached by the 28th Path)

Visualize before you a female form, voluptuous, splendid and dignified, with great radiance. There is a suggestion of the oriental in her appearance. Dark unbound hair flows loose beneath a star crown, a crown richly wrought with tier upon tier of rays of irregular length, denoting her starry origin. Around her throat, closely fitting, is a necklace of bright stones. A further necklace, hanging lower than the first, terminates in a star-like jewel which hangs just at the separation of her breasts. A diaphanous robe, open in front and having wide three-quarter length sleeves, is her only garment. This robe has jeweled and embroidered borders on the sleeves and at the lower edge. Around her waist, under the robe, is a richly jeweled girdle of emeralds, pearls and six-petaled flowers. She wears a similarly rich bracelet on each wrist and ankle. In her right hand she holds a slender wand with a globe at the base and a starburst at the tip.

Magical Image 6
(Netzach, approached by the 27th Path)

Visualize before you a female form, voluptuous but of great dignity. Upon her fair hair, which is dressed in Greek style, is a diadem of roses. About her neck is a seven-strand necklace of pearls, the lowest strand having a central pearl larger than all the others hanging between her breasts. About her waist is a richly jeweled girdle of emeralds, pearls and six-petaled flowers. She wears no robe. In her upraised left hand she holds a slender flaming torch. Her right hand is extended downwards in a graceful gesture, seeming at first glance as if about to hide her genitals, but in fact indicating her vulva with the extended middle finger. Before her bare feet a pair of doves are copulating.

Magical Image 7

(Tiphareth, Harmonized perspective)

Visualize before you a strong male figure, seated on a curule throne which has bull heads at the terminals of the arm rests, and which has eagle claws at the ends of the legs. The throne is raised upon a circular dais of four steps. The image has golden hair, longish and waving, with a full beard of moderate length. On his head is a solar crown of twelve rays. He wears a golden cloak, open to show a white robe with long white sleeves. On the breast is a winged disc, Egyptian style, with a large zircon at the center of the disc. The robe is girt with a jeweled belt, ornamented with alternate hexagrams and hexagons, each hexagon being set with a central topaz. With his left hand, the eidolon grasps a thyrsus, a slender staff surmounted by a pine cone and entwined with a trail of vine leaves, bearing bunches of grapes. The foot of the staff rests beside the base of the throne. With his right hand the figure holds a dagger, vertically, its point being plunged into the bull-head on the right arm rest. His feet are sandaled. To his right, rising up across the four steps, a serpent with open jaws looks towards the impaled bull-head.

Magical Image 8

(Binah, harmonized planetary perspective)

Visualize before you a heroic male figure with dark beard and shoulder-length hair. Upon his brow is a threefold burst of splendor, emitting rays of dazzling light. He is seated on a severely shaped, high-backed throne of onyx, a lustrous black stone with bands of white. The throne stands on a rocky eminence, as on a mountain top. The eidolon wears a draped garment, dusky in color with highlights of gold: it covers the lower part of his body to the ankles and passes over one shoulder, leaving his arms and part of his chest bare. On his arms are heavy barbaric bracelets of gold: his feet are bare. With his right hand and arm he holds the staff of a large scythe, the heel of the blade resting on the rock near his feet. In the palm of his upraised left hand he holds a large faceted diamond, which emits a dazzling radiance. An ivy plant grows up from the supporting rock, partly covering the right side of the throne.

Magical Image 9
(Malkuth, harmonized perspective)

Visualize before you the slender figure of a young maiden. Her hair is the color of corn, and flows loose under a garland of black blossoms. About her head is a large bright nimbus in which prismatic colors shimmer in concentric bands. Her eyes gaze frankly and directly before her. She wears a white opague garment, ungirded and shaped poncho style, large enough to cover her to feet and wrists in its ample draping. Her right arm is raised horizontally so that it, and the hanging folds of the garment which covers it, conceal her features below the level of the eyes: the palm of her right hand is open and is turned towards us. This same gesture, however, brings the right side of her body into relief under the fabric: its lines suggest a beautiful girlish form, immature but gracefully curved. She stands amid growing barley mingled with poppies. Amid this earthly vegetation grows a single strange flower, a ten-petaled double rose having five white petals and five black ones. Above this flower her left hand is extended, palm downwards, drawing a spiral column of flame up vertically from the rose to her hand.

Rite of Yesod
for Balancing or Resolution

After the conclusion of the Pathworking, the altar shall be covered with a violet drape. Upon the altar shall be placed the Tessera (or other chosen symbol) and either nine violet lamps or a single white lamp.

Incense should be a general compound, suitable to the Sphere of working. The following recipe is recommended; orris, galbanum, bay leaves, oil of jasmine, oil of camphor.

All being in readiness, the companions stand equally spaced in a circle about, and facing, the altar; the director stationed east of the altar.[13]

1. The director sounds the battery: a single stroke of bell or of gavel.

2. The director intones:

   I PROCLAIM A WORKING IN THE SPHERE OF YESOD, INVOKING THE SPIRITUAL POWER OF THE FOUNDATION.

3. The director sounds the battery of the Sphere: 3-3-3.

4. Incense is strewn upon the coals, and the director proceeds to the west of the altar and faces east across it. Raising his right hand, he salutes the east, then declaims:

   O MIGHTY SHADDAI EL CHAI, TO WHOM BELONG FOUNDATION AND THE INVISIBLE PLAN OF THE VISIBLE, GRANT US TO EXPERIENCE THE WONDERS OF THY SPHERE, THAT THY POWER MAY BE MADE MANIFEST WITHIN US.

5. The director resumes his station east of the altar. All link hands, right over left, and circle the altar nine times deosil.

6. Standing in their original positions, all together recite:

   STRONG AND LUMINOUS LORD OF THE WORLD OF OUR DREAMS, HAIL TO THEE! BECKONING HAND

---

13. When these balancing and resolution workings are performed by an individual operator, all is conducted as above save that he or she takes the place of the director. The plural forms in the texts should be preserved, since the individual is never truly alone in these workings.

THAT LIFTS US FROM EARTHLY BONDS, SHINING BROW THAT WINS US TO MAGICAL LIGHT, HAIL TO THEE!

7. All now face east, and visualize in that quarter the appropriate Magical Image of the Sphere of this working, as explained in Chapter 8. If desired, the director may read aloud the description of the Image to assist visualization.

8. When the Image has been powerfully envisioned, the director vibrates the divine name SHADDAI EL CHAI to invoke the energy of the god-force into the visualized image. He utters the divine name nine times, the others joining with him aloud after the first utterance.

9. All now sit, and meditate for some while upon the invoked force, reflecting upon whatever impressions rise into consciousness.

10. When the director deems it appropriate, he rises and all rise with him. All face east, and together utter the thanksgiving:

O SHADDAI EL CHAI, WE THY CHILDREN THANK THEE FOR THE MAGICK OF THY GLORIOUS PRESENCE ARISING WITHIN US. GRANT US, O MIGHTY ONE, THAT THY BLESSING MAY REMAIN WITH US WHEN WE GO FORTH FROM THIS PLACE TO DO OUR WILL IN THE WORLD.

11. All face center. The director concludes the working with the battery: 3-5-3.

Rite of Hod
for Balancing or Resolution

After the conclusion of the Pathworking, the altar shall be covered with an orange drape. Upon the altar shall be placed the Tessera (or other chosen symbol) and either eight orange lamps or a single white lamp.

Incense should be a general compound, suitable to the Sphere of working. The following recipe is recommended: lavender flowers, yellow sandalwood mastic, oil of lavender, oil of spikenard.

All being in readiness, the companions stand equally spaced in a circle about, and facing, the altar; the director stationed east of the altar.

1. The director sounds the battery: a single stroke of bell or of gavel.

2. The director intones:

   I PROCLAIM A WORKING IN THE SPHERE OF HOD, INVOKING THE SPIRITUAL POWER OF SPLENDOR.

3. The director sounds the battery of the Sphere: 2-4-2.

4. Incense is strewn upon the coals, and the director proceeds to the west of the altar and faces east across it. Raising his right hand, he salutes the east, then declaims:

   O SWIFT-WINGED ELOHIM TZABAOTH, TO WHOM BELONG SPLENDOR AND THE CONCRETION OF MIND, GRANT US TO EXPERIENCE THE WONDERS OF THY SPHERE, THAT THY POWER MAY BE MADE MANIFEST WITHIN US.

5. The director resumes his station east of the altar. All link hands, right over left, and circle the altar eight times deosil.

6. Standing in their original positions, all together recite:

   HAIL TO THEE, DIVINE BEARER OF HIGH INSPIRATION AND OF THE KNOWLEDGE WHICH BRINGS RENEWAL! BRIGHT ARE THE WINGS OF THY SPLENDOR, SWIFT IS THINE APPROACH. HAIL TO THEE!

7. All now face east, and visualize in that quarter the appropriate Magical Image of the Sphere of this working, as explained in

Chapter 8. If desired, the director may read aloud the description of the Image to assist visualization.

8. When the Image has been powerfully envisioned, the director vibrates the divine name ELOHIM TZABAOTH to invoke the energy of the god-force into the visualized image. He utters the divine name eight times, the others joining with him aloud after the first utterance.

9. All now sit, and meditate for some while upon the invoked force, reflecting upon whatever impressions rise into consciousness.

10. When the director deems it appropriate, he rises and all rise with him. All face east, and together utter the thanksgiving:

   O ELOHIM TZABAOTH, WE THY CHILDREN THANK THEE FOR THE MAGICK OF THY GLORIOUS PRESENCE ARISING WITHIN US. GRANT US, O SWIFT-WINGED ONE, THAT THY BLESSING MAY REMAIN WITH US WHEN WE GO FORTH FROM THIS PLACE TO DO OUR WILL IN THE WORLD.

11. All face center. The director concludes the working with the battery: 3-5-3.

Rite of Netzach
for Balancing or Resolution

After the conclusion of the Pathworking, the altar shall be covered with a green drape. Upon the altar shall be placed the Tessera (or other chosen symbol) and either seven green lamps or a single white lamp.

Incense should be a general compound, suitable to the Sphere of working. The following recipe is recommended: red rose buds, benzoin, lemon verbena, red storax, red sandalwood, oil of rose.

All being in readiness, the companions stand equally spaced in a circle about, and facing, the altar: the director stationed east of the altar.

1. The director sounds the battery: a single stroke of bell or of gavel.

2. The director intones:

   I PROCLAIM A WORKING IN THE SPHERE OF NET-ZACH, INVOKING THE SPIRITUAL POWER OF VICTORY.

3. The director sounds the battery of the Sphere: 2-3-2.

4. Incense is strewn upon the coals, and the director proceeds to the west of the altar and faces east across it. Raising his right hand, he salutes the east, then declaims:

   O MYSTICAL YAHVEH TZABAOTH, TO WHOM BELONG VICTORY AND THE LIFE FORCE TRIUMPHANT, GRANT US TO EXPERIENCE THE WONDERS OF THY SPHERE, THAT THY POWER MAY BE MADE MANIFEST WITHIN US.

5. The director resumes his station east of the altar. All link hands, right over left, and circle the altar seven times deosil.

6. Standing in their original positions, all together recite:

   HAIL TO THEE, QUEEN OF LOVE AND OF BEAUTY!— THE TORCH OF THY VICTORY BRINGS LIFE AND JOY TO ALL BEINGS. WITH THEE IS PEACE, FOR IN THY GOVERNANCE ALL OPPOSITES FIND THEIR HARMONY. HAIL TO THEE!

7. All now face east, and visualize in that quarter the appropriate Magical Image of the Sphere of this working, as explained in

Chapter 8. If desired, the director may read aloud the description of the Image to assist visualization.

8. When the Image has been powerfully envisioned, the director vibrates the divine name YAHVEH TZABAOTH to invoke the energy of the god-force into the visualized image. He utters the divine name seven times, the others joining with him aloud after the first utterance.

9. All now sit, and meditate for some while upon the invoked force, reflecting upon whatever impressions rise into consciousness.

10. When the director deems it appropriate, he rises and all rise with him. All face east, and together utter the thanksgiving:

    O YAHVEH TZABAOTH, WE THY CHILDREN THANK THEE FOR THE MAGICK OF THY GLORIOUS PRESENCE ARISING WITHIN US. GRANT US, O MYSTICAL ONE, THAT THY BLESSING MAY REMAIN WITH US WHEN WE GO FORTH FROM THIS PLACE TO DO OUR WILL IN THE WORLD.

11. All face center. The director concludes the working with the battery: 3-5-3.

Rite of Tiphareth
for Balancing or Resolution

After the conclusion of the Pathworking, the altar shall be covered with a yellow drape. Upon the altar shall be placed the Tessera (or other chosen symbol) and either seven yellow lamps or a single white lamp.

Incense should be a general compound, suitable to the Sphere of working. The following recipe is recommended: cinnamon, olibanum, yellow rose buds, oil of heliotrope.

All being in readiness, the companions stand equally spaced in a circle about, and facing, the altar: the director stationed east of the altar.

1. The director sounds the battery: a single stroke of bell or of gavel.

2. The director intones:

   I PROCLAIM A WORKING IN THE SPHERE OF TIPHARETH, INVOKING THE SPIRITUAL POWER OF BEAUTY.

3. The director sounds the battery of the Sphere: 2-1-1-2.

4. Incense is strewn upon the coals, and then the director proceeds to the west of the altar and faces east across it. Raising his right hand, he salutes the east, then declaims:

   O RADIANT YAHVEH ELOAH V'DAATIL TO WHOM BELONG BEAUTY AND EQUILIBRIUM, GRANT US TO EXPERIENCE THE. WONDERS OF THY SPHERE, THAT THY POWER MAY BE MADE MANIFEST WITHIN US.

5. The director resumes his station east of the altar. All link hands, right over left, and circle the altar six times deosil.

6. Standing in their original positions, all together recite:

   LORD OF OUR LIFE AND RULER OF OUR DAYS, HAIL TO THEE! THINE IS THE POWER TO LEAD US THROUGH FOLLY TO WISDOM, THROUGH DEATH TO REBIRTH, THROUGH THY LIGHT TO THY HIDDEN LIGHT. HAIL TO THEE!

7. All now face east, and visualize in that quarter the appropriate Magical Image of the Sphere of this working, as explained in

288

Chapter 8. If desired, the director may read aloud the description of the image to assist visualization.

8. When the Image has been powerfully envisioned, the director vibrates the divine name YAHVEH ELOAH V'DAATH to invoke the energy of the god-force into the visualized image. He utters the divine name six times, the others joining with him aloud after the first utterance.

9. All now sit, and meditate for some while upon the invoked force, reflecting upon whatever impressions rise into consciousness.

10. When the director deems it appropriate, he rises and all rise with him. All face east, and together utter the thanksgiving:

O YAHVEH ELOAH V'DAATH, WE THY CHILDREN THANK THEE FOR THE MAGICK OF THY GLORIOUS PRESENCE ARISING WITHIN US. GRANT US, O RADIANT ONE, THAT THY BLESSING MAY REMAIN WITH US WHEN WE GO FORTH FROM THIS PLACE TO DO OUR WILL IN THE WORLD.

11. All face center. The director concludes the working with the battery: 3-5-3.

Rite of Binah
for Balancing

After the conclusion of the Pathworking, the altar shall be covered with an indigo drape. Upon the altar shall be placed the Tessera (or other chosen symbol) and either three smoked-glass lamps or a single white lamp.

Incense should be a general compound, suitable to the Sphere of working. The following recipe is recommended: myrrh, violet leaves, lignum vitae, oil of violet.

All being in readiness, the companions stand equally spaced in a circle about, and facing, the altar; the director stationed east of the altar.

1. The director sounds the battery: a single stroke of bell or of gavel.

2. The director intones:

   I PROCLAIM A WORKING IN THE SPHERE OF BINAH, INVOKING THE SPIRITUAL POWER OF UNDERSTANDING THROUGH THE PLANETARY REALM OF SATURN.

3. The director sounds the battery of the Sphere: 1-1-1.

4. Incense is strewn upon the coals, and the director proceeds to the west of the altar and faces east across it. Raising his right hand, he salutes the east, then declaims:

   O DIVINE YAHVEH ELOHIM, TO WHOM BELONG UNDERSTANDING AND THE LIGHT SUPERNAL, GRANT US TO EXPERIENCE THE WONDERS OF THY SPHERE, THAT THY POWER MAY BE MADE MANIFEST WITHIN US.

5. The director resumes his station east of the altar. All link hands, right over left, and circle the altar three times deosil.

6. Standing in their original positions, all together recite:

   HAIL TO THEE, RULER OF THE MYSTERY OF TIME! BEHIND THEE RAGE UNSEEN THE FORMLESS FORCES OF ETERNITY. WE STAND BENEATH THY AUSTERE AND MIGHTY POWER, BUT ALSO BENEATH THE STRONG HAND OF THY PROTECTION. HAIL TO THEE!

7. All now face east, and visualize in that quarter the appropriate Magical Image of the Sphere of this working, as explained in Chapter 8. If desired, the director may read aloud the description of the image to assist visualization.

8. When the Image has been powerfully envisioned, the director vibrates the divine name YAHVEH ELOHIM to invoke the energy of the god-force into the visualized image. He utters the divine name three times, the others joining with him aloud after the first utterance.

9. All now sit, and meditate for some while upon the invoked force, reflecting upon whatever impressions rise into consciousness.

10. When the director deems it appropriate, he rises and all rise with him. All face east, and together utter the thanksgiving:

> **O YAHVEH ELOHIM, WE THY CHILDREN THANK THEE FOR THE MAGICK OF THY GLORIOUS PRESENCE ARISING WITHIN US. GRANT US, O DIVINE ONE, THAT THY BLESSING MAY REMAIN WITH US WHEN WE GO FORTH FROM THIS PLACE TO DO OUR WILL IN THE WORLD.**

11. All face center. The director concludes the working with the battery: 3-5-3.

Rite of Malkuth
for Balancing

After the conclusion of the Pathworking, the altar shall be covered with a white drape. Upon the altar shall be placed the Tessera (or other chosen symbol) and either ten white lamps or a single white lamp.

Incense should be a general compound, suitable to the Sphere of working. The following recipe is recommended; dittany, cherry wood, gum arabic, oil of geranium.

All being in readiness, the companions stand equally spaced in a circle about, and facing, the altar; the director stationed east of the altar.

1. The director sounds the battery: a single stroke of bell or of gavel.

2. The director intones:

> **I PROCLAIM A WORKING IN THE SPHERE OF MAL-KUTH, INVOKING THE SPIRITUAL POWER OF THE KINGDOM.**

3. The director sounds the battery of the Sphere: 3-4-3.

4. Incense is strewn upon the coals, and the director proceeds to the west of the altar and faces east across it. Raising his right hand, he salutes the east, then declaims:

> **O BEAUTEOUS ADONAI MELEK, TO WHOM BELONG THE KINGDOM AND THE VISION OF HOLINESS, GRANT US TO EXPERIENCE THE WONDERS OF THY SPHERE, THAT THY POWER MAY BE MADE MANIFEST WITHIN US.**

5. The director resumes his station east of the altar. All link hands, right over left, and circle the altar ten times deosil.

6. Standing in their original positions, all together recite:

> **O MAIDEN SOUL OF THE EARTH, HAIL TO THEE! O MAIDEN LIFE OF OUR LIFE, HAIL TO THEE! LOVABLE BEAUTY, POWER RE-VERED, INNOCENCE THAT WE CANNOT LOOK UPON, HAIL TO THEE!**

7. All now face east, and visualize in that quarter the appropriate Magical Image of the Sphere of this working, as explained in

Chapter 8. If desired, the director may read aloud the description of the Image to assist visualization.

8. When the Image has been powerfully envisioned, the director vibrates the divine name ADONAI HA-ARETZ to invoke the energy of the god-force into the visualized image. He utters the divine name ten times, the others joining with him aloud after the first utterance.

9. All now sit, and meditate for some while upon the invoked force, reflecting upon whatever impressions rise into consciousness.

10. When the director deems it appropriate, he rises and all rise with him. All face east, and together utter the thanksgiving:

O ADONAI MELEK, ADONAI HA-ARETZ, WE THY CHILDREN THANK THEE FOR THE MAGICK OF THY GLORIOUS PRE-SENCE ARISING WITHIN US. GRANT US, O BEAUTEOUS ONE, THAT THY BLESSING MAY REMAIN WITH US WHEN WE GO FORTH FROM THIS PLACE TO DO OUR WILL IN THE WORLD.

11. All face center. The director concludes the working with the battery: 3-5-3.

Glossary

ADEPT: One who "has attained": who has passed the Gate of Tiphareth and has entered upon, or achieved, the quest of the Holy Guardian Angel. See *Intuitive Mind* later, also see "The Magical Philosophy" Book IV, Part 1, Chapters 3, 4, 5 in particular.

AMBIVALENT: Having two sharply contrasted values, simultaneously or in alternation. Especially used of a person's emotional attitude to another person, a situation etc., as love-hate, desire-fear, attraction-repulsion.

ANDROGYNE: Having the characteristics of both male and female. The symbolic figure of the androgyne has no reference to physical hermaphroditism. In ancient times such figures were sometimes used to represent the shared experience, ranging from sensory to spiritual, of sexual partners: the Bearded Aphrodite of Amathus is an example. In later times the Androgyne has represented the bipolarity of the individual *psyche*, chiefly of the psyche in the *adept* state, integrated and regenerated. To emphasize the non-physical meaning, such figures are usually sharply divided in their characteristics, either up and down from the waist, or left and right from the vertical midline.

ANIMA: The supreme female principle as present to the unconscious levels of the *psyche*: not directly accessible to the conscious mind, and not part of the personality. The *archetype of the Supernal Mother, relating to the Neshamah* in the Qabalistic plan of the *psyche* and corresponding to the *Sephirah* Binah.

ANIMUS: The supreme male principle as present to the unconscious levels of the *psyche*: not directly accessible to the conscious mind, and not part of the personality. The *archetype* of the Supernal Father, relating to the *Chiah* in the Qabalistic plan of the *psyche* and corresponding to the *Sephirah* Chokmah.

ARCANUM (plural, ARCANA): Literally, "mystery." Each card of the *Tarot* is customarily referred to as an arcanum, a symbolic image needing interpretation. See *Tarot* later.

ARCHETYPAL IMAGE: The form in which an *archetype* is clothed by a particular culture, mythology, religion or individual.

Glossary

ARCHETYPE: A universal and, in itself, imageless concept: in the philosophies of Philo of Alexandria and Augustine of Hippo, these are discerned as subsisting within the Divine Mind: in the psychology of C.G. Jung they are discerned as present to the *Collective Unconscious* of humanity. These philosophic and psychological insights do not exclude each other, but can be taken as mutually comple-mentary.

ASCETIC: Pertaining to the "Way of Purgation," the first stage of willed spiritual evolution: austere, abstemious, self-disciplined. In the *Ogdoadic* system, this stage of development is represented by the *House of Sacrifice*.

ASSIAH: The *World* of material existence, which comprises, objectively, the whole of the physical universe. In the *Composite Tree*, the World of Assiah is represented solely by the *Sephirah* Malkuth, that is, by the planet Earth in its material manifestation.

ASSIMILATION: Absorption of an idea or entity, with its transformation to the mode of being of that which absorbs it. The unconscious mind can assimilate a new experience or concept by playing with it until it is familiar enough to be accepted: after acceptance it can be adapted, analyzed, transformed as the case may be. Another mode of assimilation is that performed in an advanced technique of "exorcism" which is also called Sublimation: the priest-magician voluntarily absorbs a noxious entity wholly into his/her own being, for the purpose of holding its components in the Light of the *Higher Self* so as to restore them to balance and harmony.

ASTRAL: Relating or belonging to the level of being which is "beyond," and causal to, the material world but is denser than the mental level: the "Astral Plane" is equivalent to the Qabalistic World of *Yetzirah*.

ATTENTION: The concentration of the conscious mind upon a single internal or external phenomenon. (So-called "divided attention" is an alternation or rotation of attention, no matter how rapidly, over two or more objects.) Attention narrows the focus of the faculties of body and psyche upon its object, magnifying and exploring the characteristics of that object to the apparent exclusion of all else. This can easily lead into an altered state of consciousness.

ATZILUTH: The highest of the Four Worlds of the *Qabalah*: the World of Divinity and, in the *Composite Tree of Life*, of the *Supernal Sephiroth*. In the human psyche, this is the world of the *Yechidah, Chiah* and *Neshamah*.

BATTERY: In magical practice, a series of percussive sounds (produced for instance with knuckles, gavel, bell or gong) whose number, rhythm and perhaps mode of production may be varied to accord with the significance of a rite. Batteries may renew the attention of participants, divide a ritual into its component sections, or emphasize salient moments in the working.

BRIAH: The Qabalistic World next below *Atziluth*: Briah is the World of Mind, the world of the *Ruach*, and essentially the world of the *adept*. It is also the world of the *archetypal images*, including those which are special vehicles of divine power and which we call "the Gods." In the *composite Tree*, Briah is represented by the *Sephiroth* Tiphareth, Geburah and Chesed.

CENTERS OF ACTIVITY: The Wheels (Chakras), Knots, or Lotuses of Eastern systems. These Centers are points in the astral body which correspond to neural or glandular centers in the physical body, but which may be said to take their origin from the non-material counterpart of the spinal column. Important practices for the benefit of the whole person depend upon the correct activation of these Centers, usually involving only a small number—up to seven—of the principal ones.

CHIAH: That function of the *Higher Self* which relates to the *Animus* of Jungian psychology and which, on the *Tree of Life*, corresponds to Chokmah, the Sphere of the Supernal Father.

COLLECTIVE UNCONSCIOUS: The repository of the totality of human experience, including the *archetypes*: evidence suggests that beyond the levels of human experience the collective unconscious extends into the experience of all life, and perhaps into the total being of the *universe*. In any case, however, the experience of the Collective Unconscious lies at greater depth than any part of the individual personality, even than the *personal unconscious*.

COMPOSITE TREE: A special formulation of the *Tree of Life* which is employed solely to indicate the *Way of Return*, but which can be traced back by inference through the writings of many centuries. In this formulation, Malkuth is experienced in the world of *Assiah*; Yesod, Hod and Netzach in the World of *Yetzirah*; Tiphareth, Geburah and Chesed in the World of *Briah*; and the Supernal Sephiroth in the World of *Atziluth*. See Chapter 2 of this book with its diagram of the Composite Tree.

COSMIC: The adjective formed from COSMOS, "Universe." In this book, the term "cosmic" is sometimes used where older works would have used "macrocosmic": that is to say, relating to the outer universe in all its material and non-material levels of being, in contrast to "microcosmic," the adjective formed from *microcosm* (which see.) Cosmic and microcosmic seems a sufficient distinction.

DESTINATION, Sphere of: The *Sephirah* to which a specified *Path* leads.

ELEMENTAL: A non-corporeal, living, and sentient being, native to the World of *Yetzirah*. Of the various Yetziratic entities, it is generally accepted that those which are termed "angels" and "intelligences" belong to the higher reaches of the astral world, nearer to the mental level, while those which are termed "spirits" and "elementals" belong to the lower reaches, nearer to materiality.

FANTASY: A "waking dream" which may be involuntary or which may be planned and guided, and which can also be aided with suitable accessories.

HIGHER SELF: That part of the psyche which comprises the "Trine of Spirit": the *Yechidah, Chiah* and *Neshamah* together, abiding (according to Qabalistic doctrine) incorruptible in the World of *Atziluth*.

HOUSE OF SACRIFICE: A formulation of the Fivefold Pattern found in Byzantine and subsequent Western art and literature, as well as elsewhere in the Near and Middle East. The Qabalistic "pattern of the psyche" is employed in different contexts to represent the human condition, the life of the *ascetic*, and the pattern of various sacrificial or sacramental acts. It is found in the *Ogdoadic* tradition—including some most effective uses in the Aurum Solis—as a very potent formula for magical ceremonial, and above all, since it is an elaboration of the pattern of the psyche itself, as a formula for *initiation*.

INITIATION: In some contexts, the beginning of anything: but especially the introduction of a person into a new phase of spiritual evolution, by means of a carefully controlled experience given in the form of a ritual or a guided meditation.

INTUITION: The direct apprehension of reality without need to "abstract" the knowledge from words, sense-perceptions or rational or imaginative processes. Properly, this direct knowing can only be performed by the *Ruach* of the *adept* when it works in conjunction with the *Intuitive Mind*. However, in some situations the *Neshamah* can operate through the *Nephesh*, which at once clothes the supernal communication with its own imagery: hence "intuitive" knowledge (in the popular sense of the word) can be sound in essentials but yet embroidered with dream-like detail.

INTUITIVE MIND: A "ray" from the Higher Self, the supernal region of the psyche, which descends by way of the Neshamah into the Ruach. The adept, who is progressing in realization of the World of Briah, can thus proportionately enjoy the supernal perceptions of the Intuitive Mind in combination with the Ruach consciousness, to lead him/her to ever greater heights of spiritual insight and growth.

LABYRINTH: Literally "the House of the Axe": a temple or other structure sacred to the axe-wielding Goddess of Crete, and having an intricate arrangement of passages. Perhaps a sophisticated form of the ancient dancing-maze, in which the dancers must perforce proceed to the center and out again: the related ideas, of dedication to the Mother and of rebirth, for the most part remain with these widely-distributed structures whether independently established or derived from the Cretan Labyrinth.

LAMEN: A "lamina": a thin plate of metal, wood or other suitable material. The word "lamen" is specifically used for a small tablet of any shape, inscribed with significant words and/or symbols, to be worn upon the breast, usually suspended about the neck: a breastplate, pentacle, or talisman of this type.

LOWER SELF: That part of a person which comprises the physical body and all the instinctual and emotional functions of the psyche, producing even the most elevated emotions; it includes also the rational mind. The term "lower" is not at all derogatory, and the Lower Self takes its natural and harmonious place in a *personality* which is governed by the *Higher Self.*

MAGICK: The control of non-material forces to produce specific and intended effects. To align this definition with present-day understanding of the matter, it is probably necessary to add that the non-material force is to be external to the psyche of the magician: for example, to cause an object to be moved by an *elemental* whom one has summoned for the purpose would be a magical act, but to move the same object by psycho-kinesis would by many people not be considered magical.

MANDALA: A concentric design of *metaphysical* significance: in its primary sense always circular (hence the name, meaning "circle" in Sanskrit), a mandala does not have that limitation in Jungian psychology, in which it can represent any state of consciousness. On basic magical principles, a mandala which is designed with understanding to represent a given state of consciousness can also be employed to produce that same state.

MEGALITH: A massive stone: particularly a massive stone of the kind used in the construction of ancient monuments. Adjective, MEGALITHIC.

METAPHYSICAL: Beyond the physical. This word was coined by Aristotle, and its usefulness has been increasingly appreciated since his day: it gives us an adjective, and the name of a subject of study (METAPHYSICS) relating to the non-material, without implying any specific cause or nature—divine, demonic, human or other—for the phenomena under consideration.

Glossary

MICROCOSM: The individual person considered as a "miniature universe." This reflection accords particularly well with Qabalistic thought, for in the individual human being we recognize the Ten *Sephiroth* and the Four *Worlds*: and the *Tree of Life* can equally be understood to show the pattern of balancing forces at the exterior, *cosmic* level, or at the interior, microcosmic level.

MYSTICISM: Strictly, Mysticism is the understanding that another faculty above reason (see *Intuitive Mind*) is needed to guide human nature into union with the Divine; and Mysticism also includes the teachings which follow from that understanding.

    The recognition that union with the Divine is the rightful comple-tion of human nature ceases to present a paradox in this context, when the existence and divine nature of the individual's own *Higher Self* is recognized.

    The adjective MYSTICAL is frequently used in a general sense to denote anything which transcends reason.

NEPHESH: That part of the *psyche* which comprises the whole emotional and instinctual nature, all that is sub-rational, both conscious and unconscious. The Nephesh is "native" to the World of *Yetzirah*: together with the physical body and the Ruach, it comprises the *Lower Self*.

NESHAMAH: One of the supernal functions of the psyche: that function of the *Higher Self* which relates to the *Anima* of Jungian psychology and which, on the *Tree of Life*, corresponds to Binah, the sphere of the Supernal Mother.

OGDOADIC: That school of the *Western Mystery Tradition* to which the Order Aurum Solis belongs, the Order upon whose teachings the contents of the present work are based. For further notes on the Ogdoadic school, see the introduction to this book.

PATH of the *Tree of Life*: On a diagram of the Tree, the 22 Paths are usually shown by parallel lines leading from one *Sephirah* to another. Progress upon any Path is marked by continuous changes in experience or in inner response: the Paths of the Tree of Life are no exception.

PATHWORKING: is a traditional form of guided meditation, planned to convey the hearer through the essential experiences of each of the Paths, and through the succession of Paths in their correct order.

PENTAGRAM: A five-pointed star. This symbol has various interpretations, the chief of which are: (1) The forces of the "five elements," Earth, Air, Fire, Water, and Spirit; (2) Human nature in equilibrium, as typified by the five senses; (3) the power of the Sphere of Mars (Geburah, the Fifth Sephirah).

PERSONALITY: In psychology, all that belongs to the individuality or identity of a specific person: the physical body, the Nephesh, the Ruach, with much of the influence imparted by the Higher Self when contact has been made with this: but not the Intuitive Mind itself, nor the Collective Unconscious, nor the Archetypes. The personal unconscious, (see *Unconscious*) even though the individual to whom it pertains may be oblivious to it, is, strictly, a part of the personality, and its contents belong thereto.

PICTOGRAPHIC: Pertaining to the "picture-writing." The drawing of various objects to convey an idea or a message is an ancient and primitive form of "writing." In the first stage of development of this art, the potential meaning of the writing was limited to what could be directly depicted; subsequently pictography could take different lines of development. Abstract meanings could be conveyed by associated images, as for instance in Chinese where the combination "bird-eye-hand" represented a word for "fear": or alternatively a sign could begin to be used to represent, wholly or in part, a word of related sound although probably unrelated meaning. This latter tendency, exemplified in the Egyptian hieroglyphic system, is the beginning of alphabetic sign-making proper.

In some alphabets, the letters function also as numerals. Thus in the Hebrew alphabet, the fourth letter (Daleth) represents both the sound D and the numeral 4; but pictographically, it represents a door. The twenty-first letter (Shin) represents the sound Sh (or in some circumstances S) and the numerical value 300: pictographically, it represents a tooth.

PLANETARY SPHERE: A Sphere, or *Sephirah*, whose character is typified by one of the "seven planets" of traditional astrology: that is, Binah (Saturn), Chesed (Jupiter), Geburah (Mars), Tiphareth (Sun), Netzach (Venus), Hod (Mercury), and Yesod (Moon). This does not imply that the character of the Sephirah coincides at every point with that of the planetary influence as the latter would be described in a book on astrology: the attributes of the Sephiroth are seen in *cosmic* terms, the astrological interpretations necessarily in *microcosmic* terms.

PSYCHE: The non-material part of a psycho-physical being. It is recognized that the powers and perceptions of the psyche extend considerably beyond the domain of the *personality*: but how far, it is impossible to say.

QABALAH: A venerable Wisdom Tradition which was formulated chiefly in Mediterranean regions: Hebrew and Greek are its principal languages. It is generally considered under two main heads: the traditional, or "theoretical" Qabalah, and the modern, or "Practical": but there is much common ground, and much exchange, between these two focal points of Qabalistic study.

RESOLUTION: (1) a firm and decisive act of the will, or habit of the mind; (2) the bringing of something to a satisfactory conclusion which accords wholly with its own nature. The present book contains two distinct examples of the latter meaning: (a) in the conclusions of the 26th and 24th Paths after the working of the 25th; and (b) in the "resolution working" to confirm the sephirothic powers of the sphere of destination after a selected Pathworking has been performed with magical intent.

RUACH: That part of the psyche which comprises the rational mind and the intellectual faculties, and which is "native" to the World of *Briah*. It is only after initiation into the Sphere of Tiphareth (whether ritually, by meditation, or by experience of life) that the rational mind progressively grows, or awakens, to its full Ruach consciousness. See "The Magical Philosophy" Book IV, Part I, Chapters 3, 4, 5.

SAURIAN: A crocodile, or an animal or entity of the general nature of the crocodile. In Egypt and other lands where saurians are found, ancient traditions have regarded them alternately as divine or demonic beings. Not only the objective qualities of crocodiles elicit awe or at least propitiation: their habit of arising from obscure waters to seize and devour their prey makes an image of the human fear that the rational consciousness may be swallowed up by the *Unconscious*. They are thus aptly associated with the dark side of the Saturnian powers.

SEPHIRAH: (plural, SEPHIROTH) One of the ten "Voices from Nothing": aspects of being, experienced by the human explorer as states of consciousness. The Sephiroth are represented as ten spheres or circles upon the Qabalistic *Tree of Life*. Their names, with literal meanings, follow: Kether (Crown), Chokmah (Wisdom), Binah (Understanding), Chesed (Mercy), Geburah (Strength), Tiphareth (Beauty), Netzach (Victory), Hod (Splendor), Yesod (Foundation), Malkuth (Kingdom).

ADOW: In Jungian psychology, a figure, usually human, of the same sex as the reamer, seen in dream as another person: in reality representing some quality, od or bad, which the dreamer does not acknowledge himself/herself to possess, which is truly part of the *personality*. A "shadow" is thus an "other self" of the er, and its function in the dream may be helpful or the reverse.

LPTURE: Work done on one's own psyche, by whatever means, to its of character which one desires, or to diminish those one finds unde-e cases, advice as to the direction of development is advantageous: graphology can be of great value here. For the "sculpture" itself, gestion, autohypnosis can be used: a very potent and effective mula of the Simulacrum" which gives the operator an assured munication with his/her emotional and instinctual nature. *actical Guide to Astral Projection,* Chapter 5.)

ly, "higher" or "from above." With reference to the *Tree of Life*, the s are the *Sephiroth* Kether, Chokmah and Binah. In the present work, of spiritual evolution in terms of the *Composite Tree*, the Supernals com-art of the Tree which is to be attained in the World of *Atziluth*: but it orne in mind that this formulation applies only to the plan of human prog-om a cosmic viewpoint, the Tree of Life exists, whole and entire, in each of ur *Worlds* according to the manner and mode of each World: thus the Super-ephiroth, with the rest of the Tree, are present in the material, the astral and tal levels of being as well as in the divine or spiritual.

T: The traditional divinatory and magical deck of 78 cards, made up of 22 Major rcana and 56 Minor Arcana. Its evolution appears to have been not only contem-orary with the medieval and modern development of the *Tree of Life*, but to have aken place in the same regions. The 22 Major Arcana are very closely related to the 22 *Paths*, and can fruitfully be used in interpreting the Paths although the cards have manifestly developed independently of the Tree in some respects.

TESSERA, The Mystica:l "The primal magical implement of Aurum Solis working." For a description of the Tessera, see Chapter 5 of the present book, Section I, item 4. The Rite for its consecration is given as Paper XXII in Book V of The Magical Philosophy.

TRANSMUTATION: The change of one material to another, as in alchemy, so as to manifest all the essential qualities of the new material. Albert the Great (1206?–1280) states that iron produced by transmutation is incapable of magnetism: the implica-tion is that in other respects (specific gravity, color, malleability, degree of hardness, tendency to rust, etc.) the alchemical iron would pass scrutiny.

TREE OF LIFE: A glyph which is basic to the *Qabalah*. It comprises ten circles arranged in a traditional diagrammatic pattern, representing ten aspects of being, the *Sephiroth*, which are discerned as existing both in the human psyche and in the *universe* at large. These ten circles are united by twenty-two *Paths* whose placement, with the priorities shown by their crossings, are likewise traditionally fixed. See diagram, Chapter 1 of this book.

UNCONSCIOUS: Those great areas of the psyche which are not within the knowledge, and so not within the direct control, of the conscious and rational mind. This term is used to comprise (a) the Higher Unconscious, the *Higher Self*, the "Supermind"; (b) the Lower Unconscious, the Deep Mind, the unconscious region of the emotional and instinctual nature; (c) the Personal Unconscious, an individual's deposit of forgotten and, often, repressed material, therefore to that extent an abnormal development in the psyche; (d) the *Collective Unconscious* (see above.)

UNIVERSE Essentially synonymous with *Cosmos* which means "the All." It is noted however that both these words are generally used to mean the totality the material level of being. In the present book we use these words to me the totality of all that is, at all levels of being: to put it in Qabalistic ter *Worlds.*

VISUALIZATION The act, or the art, of forming a mental ima Creative Visualization, which is a special method for play obtaining the fulfillment of one's wishes, simple visualizati cal and meditative practice. The seeming "externalization natural to some people, and can be acquired by others thr those to whom, as a consequence of their innate temperament wholly "in the mind's eye," visualization is no less valid and valuat point for the attention, and thus for magical purposes generally.

WAY OF RETURN: The course of the individual's spiritual evolution, "return to Source" after the long road of involution into matter. In mo listic thought there are two regular courses for the ascent, which is co as upon the *Composite Tree*: the Way of the Arrow, which is the way of th straight up the central column of the Tree of Life by the 32nd, 25th, and 14 and the Way of the Serpent, which takes in every Path of the Tree up to the due order. (It is interesting that St. John of the Cross, writing in Spain in th century, describes a spiritual ascent of ten steps, corresponding directly to the S *roth.*) This present book follows the Way of the Serpent from the 32nd Path, thro the Paths which enter Tiphareth.

WESTERN MYSTERY TRADITION: The esoteric understanding of life, and the pr tices deriving therefrom, which has accumulated and, in various formulations, ha developed, in and with Western culture. The appellation does not represent any denial of the considerable exchange of concepts, in-spirations and techniques which has taken place between East and West in all ages.

WORLDS, the Four: See *Assiah, Yetzirah, Briah, Atziluth.* A correspondence is perceived in Qabalistic thought between these four levels of being (and of consciousness) and the four Elements: material existence corresponding to Earth; the ambient, receptive astral world to Air; the world of mind, penetrating and fluidic, to Water; and the world—of divine spirit to Fire.

YECHIDAH: The supreme supernal function of the psyche, the Divine Flame within. Itself remaining a part of the Divine Mind, the Yechidah is the "nucleus" or "bud" from which our individual being develops. On the Tree of Life, the Yechidah corresponds to the *Sephirah* Kether.

YETZIRAH: That one of the four Qabalistic *Worlds* which represents the level of existence between *Assiah* and, *Briah*: the *"astral* plane." In the *Composite Tree* it comprises the *Sephiroth* Yesod, Hod, and Netzach.